Fundamentals of Computational Neuroscience

Fundamentals of Computational Neuroscience

Rebecca Sanchez

|STATES|
ACADEMIC PRESS
www.statesacademicpress.com

Published by States Academic Press,
109 South 5th Street,
Brooklyn, NY 11249, USA

ISBN: 978-1-63989-223-5

Cataloging-in-Publication Data

Fundamentals of computational neuroscience / Rebecca Sanchez.
 p. cm.
Includes bibliographical references and index.
ISBN 978-1-63989-223-5
1. Computational neuroscience. 2. Neurosciences--Data processing. 3. Computational biology.
I. Sanchez, Rebecca.
QP357.5 .F86 2022
612.8--dc23

For information on all States Academic Press publications
visit our website at www.statesacademicpress.com

Contents

Permissions

Index

Preface

The branch of neuroscience which makes use of mathematical models, abstractions and theoretical analysis of the brain is called computational neuroscience. It attempts to understand the principles which govern the structure, development, physiology and cognitive abilities of the human nervous system. Some of the important areas of research under this discipline are single neuron modeling, sensory processing, motor control, behavior of networks, memory and synaptic plasticity, consciousness, visual attention, identification, etc. The commonly used software applications for simulating the theoretical models in computational neuroscience are BRIAN, Emergent, GENESIS and NEST. This book attempts to understand the multiple branches that fall under the discipline of computational neuroscience and how such concepts have practical applications. It elucidates the concepts and innovative models around prospective developments with respect to computational neuroscience. This book aims to serve as a resource guide for students and experts alike and contribute to the growth of the discipline.

A detailed account of the significant topics covered in this book is provided below:

Chapter 1- The branch of neuroscience which makes use of mathematical models and theories to investigate the structure, development and cognitive abilities of brain is known as computational neuroscience. It involves the study of physiology of nervous system. This is an introductory chapter which will introduce briefly all the significant aspects of computational neuroscience such as neurons, holonomic brain theory, neural circuit, neural networks etc.

Chapter 2- There are various models which explain the concepts of computational neuroscience in a clear and concise manner. Some of the models explained in this chapter are single-neuron modeling, FitzHugh-Nagumo model, Hindmarsh-Rose model, Dehaene-Changeux model, Hodgkin-Huxley model, etc. This chapter has been carefully written to provide an easy understanding of these models of computational neuroscience.

Chapter 3- There are several tools and technologies used in computational neuroscience. Some of the topics discussed in this chapter are brain-computer interface, single-unit recording, Bayesian approaches to brain function, mind uploading, neurocomputational speech processing and brain-reading. All these tools and technologies used in computational neuroscience have been carefully analyzed in this chapter.

Chapter 4- The computing system designed in a way that it resembles the way of human brain to analyze and process information is known as artificial neural network. This chapter encompasses recurrent neural network, machine learning and perceptron. The topics elaborated in this chapter will help in gaining a better perspective about artificial neural networks.

Chapter 5- The assembly of instruments and methods that establish a connection between nervous system and technical devices is known as neurotechnology. In order to completely understand computational neuroscience, it is necessary to understand the processes related to it. The following chapter elucidates the varied aspects associated with this area of study such as artificial intelligence, neurophysiology and computational neuroanatomy.

I would like to make a special mention of my publisher who considered me worthy of this opportunity and also supported me throughout the process. I would also like to thank the editing team at the back-end who extended their help whenever required.

Rebecca Sanchez

Computational Neuroscience: An Introduction

The branch of neuroscience which makes use of mathematical models and theories to investigate the structure, development and cognitive abilities of brain is known as computational neuroscience. It involves the study of physiology of nervous system. This is an introductory chapter which will introduce briefly all the significant aspects of computational neuroscience such as neurons, holonomic brain theory, neural circuit, neural networks etc.

Computational neuroscience (CNS) is an interdisciplinary field for development, simulation, and analysis of multi-scale models and theories of neural function from the level of molecules, through cells and networks, up to cognition and behavior. We work closely with experimental data at these different scales - CNS models integrate these data to allow them to be understood in terms of each other, and make predictions for new experiments. Identification of scale interactions and dynamics in neural structures provides a framework for understanding the principles that govern how neural systems work, and how things can go wrong in brain disease. CNS links the diverse fields of cell and molecular biology, neuroscience, cognitive science, and psychology with electrical engineering, computer science, mathematics, and physics.

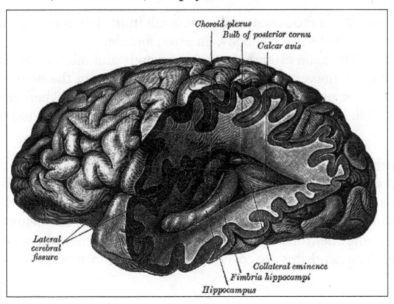

Neurons

Cells within the nervous system, called neurons, communicate with each other in unique ways. The neuron is the basic working unit of the brain, a specialized cell designed to transmit information to other nerve cells, muscle, or gland cells.

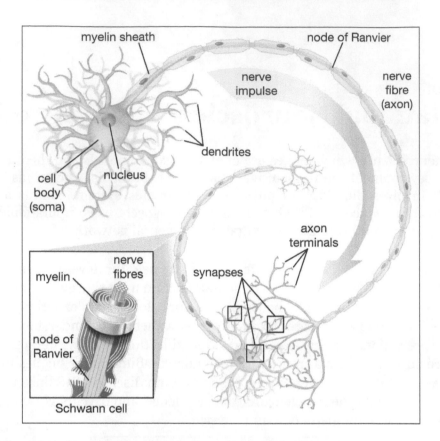

Neurons are cells within the nervous system that transmit information to other nerve cells, muscle, or gland cells. Most neurons have a cell body, an axon, and dendrites. The cell body contains the nucleus and cytoplasm. The axon extends from the cell body and often gives rise to many smaller branches before ending at nerve terminals. Dendrites extend from the neuron cell body and receive messages from other neurons. Synapses are the contact points where one neuron communicates with another. The dendrites are covered with synapses formed by the ends of axons from other neurons.

Neurons are cells within the nervous system that transmit information to other nerve cells, muscle, or gland cells. Most neurons have a cell body, an axon, and dendrites. The cell body contains the nucleus and cytoplasm. The axon extends from the cell body and often gives rise to many smaller branches before ending at nerve terminals. Dendrites extend from the neuron cell body and receive messages from other neurons. Synapses are the contact points where one neuron communicates with another. The dendrites are covered with synapses formed by the ends of axons from other neurons.

The brain is what it is because of the structural and functional properties of interconnected neurons. The mammalian brain contains between 100 million and 100 billion neurons, depending on the species. Each mammalian neuron consists of a cell body, dendrites, and an axon. The cell body contains the nucleus and cytoplasm. The axon extends from the cell body and often gives rise to many smaller branches before ending at nerve terminals. Dendrites extend from the neuron cell body and receive messages from other neurons. Synapses are the contact points where one neuron communicates with another. The dendrites are covered with synapses formed by the ends of axons from other neurons.

When neurons receive or send messages, they transmit electrical impulses along their axons, which can range in length from a tiny fraction of an inch (or centimeter) to three feet (about one meter) or more. Many axons are covered with a layered myelin sheath, which accelerates the transmission of electrical signals along the axon. This sheath is made by specialized cells called glia. In the brain, the glia that make the sheath are called oligodendrocytes, and in the peripheral nervous system, they are known as Schwann cells.

The brain contains at least ten times more glia than neurons. Glia performs many jobs. Researchers have known for a while that glia transport nutrients to neurons, clean up brain debris, digest parts of dead neurons, and help hold neurons in place.

Function of Neurons

Specialized Regions of Neurons Carry Out Different Functions

Although the morphology of various types of neurons differs in some respects, they all contain four distinct regions with differing functions: the cell body, the dendrites, the axon, and the axon terminals.

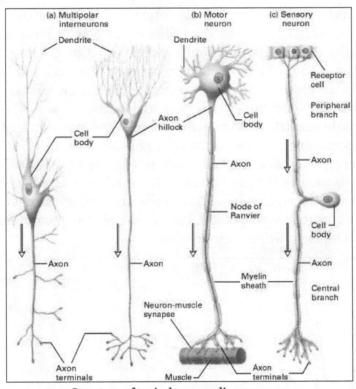

Structure of typical mammalian neurons.

In above figure, Arrows indicate the direction of conduction of action potentials in axons (red). (a) Multipolar interneurons. Each has profusely branched dendrites, which receive signals at synapses with several hundred other neurons, and a single long axon that branches laterally and at its terminus. (b) A motor neuron that innervates a muscle cell. Typically, motor neurons have a single long axon extending from the cell body to the effector cell. In mammalian motor neurons an insulating sheath of myelin usually covers all parts of the axon except at the nodes of Ranvier and the axon terminals. (c) A sensory neuron in which the axon branches just after it leaves the cell body. The peripheral branch carries the nerve impulse from the receptor cell to the cell body, which is located in the dorsal root ganglion near the spinal cord; the central branch carries the impulse from the cell body to the spinal cord or brain. Both branches are structurally and functionally axons, except at their terminal portions, even though the peripheral branch conducts impulses toward, rather than away from, the cell body.

The cell body contains the nucleus and is the site of synthesis of virtually all neuronal proteins and membranes. Some proteins are synthesized in dendrites, but no proteins are made in axons and axon terminals, which do not contain ribosomes. Proteins and membranes that are required for renewal of the axon and nerve termini are synthesized in the cell body and assembled there into membranous vesicles or multi-protein particles. By a process called anterograde transport, these materials are transported along microtubules down the length of the axon to the terminals, where they are inserted into the plasma membrane or other organelles. Axonal microtubules also are the tracks along which damaged membranes and organelles move up the axon toward the cell body; this process is called retrograde transport. Lysosomes, where such material is degraded, are found only in the cell body.

Almost every neuron has a single axon, whose diameter varies from a micrometer in certain nerves of the human brain to a millimeter in the giant fiber of the squid. Axons are specialized for the conduction of a particular type of electric impulse, called an action potential, outward, away from the cell body toward the axon terminus. An action potential is a series of sudden changes in the voltage, or equivalently the electric potential, across the plasma membrane. When a neuron is in the resting (non-stimulated) state, the electric potential across the axonal membrane is approximately −60 mV (the inside negative relative to the outside); the magnitude of this resting potential is similar to that of the membrane potential in most non-neuronal cells. At the peak of an action potential, the membrane potential can be as much as +50 mV (inside positive), a net change of ≈110 mV. This depolarization of the membrane is followed by a rapid repolarization, returning the membrane potential to the resting value. These characteristics distinguish an action potential from other types of changes in electric potential across the plasma membrane and allow an action potential to move along an axon without diminution.

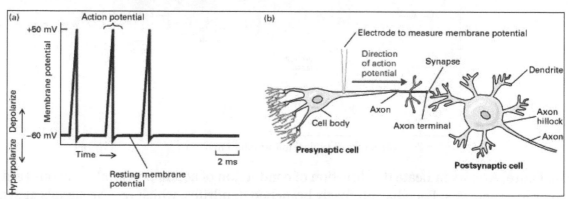

Figure above shows; (a) An action potential is a sudden, transient depolarization of the membrane followed by repolarization to the resting potential of about −60 mV. This recording of the axonal membrane potential in a presynaptic neuron shows that it is generating one action potential about every 4 milliseconds. (b) The membrane potential across the plasma membrane of a presynaptic neuron is measured by a small electrode inserted into it. Action potentials move down the axon at speeds up to 100 meters per second. Their arrival at a synapse causes release of neurotransmitters that bind to receptors in the postsynaptic cell, generally depolarizing the membrane (making the potential less negative) and tending to induce an action potential in it.

Action potentials move rapidly, at speeds up to 100 meters per second. In humans, axons may be more than a meter long, yet it takes only a few milliseconds for an action potential to move along their length. An action potential originates at the axon hillock, the junction of the axon and cell body, and is actively conducted down the axon into the axon terminals, small branches of the axon that form the synapses, or connections, with other cells. A single axon in the central nervous system can synapse with many neurons and induce responses in all of them simultaneously.

Most neurons have multiple dendrites, which extend out-ward from the cell body and are specialized to receive chemical signals from the axon termini of other neurons. Dendrites convert these signals into small electric impulses and transmit them inward, in the direction of the cell body. Neuronal cell bodies can also form synapses and thus receive signals. Particularly in the central nervous system, neurons have extremely long dendrites with complex branches. This allows them to form synapses with and receive signals from a large number of other neurons, perhaps up to a thousand. Electric disturbances generated in the dendrites or cell body spread to the axon hillock. If the electric disturbance there is great enough, an action potential will originate and will be actively conducted down the axon.

Synapses are Specialized Sites where Neurons Communicate with other Cells

Synapses generally transmit signals in only one direction: an axon terminal from the presynaptic cell sends signals that are picked up by the postsynaptic cell. There are two general types of synapse: the relatively rare electric synapse, and the chemical synapse. In this type of synapse, the axon terminal of the presynaptic cell contains vesicles filled with a particular neurotransmitter. The postsynaptic cell can be a dendrite or cell body of another neuron, a muscle or gland cell, or, rarely, even another axon. When an action potential in the presynaptic cell reaches an axon terminal, it induces a localized rise in the level of Ca^{2+} in the cytosol. This, in turn, causes some of the vesicles to fuse with the plasma membrane, releasing their contents into the synaptic cleft, the narrow space between the cells. The neurotransmitters diffuse across the synaptic cleft; it takes about 0.5 millisecond (ms) for them to bind to receptors on postsynaptic cells.

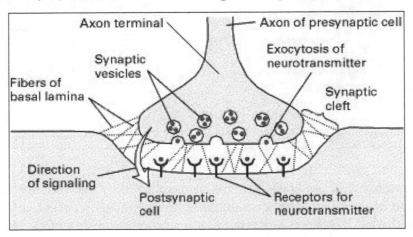

Figure shows a chemical synapse: A narrow region — the synaptic cleft — separates the plasma membranes of the presynaptic and postsynaptic cells. Transmission of electric impulses requires release of a neurotransmitter (red circles) by the presynaptic cell, its diffusion across the synaptic cleft, and its binding by specific receptors on the plasma membrane of the postsynaptic cell.

Binding of the neurotransmitter triggers changes in the ion permeability of the postsynaptic plasma membrane, which, in turn, changes the membrane's electric potential at this point. If the postsynaptic cell is a neuron, this electric disturbance may be sufficient to induce an action potential. If the postsynaptic cell is a muscle, the change in membrane potential following binding of the neurotransmitter may induce contraction; if a gland cell, the neurotransmitter may induce hormone secretion. In some cases, enzymes attached to the fibrous network connecting the cells destroy the neurotransmitter after it has functioned; in other cases, the signal is terminated when the neurotransmitter diffuses away or is transported back into the presynaptic cell.

The postsynaptic neuron at certain synapses also sends signals to the presynaptic one. Such retrograde signals can be gases, such as nitric oxide and carbon monoxide, or peptide hormones. This type of signaling, which modifies the ability of the presynaptic cell to signal the postsynaptic one, is thought to be important in many types of learning.

Neurons are Organized into Circuits

In complex multicellular animals, such as insects and mammals, various types of neurons form signaling circuits. In the simple type of circuit called a reflex arc, interneurons connect multiple sensory and motor neurons, allowing one sensory neuron to affect multiple motor neurons and one motor neuron to be affected by multiple sensory neurons; in this way interneurons integrate and enhance reflexes. For example, the knee-jerk reflex in humans involves a complex reflex arc in which one muscle is stimulated to contract while another is inhibited from contracting. Such circuits allow an organism to respond to a sensory input by the coordinated action of sets of muscles that together achieve a single purpose. However, such simple nerve systems do not directly explain higher-order brain functions such as reasoning and computation.

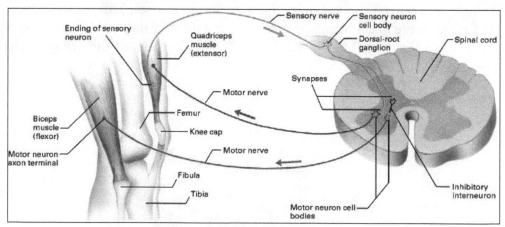

The knee-jerk reflex arc in the human.

Positioning and movement of the knee joint are accomplished by two muscles that have opposite actions: Contraction of the quadriceps muscle straightens the leg, whereas contraction of the biceps muscle bends the leg. The knee-jerk response, a sudden extension of the leg, is stimulated by a blow just below the knee cap. The blow directly stimulates sensory neurons (blue) located in the tendon of the quadriceps muscle. The axon of each sensory neuron extends from the tendon to its cell body in a dorsal root ganglion. The sensory axon then continues to the spinal cord, where it branches and synapses with two neurons: (1) a motor neuron (red) that innervates the quadriceps muscle and (2) an inhibitory interneuron (black) that synapses with a motor neuron (green) innervating the biceps muscle. Stimulation of the sensory neuron causes a contraction of the quadriceps and, via the inhibitory neuron, a simultaneous inhibition of contraction of the biceps muscle. The net result is an extension of the leg at the knee joint. Each cell illustrated here actually represents a nerve, that is, a population of neurons.

The sensory and motor neurons of circuits such as the knee-jerk reflex are contained within the peripheral nervous system. These circuits send information to and receive information from the central nervous system (CNS), which comprises the brain and spinal cord and is composed mainly of interneurons. Highly specialized sensory receptor cells, which respond to specific environmental stimuli, send their outputs either directly to the brain (e.g., taste and odorant receptors) or to peripheral sensory neurons (e.g., pain and stretching receptors). The peripheral nervous system contains two broad classes of motor neurons. The somatic motor neurons stimulate voluntary muscles, such as those in the arms, legs, and neck; the cell bodies of these neurons are located inside the central nervous system, in either the brain or the spinal cord. The autonomic motor neurons innervate glands, heart muscle, and smooth muscles not under conscious control, such as the muscles that surround the intestine and other organs of the gastrointestinal tract. The two classes of autonomic motor neurons, sympathetic and parasympathetic, generally have opposite effects: one class stimulates a muscle or gland, and the other inhibits it. Somatic sensory neurons, which convey information to the central nervous system, have their cell bodies clustered in ganglia, masses of nerve tissue that lie just outside the spinal cord. The cell bodies of the motor neurons of the autonomic nervous system also lie in ganglia. Each peripheral nerve is actually a bundle of axons; some are parts of motor neurons; others are parts of sensory neurons.

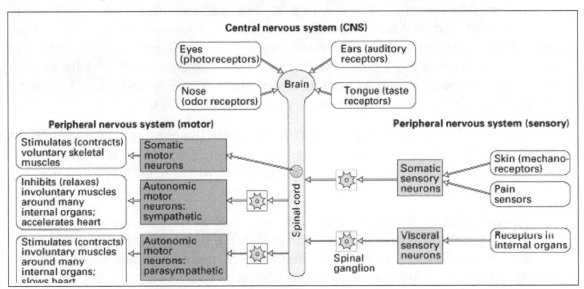

A highly schematic diagram of the vertebrate nervous system.

The central nervous system (CNS) comprises the brain and spinal cord. It receives direct sensory input from the eyes, nose, tongue, and ears. The peripheral nervous system (PNS) comprises three sets of neurons: (1) somatic and visceral sensory neurons, which relay information to the CNS from receptors in somatic and internal organs; (2) somatic motor neurons, which innervate voluntary skeletal muscles; and (3) autonomic motor neurons, which innervate the heart, the smooth involuntary muscles such as those surrounding the stomach and intestine, and glands such as the liver and pancreas. The sympathetic and parasympathetic autonomic motor neurons frequently cause opposite effects on internal organs. The cell bodies of somatic motor neurons are within the CNS; those of somatic sensory neurons and of autonomic motor neurons are in ganglia adjacent to the CNS. Having surveyed the general features of neuron structure, interactions, and simple circuits, let us turn to the mechanism by which a neuron generates and conducts electric impulses.

Types of Neurons

There are different types of neurons; the functional role of a given neuron is intimately dependent on its structure. There is an amazing diversity of neuron shapes and sizes found in different parts of the nervous system (and across species):

- Sensory neurons: Sensory neurons are the nerve cells that are activated by sensory input from the environment - for example, when you touch a hot surface with your fingertips, the sensory neurons will be the ones firing and sending off signals to the rest of the nervous system about the information they have received.

  The inputs that activate sensory neurons can be physical or chemical, corresponding to all five of our senses. Thus, a physical input can be things like sound, touch, heat, or light. A chemical input comes from taste or smell, which neurons then send to the brain. Most sensory neurons are pseudo unipolar, which means they only have one axon which is split into two branches.

- Motor neurons: Motor neurons of the spinal cord are part of the central nervous system (CNS) and connect to muscles, glands and organs throughout the body. These neurons transmit impulses from the spinal cord to skeletal and smooth muscles (such as those in your stomach), and so directly control all of our muscle movements. There are in fact two types of motor neurons: those that travel from spinal cord to muscle are called lower motor neurons, whereas those that travel between the brain and spinal cord are called upper motor neurons. Motor neurons have the most common type of 'body plan' for a nerve cell - they are multipolar, each with one axon and several dendrites.

- Interneurons: As the name suggests, interneurons are the ones in between - they connect spinal motor and sensory neurons. As well as transferring signals between sensory and motor neurons, interneurons can also communicate with each other, forming circuits of various complexities. They are multipolar, just like motor neurons.

- Neurons in the brain: In the brain, the distinction between types of neurons is much more complex. Whereas in the spinal cord we could easily distinguish neurons based on their function, that isn't the case in the brain. Certainly, there are brain neurons involved in sensory processing – like those in visual or auditory cortex – and others involved in motor processing – like those in the cerebellum or motor cortex. However, within any of these sensory or motor regions, there are tens or even hundreds of different types of neurons. In fact, researchers are still trying to devise a way to neatly classify the huge variety of neurons that exist in the brain.

Holonomic Brain Theory

The Holonomic Brain Theory describes a type of process that occurs in fine fibered neural webs. The process is composed of patches of local field potentials described mathematically as windowed Fourier transforms or wavelets. The Fourier approach to sensory perception is the basis for the holonomic theory of brain function. Holonomy, as its name implies, is related to the unconstrained Fourier co-ordinate system described by holography. The Fourier transformation changes a space-time coordinate system into a spectral coordinate system within which the properties of our ordinary images are spread throughout the system. Fourier transformations are routinely performed on electrical recordings from the brain such as EEG and local field potentials.

The term "holonomy" to describe a constrained, windowed, Fourier process, was borrowed from Hertz who used it to express in more generally applicable co-ordinates a specific co-ordinate system. Holonomic processes have more recently been called "Quantum Holography" by Walter Schempp in their application to image processing in tomography as in PET scans and functional Magnetic Resonance (fMRI) and even more recently for processing images in digital cameras. Dennis Gabor had pioneered the use of windowed Fourier processes for use in communication theory and noted its similarity to its use in describing quantum processes in subatomic physics. Gabor therefore called his units of communication "quanta of information". Karl Pribram's holonomic theory is based on evidence that the dendritic receptive fields in sensory cortexes are described mathematically by Gabor functions.

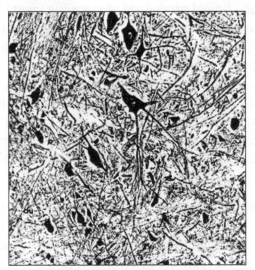

Taking the visual system as an example, the form of an optical image is transformed by the retina into a quantum process that is transmitted to the visual cortex. Each dendritic receptive field thus represents the "spread" of the properties of that form originating from the entire retina. Taken together, cortical receptive fields form patches of dendritic local field potentials described mathematically by Gabor functions. Note that the spread of properties occurs within each patch; there is no spread of the Fourier process over the large extent of the entire cortex. In order to serve the perceptual process the patches must become assembled by the operation of nerve impulses in axonal circuits. Processing the vibratory sensory inputs in audition and in tactile sensation proceeds somewhat similarly.

But Gabor and similar wavelet functions, though useful in communication and computations, fail to serve as the properties of images and objects that guide us in the space-time world we navigate. In order to attain such properties an inverse Fourier transformation has to occur. Fortunately the Fourier process is readily invertible; the same transformation that begets the holographic domain gets us back into space-time. The inverse Fourier transformation is accomplished by movement. In vision, nystagmoid movements define pixels, points which are mathematically defined by "Point Attractors". Larger eye and head movements define groupings of points which can readily be recognized as moving space-time figures. Such groupings are mathematically defined as "Symmetry Groups". The brain processes involved are organized by a motor cortex immediately adjacent to the primary visual cortex. Similar motor strips are located adjacent to other sensory input systems.

Roots of the Holonomic Theory

The holonomic theory of brain function has two roots:

- The experimental evidence accrued during the 1960s and 1970s that mapped certain brain processes as local field potentials as well as bursts of electrical discharges traversing circuits.

- The mathematical insights of dennis gabor in the 1940s as realized in optical imaging by emmett leith in the early 1960s.

The experimental mapping procedure originated with Stephen Kuffler. Kuffler, working with the visual system took the common clinical procedure of mapping visual fields into the microelectrode laboratory. A visual field is described as the part of the environment that a person can see with one eye without moving that eye. Maps of this field are routinely recorded by means of the verbal response of the person to a spot of light on an appropriate medium such as graph paper. For the verbal response of the human, Kuffler substituted the response of a single neuron recorded from a microelectrode implanted in the visual system of an animal. Because the record was made from the domain of a single neuron rather than the whole visual system, the map portrayed what was going on in the dendritic arbor of that neuron. The map was no longer a map of what was "seen" by the whole visual system but only that part, the receptive dendritic field, "viewed" by the particular neuron.

The dendritic arbor is made up of fibers for the most part too fine to support propagated action potentials, spikes. Rather the local field potential changes oscillate between moderate excitation (postsynaptic depolarization) and inhibition (post-synaptic hyper-polarization). The maps therefore represent a distribution of oscillations of electrical potentials within a particular dendritic arbor.

Hubel and Wiesel, working in Kufler's laboratory discovered that the visual cortex responded more effectively to an elongated line or bar presented at a specific orientation rather than to a spot of light. However, a decade later many laboratories especially those of Fergus Campbell at The University of Cambridge, England; and Russel and Karen DeValois at The University of California at Berkeley found that oriented gratings composed of lines at different spacing, rather than single lines were the effective stimulus to engage a neuron in the visual cortex. These gratings were characterized by their spatial frequency: scanning the grating produces an alternation between light and dark, the frequency of alternation depending on the spacing of the grating. An example in the somatosensory cortex of three receptive fields and their contour maps produced by a tactile grating is presented in Figure.

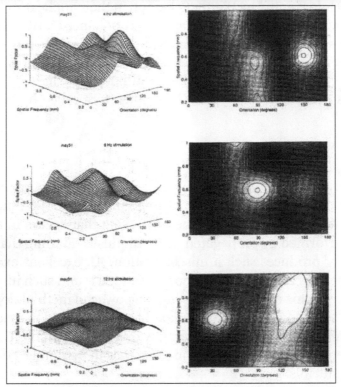

An example of the three dimensional representation of the surface distribution and associated contour map of the electrical response to buccal nerve stimulation.

Theories of visual perception built on the finding of oriented lines gave rise to what may be called a two dimensional "stick figure" view of how we come to perceive images of objects based on Euclidian Geometry. Theories of perception based on frequencies gave rise to a transformational view of the processing of visual signals.

Mathematically, this transformational view is based on the Fourier theorem. This theorem states that any space-time pattern can be transformed into a spectrum based on waveforms that encode amplitudes, frequencies and the relationships among their phases. Usefully, we can invert the process to regain the space-time pattern from the spectrum.

A fast Fourier procedure (FFT) is commonly used in statistics to make correlations. The Fourier procedure is also routinely found useful in electroencephalography (EEG) to distinguish individual frequencies and frequency bands among the recorded electrical waveforms. Russ and Karen De-Valois in their 1998 book "Spatial Vision" expressed what Fergus Campbell at Cambridge University, Vadim Glezer at the Pavlov Institute at Leningrad and many others of us were experiencing: "Linear systems analysis originated in a striking mathematical discovery by a French physicist, Baron Jean Fourier, in 1822 which has found a wide application in physics and engineering for a century and a half. It has also served as a principle basis for understanding hearing ever since its application by Ohm and Helmholtz. The successful application of these procedures to the study of visual processes has come only in the last two decades.

The Fourier approach to sensory perception is the basis for the holonomic theory of brain function. The term "holonomy" was borrowed from Hertz who used it to express in more generally applicable co-ordinates a specified co-ordinate system. Holonomic processes have more recently been called "Quantum Holography" by Walter Schempp in their application to image processing in tomography as in PET scans and functional Magnetic Resonance (fMRI). Holonomy, as its name implies, is related to the less constrained co-ordinate system described by holography. Quantum holography, holonomy, uses windowed Fourier transformations, often called "wavelets". Gabor had pioneered this use in communication theory and noted its similarity to its use in describing quantum processes in subatomic physics. Gabor therefore called his units of communication "quanta of information".

Misconceptions

There are four common misconceptions about the application of holographic and holonomic theories – that is, holonomic procedures -- to brain function. The first and most important of these is that, contrary to what is shown in Figure, the processing that occurs in the dendritic arbor, in the receptive field, is performed by propagated nerve impulses. Finding that impulses do occur in certain dendrites readily produces such a misconception. An excellent example appears in Eric Kandell's 2006 biographical "In Search of Memory." Kandell found such impulses in the dendrites of the hippocampus early in his career: By applying the powerful methodologies of cell biology, Alden and I easily picked some low hanging intellectual fruit. We found that action potentials [nerve impulses] in the pyramidal cells of the hippocampus originated at more than one site within the cell. We had good evidence to suggest that action potentials in pyramidal cells of the hippocampus can also begin in the dendrites.

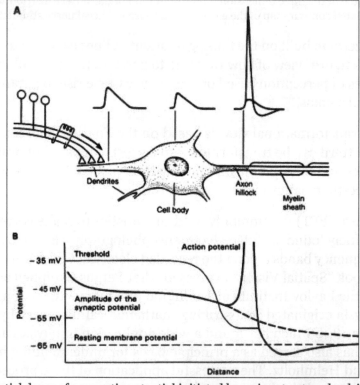

Satial decay of a synaptic potential initiated by an input onto a dendrite.

This proved to be an important discovery. Up to that time most scientists including Dominick Purpura and Harry Grundfest, thought that dendrites could not be excited and therefore could not generate action potentials. Willifred Rall, a major theorist and model builder at NIH, had developed a mathematical model showing how dendrites of motor neurons function. This model was based on the fundamental assumption that the cell membrane of dendrites is passive: it does not contain voltage-gated sodium channels and therefore cannot support an action potential. The intracellular signals we recorded were the first evidence to the contrary, and our finding later proved to be a general principle of neuronal function.

The problem that Kandell's finding poses can be called "The tyranny of names". Those of us who have been concerned with processes occurring in fine-fibered webs have been too prone to focus on dendrites per se. Kandell's finding has been repeatedly confirmed as has his conclusion which has been restated in his (as well as other) otherwise excellent neuroscience texts. Dendrites, defined as afferents to neural cell bodies, come in all sizes. The biggest of them all are the afferent peripheral nerves entering the spinal cord. Such large fibers readily support the propagation of nerve impulses. Large diameter fibers occur both as afferent (dendritic) and efferent (axonal) fibers in neural circuits.The hippocampal dendrites, though not as large as peripheral nerves, have sizable diameters. The very fact that Kandell and others can make intracellular recordings from these hippocampal dendrites attests to their considerable size. The webs wherein holonomic processes occur (in the hippocampus and elsewhere) are made up of pre- and postsynaptic slim branches of larger fibers. Fine fibered webs occur in the brain, both at the ends of branching axons and within dendritic arbors. The holonomic brain theory is founded in the processing that occurs in fine fiber webs wherever they occur.

The tyranny of names was called to attention when, in the early 1950s it is found that responses in the precentral motor cortex of the brain evoked by sciatic stimulation. It took much subsequent research and weeks of phone conversations and visits by neuroscience friends Clint Woolsey and Wade Marshall to witness demonstrations in laboratory to convince them that the precentral cortex is actually a sensory cortex for intentional action, not just an efferent path to muscles from the brain.

Contrast Kandell's statement with another, made repeatedly over the decades by Ted Bullock: "In 1957 it was possible to say 'These considerations also lead us to the suggestion that much of normal nervous function occurs without impulses [emphasis in the original] but mediated by graded activity, not only as response but also as stimulus'. The far-reaching implications of the assumption that neurons can affect each other by means distinct from classical impulses in synaptic pathways are obvious'. I referred to Bremer and Gerard who influenced me most in this view, which remained for a long time ignored in the conventional orthodoxy. [Currently therefore,] I propose that a 'circuit' in our context of nervous tissue is an oversimplified abstraction involving a limited subset of communicated signals That, in fact, there are many parallel types of signals and forms of response, often skipping over neighbors [that are] indirect contact and acting upon more or less specified classes of nearby or even remote elements. Thus the true picture of what is going on could not be drawn as a familiar circuit; and specified influence would not be properly called connectivity, except for a very limited subset of neighbors. Instead of the usual terms 'neural net' or 'local circuit' I would suggest we think of a 'neural throng', that is a form of densely packed social gathering with more structure and goals than a mob."

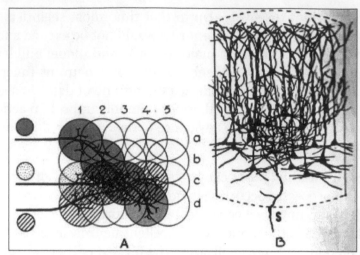

Diagram of microstructure of synaptic domains in cortex. The ensemble of overlapping circles represents the junctions between branches of input axons and cortical dendrites.

Hopefully, things are changing in the current century. Or take author's statements in 1991 "Brain and Perception." Pribram describes one example of properties of the manner in which some cortical dendrites interact: Receptive fields in the sensory cortex are composed of polarizations occurring in dendritic arbors of cortical neurons. According to the holonomic brain theory these polarizations collectively interact to produce the receptive field properties mapped during single neuron recording. The recording electrode, that is, the relevant the axon, samples that interaction. Dendrites are fitted with spines that resemble little cilia, or hairs, protruding perpendicularly from the dendritic fiber. These spines have bulbs at their endings, knob-like heads that make contact with branches of axons and other dendrites to form synapses. Activity in axons and in other dendrites such as those stemming from reciprocal synapses produce depolarizations and hyperpolarizations in the dendritic spines.

Shepherd, Rall, Perkel and their colleagues modeled the process whereby these postsynaptic events occurring in the spine heads interact. The issue is this: The stalks of the spines are narrow and therefore impose a high resistance to conduction (active or passive) toward the dendritic branch. Spine head depolarizations (as well as hyperpolarizations) must therefore interact with one another if they are to influence the action potentials generated at the axon hillock of the parent cell of the dendrite. The interactions (dromic and antidromic) among dendritic potentials (by means of which the signal becomes effective at the next stage of processing) thus depend on the simultaneous activation of both pre and postsynaptic sites.

According to Shepherd: "The relative efficacy of distal dendritic inputs would [in this manner] be greatly enhanced information might thus be processed through precise timing of specific inputs to different neighboring spines. These precise interactions would greatly increase the complexity of information processing that can take place in distal dendrites".

Holonomy is Patch Holography

Another common misconception is that the Fourier transformation is globally spread across the entire brain cortex. This has led to misleading statements such as "The brain is a hologram." Only one particular brain process is holonomic, the one taking place in the transactions occurring in its fine fibered web. From the outset in the early 1960s when Pribram proposed the theory, he noted that the spread function (as it is appropriately called) is limited to a receptive field of an individual neuron in a cortical sensory system — and he actually thought that this was a serious problem for the theory until it was shown by radio-astronomers that such limited regions could be patched together to encompass large regions of observations.

Despite these precise early descriptions, psychophysicists and others in the scientific community spent much time and effort to show that a global Fourier transformation would not work to explain sensory function. Few paid heed to patch holography -- which Pribram had dubbed holonomy and which engineers and mathematicians call a "windowed Fourier Transformation".

Interference Patterns

The third common misconception regarding holography and holonomy is that these processes deal with waves. Waves occur in space and in time. The Fourier transformation deals with the intersections among waves, their interference patterns created by differences among their phases. The amplitudes of these intersections are Fourier coefficients, discrete numbers that are used for computation. These numbers are useful in statistical calculations. The statistical and the spectral computations are readily convertible into one another: successive terms in the Fourier series correspond to "orders" in statistics and thus can serve as vectors in graphs. [For instance it takes 4th order statistics to adequately analyze the waveforms of an EEG by Independent Component Analysis (ICA)]. Convertibility raises the question of the value of having multiple mathematical representations of data. The spectral representation displays a more nuanced ("Anschaulichkeit" in German) representation while the statistical/vector representation is more computationally friendly.

Deep and Surface Structures of Memory

A final common misconception that needs to be dealt with is that all memory storage is holonomic (holographic). This misconception stems from juxtaposing memory storage to memory retrieval. However, in order for retrieval to occur, the memory must be stored in such a way that it can become retrieved. In other words, retrieval is dependent on storing a code. The retrieval process, the encoding, is stored in the brain's circuitry. We can, therefore, distinguish a deep holonomic store (which can be content addressable) from a surface pattern (such as naming) of stored circuitry. Thus the deep dis-membered holonomic store can be re-membered.

Neural Circuit

Neurons never function in isolation; they are organized into ensembles or circuits that process specific kinds of information. Although the arrangement of neural circuits varies greatly according to the intended function, some features are characteristic of all such ensembles. The synaptic connections that define a circuit are typically made in a dense tangle of dendrites, axons terminals, and glial cell processes that together constitute neuropil. Thus, the neuropil between nerve cell bodies is the region where most synaptic connectivity occurs. The direction of information flow in any particular circuit is essential to understanding its function. Nerve cells that carry information toward the central nervous system (or farther centrally within the spinal cord and brain) are called afferent neurons; nerve cells that carry information away from the brain or spinal cord (or away from the circuit in question) are called efferent neurons. Nerve cells that only participate in the local aspects of a circuit are called interneurons or local circuit neurons. These three classes—afferent neurons, efferent neurons, and interneurons—are the basic constituents of all neural circuits.

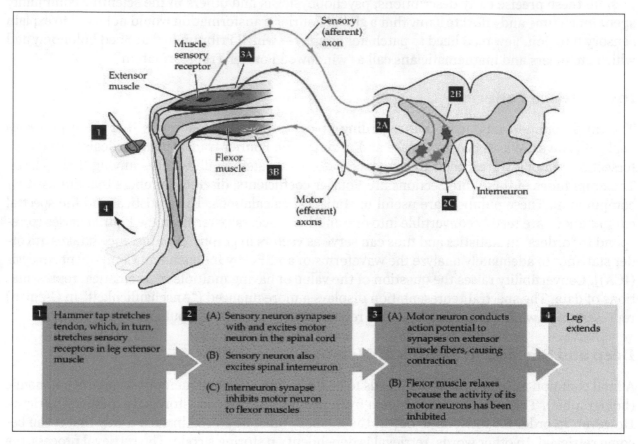

| 1 | Hammer tap stretches tendon, which, in turn, stretches sensory receptors in leg extensor muscle | 2 | (A) Sensory neuron synapses with and excites motor neuron in the spinal cord

(B) Sensory neuron also excites spinal interneuron

(C) Interneuron synapse inhibits motor neuron to flexor muscles | 3 | (A) Motor neuron conducts action potential to synapses on extensor muscle fibers, causing contraction

(B) Flexor muscle relaxes because the activity of its motor neurons has been inhibited | 4 | Leg extends |

A simple reflex circuit, the knee-jerk response (more formally, the myotatic reflex), illustrates several points about the functional organization of neural circuits. Stimulation of peripheral sensors (a muscle stretch receptor in this case) initiates receptor potentials that trigger action potentials that travel centrally along the afferent axons of the sensory neurons. This information stimulates spinal motor neurons by means of synaptic contacts. The action potentials triggered by the synaptic potential in motor neurons travel peripherally in efferent axons, giving rise to muscle contraction and a behavioral response. One of the purposes of this particular reflex is to help maintain an upright posture in the face of unexpected changes.

Neural circuits are both anatomical and functional entities. A simple example is the circuit that subserves the myotatic (or "knee-jerk") spinal reflex. The afferent limb of the reflex is sensory neurons of the dorsal root ganglion in the periphery. These afferents target neurons in the spinal cord. The efferent limb comprises motor neurons in the ventral horn of the spinal cord with different peripheral targets: One efferent group projects to flexor muscles in the limb, and the other to extensor muscles. The third element of this circuit is interneurons in the ventral horn of the spinal cord. The interneurons receive synaptic contacts from the sensory afferent neurons and make synapses on the efferent motor neurons that project to the flexor muscles. The synaptic connections between the sensory afferents and the extensor efferent are excitatory, causing the extensor muscles to contract; conversely, the interneurons activated by the afferents are inhibitory, and their activation by the afferents diminishes electrical activity in motor neurons and causes the flexor muscles to become less active. The result is a complementary activation and inactivation of the synergist and antagonist muscles that control the position of the leg.

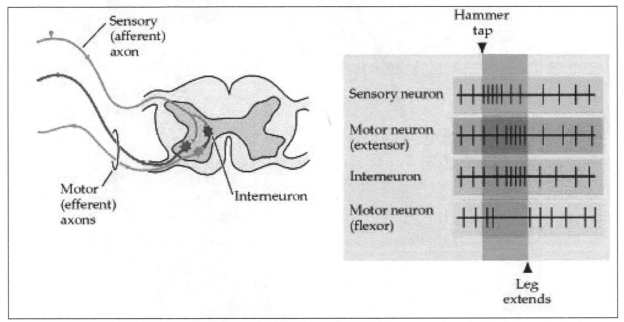

Relative frequency of action potentials in different components
of the myotatic reflex as the reflex pathway is activated.

A more detailed picture of the events underlying the myotatic or any other circuit can be obtained by electrophysiological recording. There are two basic approaches to measuring electrical activity: extracellular recording where an electrode is placed near the nerve cell of interest to detect activity, and intracellular recording where the electrode is placed inside the cell. Such recordings detect two basic types of signals. Extracellular recordings primarily detect action potentials, the all-or-nothing changes in the potential across nerve cell membranes that convey information from one point to another in the nervous system.

Intracellular recordings can detect the smaller graded potential changes that serve to trigger action potentials. These graded triggering potentials can arise at either sensory receptors or synapses and are called receptor potentials or synaptic potentials, respectively. For the myotatic circuit, action potential activity can be measured from each element (afferents, efferent, and interneurons) before, during, and after a stimulus. By comparing the onset, duration, and frequency of action potential activity in each cell, a functional picture of the circuit emerges. As a result of the stimulus, the sensory neuron is triggered to fire at higher frequency (i.e., more action potentials per unit time). This increase triggers in turn a higher frequency of action potentials in both the extensor motor neurons and the interneurons. Concurrently, the inhibitory synapses made by the interneurons onto the flexor motor neurons cause the frequency of action potentials in these cells to decline. Using intracellular recording, it is possible to observe directly the potential changes underlying the synaptic connections of the myotatic reflex circuit.

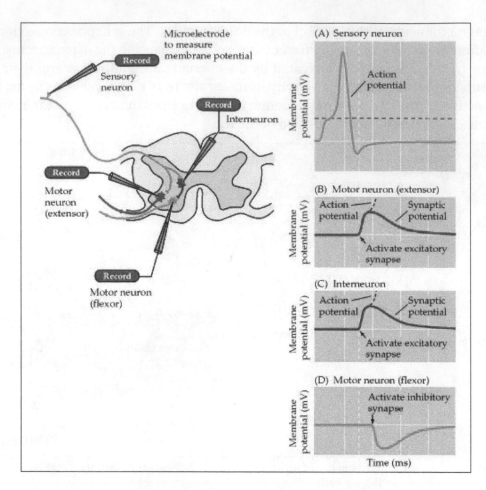

Figure shows intracellularly recorded responses underlying the myotatic reflex: (A) Action potential measured in a sensory neuron. (B) Postsynaptic triggering potential recorded in an extensor motor neuron. (C) Postsynaptic triggering potential in an interneuron. (D) Postsynaptic inhibitory potential in a flexor motor neuron. Such intracellular recordings are the basis for understanding the cellular mechanisms of action potential generation, and the sensory receptor and synaptic potentials that trigger these conducted signals.

Neural Networks

Neural networks, also known as artificial neural networks (ANNs) or simulated neural networks (SNNs) are a subset of machine learning and are at the heart of deep learning algorithms. Their name and structure are inspired by the human brain, mimicking the way that biological neurons signal to one another.

Artificial neural networks (ANNs) are comprised of a node layers, containing an input layer, one or more hidden layers, and an output layer. Each node, or artificial neuron, connects to another and has an associated weight and threshold. If the output of any individual node is above the specified threshold value, that node is activated, sending data to the next layer of the network. Otherwise, no data is passed along to the next layer of the network.

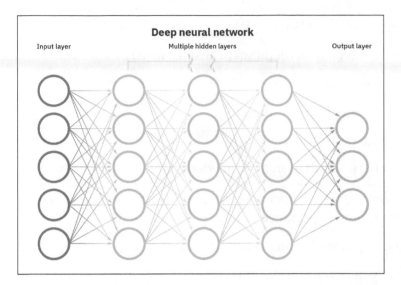

Neural networks rely on training data to learn and improve their accuracy over time. However, once these learning algorithms are fine-tuned for accuracy, they are powerful tools in computer science and artificial intelligence, allowing us to classify and cluster data at a high velocity. Tasks in speech recognition or image recognition can take minutes versus hours when compared to the manual identification by human experts. One of the most well-known neural networks is Google's search algorithm.

Working of Neural Networks

Think of each individual node as its own linear regression model, composed of input data, weights, a bias (or threshold), and an output. The formula would look something like this:

$$\sum_{i=1}^{m} w_i x_i + \text{bias} = w_1 x_1 + w_2 x_2 + w_3 x_3 + \text{bias}$$

$$\text{Output} = f(x) = \begin{cases} 1 \text{ if } \sum w_i x_i + b \geq 0 \\ 0 \text{ if } \sum w_i x_i + b < 0 \end{cases}$$

Once an input layer is determined, weights are assigned. These weights help determine the importance of any given variable, with larger ones contributing more significantly to the output compared to other inputs. All inputs are then multiplied by their respective weights and then summed. Afterward, the output is passed through an activation function, which determines the output. If that output exceeds a given threshold, it "fires" (or activates) the node, passing data to the next layer in the network. This results in the output of one node becoming in the input of the next node. This process of passing data from one layer to the next layer defines this neural network as a feed forward network.

Let's break down what one single node might look like using binary values. We can apply this concept to a more tangible example, like whether you should go surfing (Yes: 1, No: 0). The decision to go or not to go is our predicted outcome, or y-hat. Let's assume that there are three factors influencing your decision-making:

- Are the waves good? (Yes: 1, No: 0).

- Is the line-up empty? (Yes: 1, No: 0).

- Has there been a recent shark attack? (Yes: 0, No: 1).

Then, let's assume the following, giving us the following inputs:

- $X1$ = 1, since the waves are pumping.

- $X2$ = 0, since the crowds are out.

- $X3$ = 1, since there hasn't been a recent shark attack.

Now, we need to assign some weights to determine importance. Larger weights signify that particular variables are of greater importance to the decision or outcome.

- $W1$ = 5, since large swells don't come around often.

- $W2$ = 2, since you're used to the crowds.

- $W3$ = 4, since you have a fear of sharks.

Finally, we'll also assume a threshold value of 3, which would translate to a bias value of −3. With all the various inputs, we can start to plug in values into the formula to get the desired output.

$$Y\text{-hat} = (1*5) + (0*2) + (1*4) - 3 = 6$$

If we use the activation function from the beginning of this section, we can determine that the output of this node would be 1, since 6 is greater than 0. In this instance, you would go surfing; but if we adjust the weights or the threshold, we can achieve different outcomes from the model. When we observe one decision, like in the above example, we can see how a neural network could make increasingly complex decisions depending on the output of previous decisions or layers.

In the example above, we used perceptron's to illustrate some of the mathematics at play here, but neural networks leverage sigmoid neurons, which are distinguished by having values between 0 and 1. Since neural networks behave similarly to decision trees, cascading data from one node to another, having x values between 0 and 1 will reduce the impact of any given change of a single variable on the output of any given node, and subsequently, the output of the neural network.

As we start to think about more practical use cases for neural networks, like image recognition or classification, we'll leverage supervised learning, or labeled datasets, to train the algorithm. As we train the model, we'll want to evaluate its accuracy using a cost (or loss) function. This is also commonly referred to as the mean squared error (MSE). In the equation below:

- i represents the index of the sample,

- y-hat is the predicted outcome,

- y is the actual value,

- m is the number of samples.

$$\text{Cost Function} = \text{MSE} = \frac{1}{2m}\sum_{i=1}^{m}\left(\hat{y}-y\right)^2$$

Ultimately, the goal is to minimize our cost function to ensure correctness of fit for any given observation. As the model adjusts its weights and bias, it uses the cost function and reinforcement learning to reach the point of convergence, or the local minimum. The process in which the algorithm adjusts its weights is through gradient descent, allowing the model to determine the direction to take to reduce errors (or minimize the cost function). With each training example, the parameters of the model adjust to gradually converge at the minimum.

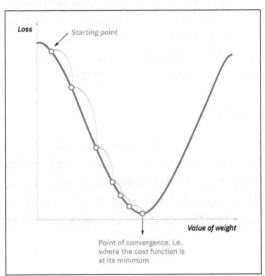

Most deep neural networks are feedforward, meaning they flow in one direction only, from input to output. However, you can also train your model through backpropagation; that is, move in the opposite direction from output to input. Backpropagation allows us to calculate and attribute the error associated with each neuron, allowing us to adjust and fit the parameters of the model(s) appropriately.

Types of Neural Networks

Neural networks can be classified into different types, which are used for different purposes. While this isn't a comprehensive list of types, the below would be representative of the most common types of neural networks that you'll come across for its common use cases: The perceptron is the oldest neural network, created by Frank Rosenblatt in 1958. It has a single neuron and is the simplest form of a neural network.

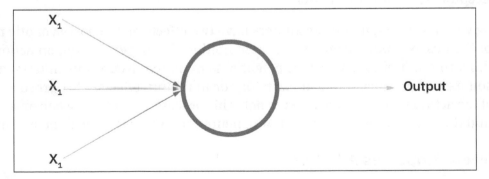

Feedforward neural networks, or multi-layer perceptrons (MLPs), are what we've primarily been focusing. They are comprised of an input layer, a hidden layer or layers, and an output layer. While these neural networks are also commonly referred to as MLPs, it's important to note that they are actually comprised of sigmoid neurons, not perceptrons, as most real-world problems are nonlinear. Data usually is fed into these models to train them, and they are the foundation for computer vision, natural language processing, and other neural networks.

Convolutional neural networks (CNNs) are similar to feedforward networks, but they're usually utilized for image recognition, pattern recognition, and/or computer vision. These networks harness principles from linear algebra, particularly matrix multiplication, to identify patterns within an image. Recurrent neural networks (RNNs) are identified by their feedback loops. These learning algorithms are primarily leveraged when using time-series data to make predictions about future outcomes, such as stock market predictions or sales forecasting.

Neural Networks vs. Deep Learning

Deep Learning and neural networks tend to be used interchangeably in conversation, which can be confusing. As a result, it's worth noting that the "deep" in deep learning is just referring to the depth of layers in a neural network. A neural network that consists of more than three layers—which would be inclusive of the inputs and the output—can be considered a deep learning algorithm. A neural network that only has two or three layers is just a basic neural network.

Neurotransmission

Neurotransmission is the process by which neurons communicate with one another across synapses using neurotransmitters. Also known as synaptic transmission. From the neuron, the neurotransmitter is released (particularly from its axon) and interacts with the dendrites of another neuron. They are produced in the ribosomes of the presynaptic neuron. They are stored in vesicles. These vesicles' location is cytoplasm of a neuron. When an action potential arrives at the pre-synaptic terminal, there is the entry of the calcium ions in pre-synaptic neurons.

Now, after calcium ions entry into the cell, synaptic vesicles merges with pre-synaptic membrane and neurotransmitter is released into the synaptic cleft. When neurotransmitter arrives at the cell membrane of a post-synaptic neuron, certain protein molecules are activated. These protein molecules are receptors for neurotransmitters.

After binding with receptors, neurotransmitters have two effects on the post-synaptic membrane. Excitation of the postsynaptic membrane or its inhibition. During excitation, an action potential is generated. During inhibition, an action potential is inhibited. Neurotransmitters are released in small amounts and produce minimal excitatory or inhibitory effects. This process takes place regardless of the action potential generated or not. This process is amplified when an action potential arrives and the required message is sent from neuron to its target through neurotransmission.

How Different Impulses Add up?

Neurons are connected with multiple other neurons. They receive impulses from them. These impulses can sum up together to cause the desired effects. This is called summation.

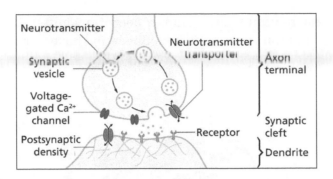

Types of Summation

There are two ways by which summation occurs:

- Spatial summation: It happens when multiple action potentials arrive at the presynaptic terminal and cause the release of the amount of neurotransmitter enough to exceed the trigger point of the postsynaptic neuron.

- Temporal summation occurs when multiple action potentials are generated in a short period to reach the desired threshold of the postsynaptic neuron.

Convergence and Divergence

Both convergence and divergence are important aspects of neurotransmission. By taking input from multiple neurons, neurons converge the information. By sending signals to different neurons, they diverge information.

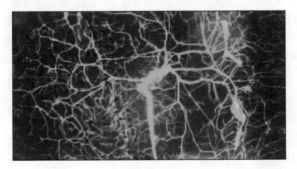

Co-Transmission

Sometimes many neurotransmitters are released from a single neuron (presynaptic terminal). This phenomenon is called co-transmission. For example, Glycine and GABA are released together. The same is true for dopamine and glutamate.

Types

There are two types of neurotransmission:

- Chemical transmission,

- Electrical transmission.

The main component of the neurotransmission is a neurotransmitter. There are several types of neurotransmitters. Most common those are in abundance and have a great impact on the body are Acetylcholine, Dopamine, Norepinephrine, Serotonin, GABA, endorphins, glycine, and glutamate.

Acetylcholine

Acetylcholine is the most abundant neurotransmitter in the brain. It is responsible for producing the effects of the parasympathetic nervous system. Acetylcholine causes contraction of muscles. It causes activates of receptors for pain. Acetylcholine is involved in the normal functioning of many glands. It controls many stages of sleep especially the REM sleep stage. Acetylcholine acts as a vasodilator. It increases sweating, lacrimation, and all body secretions. It can be a culprit for causing a decrease in heart rate.

Norepinephrine

Norepinephrine is an important neurotransmitter. Now why you remain attentive has something to do with norepinephrine levels. Our emotional IQ is dependent on nor-epinephrine levels. It regulates sleeping, dreaming, and learning. The neurotransmitter nor-epinephrine along with epinephrine is involved in fight or flight response. Norepinephrine causes an increase in blood pressure. Similarly, heart rate and blood glucose levels are affected by it.

Dopamine

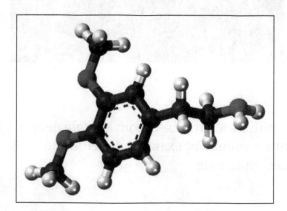

Dopamine is an important neurotransmitter. It is the neurotransmitter of the reward center. It has a role in administrative functions. It has control over movements of that body that are involved in muscle coordination, arousal, positive and negative reinforcement, motivation and reward. It is involved in lactation and sexual gratification.

GABA

GABA is the most important inhibitory neurotransmitter because it inhibits the transmission of nerve impulses which reduces activity in our brain. Alcohol euphoric effects depend on its interaction with GABA receptors. Lack of GABA neurotransmitters results in loss of inhibition. Loss of inhibition causes hyperactivity in the nervous system leading to seizures and mood disorders. Raised levels of GABA can lead to sleepiness. These inhibitory effects of GABA are significant as this effect can be utilized in treating diseases that are caused by hyperactivity of neurons like epilepsy and Huntington's disease. They help to relieve pain, give a feeling of relaxation and fight with stress.

Serotonin

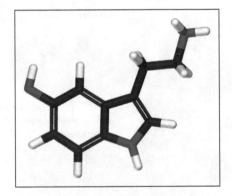

A hormone that keeps you high and happy is Serotonin. So, one need to take good cares of his/her serotonin levels. Your quality of sleep, your sexual drive and memory depend on circulating levels of serotonin. Serotonin has a defense mechanism in our digestive system. In response to toxins or irritants intake, it increases gut motility and protects the body. A blood clot is formed after injury due to vasoconstriction that is mediated by serotonin.

Glutamate

Glutamate is an excitatory neurotransmitter that is present in abundance in vertebrate nervous system. It regulates learning and memory. It plays a role in GABA neurotransmitter production.

It helps in the development of the brain. The brain appears to need glutamate to form memories. Glutamate provides energy to the muscle during strenuous exercise. A study reveals that this neurotransmitter further delays dystrophy of muscles in animals that lack vitamin D. The presence of Glutamate receptors on macrophages, T cells and B cells suggests their role in innate immunity.

Impairment in Neurotransmission

Our whole-body control depends upon neurotransmission. So any impairment in neurotransmission results in diseases that affect our body.

Diseases due to Dysfunction in Neurotransmission

Myasthenia gravis is a disease that affects muscle functioning. It is caused by decreased levels of the neurotransmitter acetylcholine. In this disease, antibodies have formed that damage the receptor for acetylcholine at the neuromuscular junction. The patient presents with drooping of eyelids and difficulty in performing daily activities like walking, talking, etc. Nerve conduction study is diagnostic for this disease.

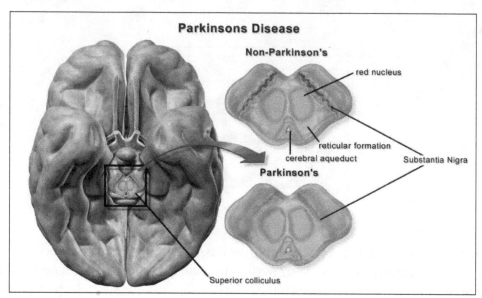

Parkinson's disease is caused by low levels of the neurotransmitter dopamine in the brain. In this disease, there is a loss of neurons in basal ganglia that are producing dopamine. The patient presented to us with tremors (hallmark of this disease) bradykinesia, stooped posture and masked faces. This disease is diagnosed on clinical examination. Generalized anxiety disorder, stress, and depression are caused by low levels of serotonin. They are diagnosed with a medical history and in severe cases when leading to suicidal tendencies. In Alzheimer's disease, there is a loss of memory and the patient can't take care of himself. In this disease, there are low levels of acetylcholine in the brain.

Significance of Neurotransmission Impairment in Pharmacology

Our medicine industry is dependent on knowledge of neurotransmission to treat treating various diseases. They manage concentrations of certain neurotransmitters by either increasing or decreasing them, thus treating certain diseases. For example, Myasthenia gravis is treated by acetylcholinesterase inhibitors which increase the level of acetylcholine. They do so by inhibiting the degradation of ace-tylcholine by the enzyme acetylcholinesterase. Neostigmine is an example of such a drug.

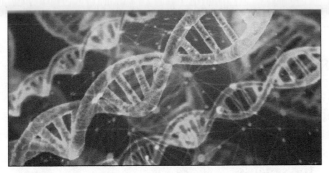

Figure shows another one, Parkinson's disease is treated by Levodopa which is given along with carbidopa to increase dopamine availability to the brain. This combination improved a lot of symp-toms. Similarly, Selective serotonin reuptake inhibitors increase the concentration of neurotrans-mitter serotonin thus helping in the treatment of generalized anxiety disorder and depression. Epilepsy treatment is based on reducing the hyperactivity of the brain by giving medication that interacts with GABA receptors. Beta-blockers work by controlling the concentration of nor-epi-nephrine. They are used in the treatment of migraine, heart diseases, and glaucoma.

The Bottom Line

When we want to understand the diverse world of our body which is controlled by our brain, we need to know about neurotransmission. Due to neurotransmission, billions of neurons are con-nected chemically.

Neurotransmitter

Neurotransmitter, also called chemical transmitter or chemical messenger is any of a group of chem-ical agents released by neurons (nerve cells) to stimulate neighbouring neurons or muscle or gland cells, thus allowing impulses to be passed from one cell to the next throughout the nervous system.

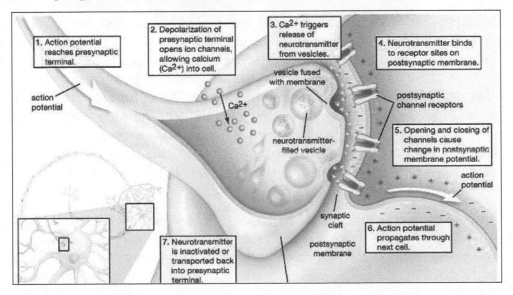

Synapse neuron: Chemical transmission of a nerve impulse at the synapse. The arrival of the nerve impulse at the presynaptic terminal stimulates the release of neurotransmitter into the synaptic gap. The binding of the neurotransmitter to receptors on the postsynaptic membrane stimulates the regeneration of the action potential in the postsynaptic neuron.

Neurotransmitter Signaling

Neurotransmitters are synthesized by neurons and are stored in vesicles, which typically are located in the axon's terminal end, also known as the presynaptic terminal. The presynaptic terminal is separated from the neuron or muscle or gland cell onto which it impinges by a gap called the synaptic cleft. The synaptic cleft, presynaptic terminal and receiving dendrite of the next cell together form a junction known as the synapse.

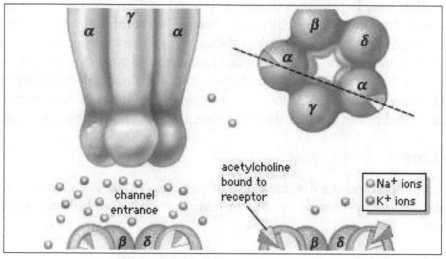

Nicotinic receptor.

The nicotinic receptor, composed of two α-subunits and β-, γ-, and δ-subunits arranged symmetrically around a central channel, binds acetylcholine, which causes the channel to open and allows diffusion of sodium (Na⁺) and potassium (K⁺) ions into the cell interior.

When a nerve impulse arrives at the presynaptic terminal of one neuron, neurotransmitter-filled vesicles migrate through the cytoplasm and fuse with the presynaptic terminal membrane. The neurotransmitter molecules are then released through the presynaptic membrane and into the synaptic cleft. In milliseconds, they travel across the synaptic cleft to the postsynaptic membrane of the adjoining neuron, where they then bind to receptors. Receptor activation results in either the opening or the closing of ion channels in the membrane of the second cell, which alters the cell's permeability. In many instances, the change in permeability results in depolarization, causing the cell to produce its own action potential, thereby initiating an electrical impulse. In other cases, the change leads to hyperpolarization, which prevents the generation of an action potential by the second cell.

The termination of neurotransmitter activity happens in several different ways. The molecules may diffuse out of the synaptic cleft, away from the receptive cell. They also can be taken back up into the presynaptic terminal via transporter molecules, or they may be metabolized by enzymes in the synaptic cleft.

Types of Neurotransmitters

Different types of neurotransmitters have been identified. Based on chemical and molecular properties, the major classes of neurotransmitters include amino acids, such as glutamate and glycine; monoamines, such as dopamine and norepinephrine; peptides, such as somatostatin and opioids; and purines, such as adenosine triphosphate (ATP). Some gaseous substances, such as nitric oxide, can also act as neurotransmitters, as can endogenous substances known as trace amines, which are related chemically to the monoamines; examples include tryptamine and the phenethylamines.

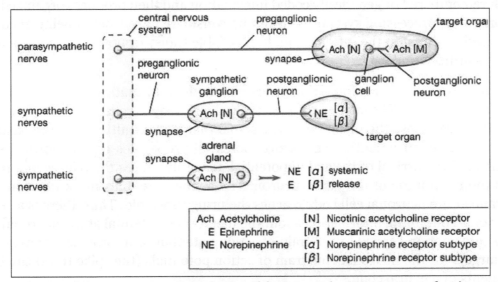

Autonomic nervous system: Organization of the autonomic nervous system, showing the key role of acetylcholine in the transmission of nervous impulses.

Acetylcholine, a substance synthesized by neurons, is the primary neurotransmitter of the parasympathetic nervous system, which controls smooth muscle contraction and blood vessel dilation and slows heart rate. The major inhibitory neurotransmitter of the nervous system is GABA (gamma-aminobutyric acid), which acts to dampen neuronal activity.

Abnormalities in neurotransmitter release and activity have been linked to various diseases and disorders, particularly neuropsychiatric and neurodegenerative disorders. For example, dysfunction of the neurotransmitters dopamine, glutamate, and GABA has been reported in schizophrenia, while reductions in levels and activity of norepinephrine and serotonin have been reported in persons with depression. Decreased levels of dopamine, attributed to the loss of so-called dopaminergic neurons, is a central feature of Parkinson disease.

Neural Coding

Neural coding describes the study of information processing by neurons. Such studies seek to learn what information is used, and how information is transformed as it passes from one processing stage to another. The field of neural coding seeks to synthesize information arising from many levels of analysis and to explain how integrated behavior arises from the cooperative activity of the neurons in the brain.

Much is known about the biophysics of neuronal responses – that is, how a spike is generated, how the spike acts on the axonal terminal to cause transmitter release, and how transmitters act on the target neuronal receptors. However, the impact of series of spikes is not well known, and it is even less clear what information has been encoded and how that information will be utilized in subsequent processing stages.

It is natural to consider the brain as an information processing machine. It takes in information from physical changes in the environment, including light, touch, and sound, integrates this information with remembered or genetically coded information and then produces organized behavior. In any information processing system, issues to be considered are what is being encoded, what is the code used to transmit the information, how reliable (noisy or not) is the code, and how the information is utilized or decoded.

At the base of this cascade of information processing is the information transformed and transmitted by single neurons. The signal on dendrites and cell body is reflected in fluctuations in the potential difference across the membrane. The signal that is transmitted down the axon is quite different; it is the action potential. This action potential propagates rapidly down the axon. At the axon terminal the arrival of the action potential generally causes the release of a transmitter that affects the membrane of the target neuron. The action potentials mark times at which the cell membrane at the neuronal cell body reaches the firing threshold. Thus, there is a sequence of action potentials containing information about the membrane potential at the neuronal cell body, and it is the information carried by the train of action potentials that provides information at the projection targets for the neurons. This train of action potentials (the spike train) can be considered as elements of a neural code.

Neural Encoding

Neural encoding is the study of how neurons represent information with electrical activity (action potentials) at the level of individual cells or in networks of neurons. Studies of neural encoding aim to characterize the relationship between sensory stimuli or behavioural output and neural signals.

Neural Decoding

Neural decoding is an important tool for understanding how neural activity relates to the outside world and for engineering applications such as brain-machine interfaces. Despite many advances in machine learning, it is still common to use traditional linear methods for decoding.

Neural decoding uses activity recorded from the brain to make predictions about variables in the outside world. For example, researchers predict movements based on activity in motor cortex, decisions based on activity in prefrontal and parietal cortices, and spatial locations based on activity in the hippocampus. These decoding predictions can be used to control devices (e.g., a robotic limb) or to better understand how areas of the brain relate to the outside world. Decoding is a central tool in neural engineering and for neural data analysis.

In essence, neural decoding is a regression (or classification) problem relating neural signals to particular variables. When framing the problem in this way, it is apparent that there is a wide range of methods that one could apply. However, despite the recent advances in machine learning (ML) techniques for regression, it is still common to decode activity with traditional methods such as linear regression. Using modern ML tools for neural decoding has the potential to boost performance significantly and might allow deeper insights into neural function.

Code Generation in Computational Neuroscience

All brains are composed of a huge variety of neuron and synapse types. In computational neuroscience we use models for mimicking the behavior of these elements and to gain an understanding of the brain's behavior by conducting simulation experiments in neural simulators. These models are usually defined by a set of variables which have either concrete values or use functions and differential equations that describe the temporal evolution of the variables.

A simple but instructive example is the integrate-and-fire neuron model, which describes the dynamics of the membrane potential V in the following way: when V is below the spiking threshold θ, which is typically at around −50 mV, the time evolution is governed by a differential equation of the type:

$$\frac{d}{dt}V = f(V)$$

Where, f is a function that is possibly non-linear.

Once V reaches its threshold θ, a spike is fired and V is set back to E_L for a certain time called the refractory period. E_L is called the resting potential and is typically around −70 mV. After this time the evolution of the equation starts again. An important simplification compared to biology is that the exact course of the membrane potential during the spike is either completely neglected or only partially considered in most models. Threshold detection is rather added algorithmically on top of the modeled sub-threshold dynamics.

Two of the most common variants of this type of model are the current-based and the conductance-based integrate-and-fire models. For the case of the current-based model we have the following general form:

$$\frac{d}{dt}V(t) = \frac{1}{\tau}\left(E_L - V(t)\right) + \frac{1}{C}I(t) + F\left(V(t)\right)$$

Here C is the membrane capacitance, τ the membrane time constant, and I the input current to the neuron. Assuming that spikes will be fixed to temporal grid points, I(t) is the sum of currents generated by all incoming spikes at all grid points in time $t_i \leq t$ scaled by their synaptic weight plus a piecewise constant function I_{ext} that models an external input:

$$I(t) = \sum_{i \in N, t_i \leq t} \sum_{k \in S_{t_i}} I_k\left(t - t_i\right) + I_{ext}\left(t\right)$$

S_t is the set of synapses that deliver a spike to the neuron at time t and I_k is the current that enters the neuron through synapse k. F is some non-linear function of V that may be zero.

One concrete example is the simple integrate-and-fire neuron with alpha-shaped synaptic input, where $F(V) \equiv 0$, $F(V) \equiv 0$, $I_k(t) = \dfrac{e}{\tau_{syn}} t e^{-t}/\tau_{syn}$ and τ_{syn} is the rise time, which is typically around 0.2–2.0 ms.

When implementing such models in neural simulators their differential equations must be solved as part of the neuron model implementation. One typical approach is to use a numeric integrator, e.g., a simple Euler method.

For a simulation stepsize h and some given approximation V_t of V(t), using an Euler method would lead to the following approximation V_{t+h} of V(t+h):

$$V_{t+h} = V_t + h\left(\frac{1}{\tau}(E_L - V_t) + \frac{1}{C}I(t)\right)$$

Publications in computational neuroscience mostly contain descriptions of models in terms of their mathematical equations and the algorithms to add additional behavior such as the mechanism for threshold detection and spike generation. However, if looking at a model implementation and comparing it to the corresponding published model description, one often finds that they are not in agreement due to the complexity and variety of available forms of abstractions of such a transformation. Using a general purpose programming language to express the model implementation even aggravates this problem as such languages provide full freedom for model developers while lacking the means to guide them in their challenging task due to the absence of neuroscience domain concepts.

Furthermore, the complexity of the brain enforces the use of a heterogeneous set of models on different abstraction levels that, however, need to efficiently cooperate upon execution. Model compositionality is needed on the abstract mathematical side as well as on the implementation level.

The use of problem-tailored model description languages and standardized simulators is often seen as a way out of the dilemma as they can provide the domain-specificity missing in a general programming language, however often at the cost of restricting the users in their freedom to express arbitrary algorithms.

In other words, engineering complex software systems introduces a conceptual gap between problem domains and solution domains. Model driven development aims at closing this gap by using abstract models for the description of domain problems and code generation for creating executable software systems. Early MDD techniques have been already successfully applied in computer science for decades. These techniques ensure reduced development costs and increased software quality of resulting software systems. MDD also provides methodological concepts to increase design and development speed of simulation code.

It turns out that MDD is not restricted to the software engineering domain, but can be applied in many science and also engineering domains. For example, the Systems Biology Markup Language from the domain of biochemistry enables modeling of biochemical reaction networks, like cell signaling pathways, metabolic pathways, and gene regulation, and has several software tools that support users with the creation, import, export, simulation, and further processing of models expressed in SBML.

MDD works best if the underlying modeling language fits to the problem domain and thus is specifically engineered for that domain. The modeling language must provide modularity in several domains: individual neurons of different behavior must be modeled, time, and geometric abstractions should be available, composition of neurons to large networks must be possible and reuse of neuron models or neuron model fragments must be facilitated.

In the context of computational neuroscience the goal of MDD is to transform complex and abstract mathematical neuron, synapse, and network specifications into efficient platform-specific executable representations. There is no lack of neural simulation environments that are able to simulate models efficiently and accurately, each specializing on networks of different size and complexity. Some of these simulators have included optimized neural and synaptic models written in low-level code without support for more abstract, mathematical descriptions. Others have provided a separate model description language together with tools to convert these descriptions into reusable model components. Recently, such support has also been added to the NEST simulator via NESTML. Finally, other simulators include model descriptions as integral parts of the simulation script, transparently converting these descriptions into executable code.

These approaches to model descriptions have been complemented in recent years by various initiatives creating simulator-independent model description languages. These languages completely separate the model description from the simulation environment and are therefore not directly executable. Instead, they provide code generation tools to convert the descriptions into code for target environments such as the ones mentioned above, but also for more specialized target platforms such as GPUs, or neuromorphic chips like SpiNNaker or the BrainScaleS System. Prominent description languages include NineML, NeuroML, and LEMS. These languages are often organized hierarchically, for example LEMS is the low-level description language for neural and synaptic models that can be assembled into a network with a NeuroML description. Another recently developed description language, SpineML builds upon LEMS descriptions as well.

A new generation of centralized collaboration platforms like Open Source Brain and the Human Brain Project Collaboratory are being developed to allow greater access to neuronal models for both computationally proficient and non-computational members of the neuroscience community. Here, code generation systems can serve as a means to free the user from installing their own software while still giving them the possibility to create and use their own neuron and synapse models.

Tools and Code Generation Pipelines

Brian

All versions of the Brian simulator have used code generation, from the simple pure Python code generation for some model components in its earliest versions, through the mixed Python/C++ code generation in later versions, to the exhaustive framework in its latest version (2.x) that will be described here. It now uses a consistent code generation framework for all model components, and allows for multiple target languages and devices. Brian 2 had code generation as a major design goal, and so the user model, data model, and execution model were created with this in mind.

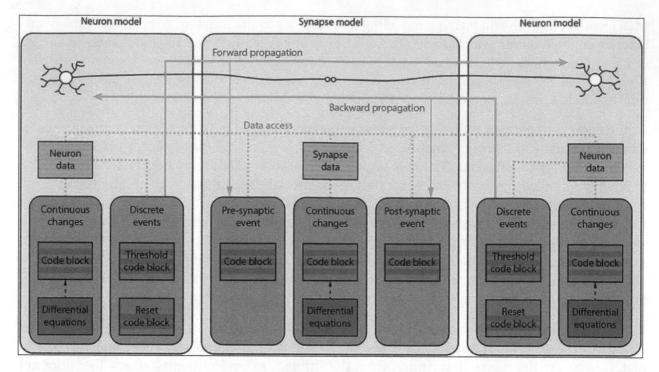

Figure shows Brian model structure. Brian users define models by specifying equations governing a single neuron or synapse. Simulations consist of an ordered sequence of operations (code blocks) acting on neuronal or synaptic data. A neuronal code block can only modify its own data, whereas a synaptic code block can also modify data from its pre- or post-synaptic neurons. Neurons have three code blocks: one for its continuous evolution (numerical integration), one for checking threshold conditions and emitting spike events, and one for post-spike reset in response to those events. Synapses have three code blocks: two event-based blocks for responding to pre- or postsynaptic spikes (corresponding to forward or backward propagation), and one continuous evolution block. Code blocks can be provided directly, or can be generated from pseudo-code or differential equations.

Main Modeling Focus

Brian focuses on modeling networks of point neurons, where groups of neurons are described by the same set of equations (but possibly differ in their parameters). Depending on the equations, such models can range from variants of the integrate-and-fire model to biologically detailed models incorporating a description of multiple ion channels. The same equation framework can also be used to model synaptic dynamics (e.g., short- and long-term plasticity) or spatially extended, multi-compartmental neurons.

Model Notation

From the user point of view, the simulation consists of components such as neurons and synapses, each of which is defined by equations given in standard mathematical notation. For example, a leaky integrate-and-fire neuron evolves over time according to the differential equation $dv/dt = -v/\tau$. In Brian this would be written as the Python string 'dv/dt=-v/tau : volt' in which the part after the colon defines the physical dimensions of the variable v. All variables and constants have physical dimensions, and as part of the code generation framework, all operations are checked for dimensional consistency.

Since all aspects of the behavior of a model are determined by user-specified equations, this system offers the flexibility for implementing both standard and non-standard models. For example, the effect of a spike arriving at a synapse is often modeled by an equation such as $v_{post} \leftarrow v_{post} + w$ where vpost is the postsynaptic membrane potential and w is a synaptic weight. In Brian this would be rendered as part of the definition of synapses as (..., `on_pre='v_post += w'`). However, the user could as well also change the value of synaptic or presynaptic neuronal variables. For the example of STDP, this might be something like `Synapses(..., on_pre='v_post+=w; Am+=dAm; w=-clip(w+Ap, 0, wmax)')`, where Am and Ap are synaptic variables used to keep a trace of the pre- and post-synaptic activity, and `clip(x, y, z)` is a pre-defined function (equivalent to the NumPy function of the same name) that returns x if it is between y and z, or y or z if it is outside this range.

Code Generation Pipeline

The code generation pipeline in Brian is illustrated in figure. Code generation will typically start with a set of (potentially stochastic) first order ordinary differential equations. Using an appropriate solver, these equations are converted into a sequence of update rules. As an example, consider the simple equation $dv/dt = -v/\tau$ mentioned above. Brian will detect that the equation is linear and can be solved exactly, and will therefore generate the following update rule: `v_new = v_old * exp(-dt/tau)`.

Brian code:

```
G = NeuronGroup(1, 'dv/dt = -v/tau : 1')
```

"Abstract code" (internal pseudo-code representation)

```
_v = v*exp(-dt/tau)
v = _v
```

C++ code snippet (scalar part)

```
const double dt = _ptr_array_defaultclock_dt[0];
const double _lio_1 = exp((-dt)/tau);
```

C++ code snippet (vector part)

```
double v = _ptr_array_neurongroup_v[_idx];
const double _v = _lio_1*v;
v = _v;
_ptr_array_neurongroup_v[_idx] = v;
```

Compilable C++ code excerpt:

```
// scalar code
const double dt = _ptr_array_defaultclock_dt[0];
const double _lio_1 = exp((-dt)/tau);
for(int _idx=0; _idx<_N; idx++)
{
    // vector code
    double v = _ptr_array_neurongroup_v[_idx];
    const double _v = _lio_1*v;
    v = _v;
    _ptr_array_neurongroup_v[_idx] = v;
}
```

Figure shows Brian code generation pipeline. Code is transformed in multiple stages: the original Brian code (in Python), with a differential equation given in standard mathematical form; the internal pseudocode or "abstract code" representation (Python syntax), in this case an exact numerical solver for the equations; the C++ code snippets generated from the abstract code; the compilable C++ code. Note that the C++ code snippets include a scalar and vector part, which is automatically computed from the abstract code. In this case, a constant has been pulled out of the loop and named `_lio_1`.

Such strings or sequences of strings form a sort of mathematical pseudocode called an abstract code block. The user can also specify abstract code blocks directly. For example, to define the operation that is executed upon a spike, the user might write `v_post += w` as shown above.

From an abstract code block, Brian transforms the statements into one of a number of different target languages. The simplest is to generate Python code, using NumPy for vectorized operations. This involves relatively few transformations of the abstract code, mostly concerned with indexing. For example, for a reset operation $v \leftarrow v_r$ that should be carried out only on those neurons that have spiked, code equivalent to `v[has_spiked] = v_r` is generated, where `has_spiked` is an array of integers with the indices of the neurons that have spiked. The direct C++ code generation target involves a few more transformations on the original code, but is still relatively straightforward. For example, the power operation ab is written as `a**b` in Python, whereas in C++ it should be written as `pow(a, b)`. This is implemented using Python's built-in AST module, which transforms a string in Python syntax into an abstract syntax tree that can be iterated. Finally, there is the Cython code generation target. Cython is a Python package that allows users to write code in a Python-like syntax and have it automatically converted into C++, compiled and run. This allows Python users to maintain easy-to-read code that does not have the performance limitations of pure Python.

The result of these transformations is a block of code in a different target language called a snippet, because it is not yet a complete compilable source file. This final transformation is carried out by the widely used Python templating engine Jinja2, which inserts the snippet into a template file.

The final step is the compilation and execution of the source files. Brian operates in one of two main modes: runtime or standalone mode. The default runtime mode is managed directly by Python. Source files are compiled into separate Python modules which are then imported and executed in sequence by Brian. This allows users to mix arbitrary pure Python code with compiled code, but comes with a performance cost, namely that each function call has an associated Python overhead. For large numbers of neurons this difference is relatively little because the majority of time is spent inside compiled code rather than in Python overheads (which are a fixed cost not depending on the number of neurons). However, for smaller networks that might need to be run repeatedly or for a long duration, these overheads can be significant. Brian therefore also has the standalone mode, in which it generates a complete C++ project that can be compiled and run entirely independently of Python and Brian. This is transparent for the users and only requires them to write `set_de-vice('cpp_standalone')` at the beginning of their scripts. While this mode comes with the advantage of increased performance and portability, it also implies some limitations as user-specified Python code and generated code cannot be interspersed.

Brian's code generation framework has been designed in a modular fashion and can be extended on multiple levels. For specific models, the user might want to integrate a simulation with hand-written code in the target programming language, e.g., to feed real-time input from a sensor into the simulation. Brian supports this use case by allowing references to arbitrary user-defined functions in the model equations and statements, if its definition in the target language and the physical dimensions of its arguments and result are provided by the user. On a global level, Brian supports the definition of new target languages and devices. This mechanism has for example been used to provide GPU functionality through the Brian2GeNN interface, generating and executing model code for the GeNN simulator.

Numerical Integration

As stated above, Brian converts differential equations into a sequence of statements that integrate the equations numerically over a single time step. If the user does not choose a specific integration method, Brian selects one automatically. For linear equations, it will solve the equations exactly according to their analytic solution. In all other cases, it will choose a numerical method, using an appropriate scheme for stochastic differential equations if necessary. The exact methods that will be used by this default mechanism depend on the type of the model. For single-compartment neuron and synapse models, the methods exact, euler, and heun will be tried in order, and the first suitable method will be applied. Multicompartmental neuron models will chose from the methods exact, exponential euler, rk2, and heun.

The following integration algorithms are provided by Brian and can be chosen by the user:

- Exact (named linear in previous versions): Exact integration for linear equations.

- Exponential euler: Exponential Euler integration for conditionally linear equations.

- Euler: Forward Euler integration (for additive stochastic differential equations using the Euler-Maruyama method).

- rk2: Second order Runge-Kutta method (midpoint method).

- rk4: Classical Runge-Kutta method (RK4).

- Heun: Stochastic Heun method for solving Stratonovich stochastic differential equations with non-diagonal multiplicative noise.

- Milstein: Derivative-free Milstein method for solving stochastic differential equations with diagonal multiplicative noise.

In addition to these predefined solvers, Brian also offers a simple syntax for defining new solvers.

Data and Execution Model

In terms of data and execution, a Brian simulation is essentially just an ordered sequence of code blocks, each of which can modify the values of variables, either scalars or vectors (of fixed or dynamic size). For example, N neurons with the same equations are collected in a `NeuronGroup` object. Each variable of the model has an associated array of length N. A code block will typically consist of a loop over indices i = 0, 1, 2, ..., N-1 and be defined by a block of code executing in a namespace (a dictionary mapping names to values). Multiple code objects can have overlapping namespaces. So for example, for neurons there will be one code object to perform numerical integration, another to check threshold crossing, another to perform post-spike reset, etc. This adds a further layer of flexibility, because the user can choose to re-order these operations, for example to choose whether synaptic propagation should be carried out before or after post-spike reset.

Each user defined variable has an associated index variable that can depend on the iteration variable in different ways. For example, the numerical integration iterates over i = 0, 1, 2, ..., N−1. However, post-spike reset only iterates over the indices of neurons that spiked. Synapses are handled in the same way. Each synapse has an associated presynaptic neuron index, postsynaptic neuron index, and synaptic index and the resulting code will be equivalent to `v_post[postsynaptic_index[i]] += w[synaptic_index[i]]`.

Brian assumes an unrestricted memory model in which all variables are accessible, which gives a particularly flexible scheme that makes it simple to implement many non-standard models. This flexibility can be achieved for medium scale simulations running on a single CPU (the most common use case of Brian). However, especially for synapses, this assumption may not be compatible with all code generation targets where memory access is more restrictive (e.g., in MPI or GPU setups). As a consequence, not all models that can be defined and run in standard CPU targets will be able to run efficiently in other target platforms.

GeNN

GeNN (GPU enhanced Neuronal Networks) is a C++ and NVIDIA CUDA based framework for facilitating neuronal network simulations with GPU accelerators. It was developed because optimizing simulation code for efficient execution on GPUs is a difficult problem that distracts computational neuroscience researchers from focusing on their core research. GeNN uses code generation to achieve efficient GPU code while maintaining maximal flexibility of what is being simulated and which hardware platform to target.

Main Modeling Focus

The focus of GeNN is on spiking neuronal networks. There are no restrictions or preferences for neuron model and synapse types, albeit analog synapses such as graded synapses and gap junctions do affect the speed performance strongly negatively.

GeNN expects users to define their own code for neuron and synapse model time step updates as C++ strings. In the example above, the neurons are standard Izhikevich neurons and synaptic connections are pulse coupling with delay. GeNN works with the concept of neuron and synapse types and subsequent definition of neuron and synapse populations of these types.

Code Generation Pipeline

The model description provided by the user is used to generate C++ and CUDA C code for efficient simulation on GPU accelerators. For maximal flexibility, GeNN only generates the code that is specific to GPU acceleration and accepts C/C++ user code for all other aspects of a simulation, even though a number of examples of such code are available to copy and modify. The basic strategy of this workflow is illustrated in figure. Structuring the simulator framework in this way allows achieving key goals of code generation in the GPU context. First, the arrangement of neuron and synapse populations into kernel blocks and grids can be optimized by the simulator depending on the model and the hardware detected at compile time. This can lead to essential improvements in the simulation speed. The approach also allows users and developers to define a practically unlimited number of neuron and synapse models, while the final, generated code only contains what is being used and the resulting executable code is lean. Lastly, accepting the users' own code for the input-output and simulation control allows easy integration with many different usage scenarios, ranging from large scale simulations to using interfaces to other simulation tools and standards and to embedded use, e.g., in robotics applications.

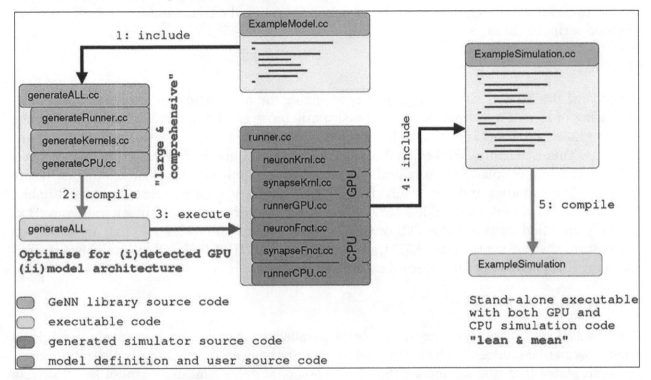

Figure shows schematic of the code generation flow for the GPU simulator framework GeNN. Neural models are described in a C/C++ model definition function ("ExampleModel.cc"), either hand-crafted by a user or generated from a higher-level model description language such as SpineML or Brian 2. The neuron model description is included into the GeNN compiler that produces optimized CUDA/C++ code for simulating the specified model. The generated code can then be used by hand-crafted or independently generated user code to form the final executable. The framework is minimalistic in generating only optimized CUDA/C++ code for the core model and not the simulation workflow in order to allow maximal flexibility in the deployment of the final executable. This can include exploratory or large scale simulations but also real-time execution on embedded systems for robotics applications. User code in blue, GeNN components in gray, generated CUDA/C++ code in pink.

Numerical Integration

Unlike for other simulators, the numerical integration methods, and any other time-step based update methods are for GeNN in the user domain. Users define the code that performs the time step update when defining the neuron and synapse models. If they wish to use a numerical integration method for an ODE based neuron model, users need to provide the code for their method within the update code. This allows for maximal flexibility and transparency of the numerical model updates.

However, not all users may wish to use the C++ interface of GeNN or undertake the work of implementing the time step updates for their neuron models from scratch. For these users there are additional tools that allow connecting other model APIs to GeNN. Brian2GeNN allows to execute Brian 2 scripts with GeNN as the backend and there is a separate toolchain connecting SpineCreator and SpineML to GeNN to achieve the same. Although there can be a loss in computing speed and the range of model features that can be supported when using such interfaces, using GPU acceleration through Brian2GeNN can be as simple as issuing the command set_device('genn') in a Python script for Brian 2.

Myriad

The goal of the Myriad simulator project is to enable the automatic parallelization and multi-processing of any compartmental model, particularly those exhibiting dense analog interactions such as graded synapses and mass diffusion that cannot easily be parallelized using standard approaches. This is accomplished computationally via a shared-memory architecture that eschews message-passing, coupled with a radically granular design approach that flattens hierarchically defined cellular models and can subdivide individual isometric compartments by state variable. Programmatically, end-user models are defined in a Python-based environment and converted into fully-specified C99 code (for CPU or GPU) via code generation techniques that are enhanced by a custom abstract syntax tree (AST) translator and, for NVIDIA GPUs, a custom object specification for CUDA enabling fully on-card execution.

Main Modeling Focus

Myriad was conceived as a strategy to enable the parallelization of densely integrated mechanisms in compartmental models. Under traditional message-passing approaches to parallelization, compartment states that update one another densely—e.g., at every timestep—cannot be effectively parallelized. However, such dense analog interactions are common in compartmental models; examples include graded synapses, gap junctions, and charge or mass diffusion among adjacent compartments. In lieu of message passing, Myriad uses a shared memory strategy with barrier synchronization that parallelizes dense models as effectively as sparsely coupled models. This strategy imposes scale limitations on simulations based on available memory, though these limitations are being somewhat eased by new hardware developments.

Model Notation

The core of Myriad is a parallel solver layer designed so that all models that can be represented as a list of isometric, stateful nodes (compartments), can be connected pairwise by any number of arbitrary mechanisms and executed with a high degree of parallelism on CPU threads. No hierarchical relationships among nodes are recognized during execution; hierarchies that exist in user-defined models are flattened during code generation. This flat organization facilitates thread-scaling to any number of available threads and load-balancing with very fine granularity to maximize the utilization of available CPU or GPU cores. Importantly, analog coupling mechanisms such as cable equations, Hodgkin-Huxley membrane channels, mass diffusion, graded synapses, and gap junctions can be parallelized in Myriad just as efficiently as sparse events. Because of this, common hierarchical relationships in neuronal models, such as the positions of compartments along an extended dendritic tree, can be flattened and the elements distributed arbitrarily across different compute units. For example, two nodes representing adjacent compartments are coupled by "adjacency" mechanisms that pass appropriate quantities of charge and mass between them without any explicit or implicit hierarchical relationship. This solver comprises the lowest layer of a three-layer simulator architecture.

A top-level application layer, written in idiomatic Python 3 enriched with additional C code, defines the object properties and primitives available for end-user model development. It is used to specify high-level abstractions for neurons, sections, synapses, and network properties. The mechanisms (particles, ions, channels, pumps, etc.) are user-definable with object-based inheritance, e.g., channels inherit properties based on their permeant ions. Simulations are represented as objects to facilitate iterative parameter searches and reproducibility of results. The inheritance functionality via Python's native object system allows access to properties of parent component and functionality can be extended and overridden at will.

The intermediate interface layer flattens and translates the model into non-hierarchical nodes and coupling mechanisms for the solver using AST-to-AST translation of Python code to C. Accordingly, the top-level model definition syntax depends only on application-layer Python modules; in principle, additional such modules can be written for applications outside neuroscience, or to mimic the model definition syntax of other Python-based simulators. For the intended primary application of solving dense compartmental models of neurons and networks, the models are defined in terms of their cellular morphologies and passive properties (e.g., lengths, diameters, cytoplasmic resistivity) and their internal, transmembrane, and synaptic mechanisms. State variables include potentials, conductances, and (optionally) mass species concentrations. Equations for mechanisms are arbitrary and user-definable.

Code Generation Pipeline

To achieve an efficient parallelization of dense analog mechanisms, it was necessary to eschew message-passing. Under message-based parallelization, each data transfer between compute units generates a message with an uncertain arrival time, such that increased message densities dramatically increase the rollback rate of speculative execution and quickly become rate-limiting for simulations. Graded connections such as analog synapses or cable equations yield new messages at every timestep and hence parallelize poorly. This problem is generally addressed by maintaining coupled analog mechanisms on single compute units, with parallelization being limited to model elements that can be coupled via sparse boolean events, such as action potentials. Efficient simulations therefore require a careful, platform-specific balance between neuronal complexity and synaptic density. The unfortunate consequence is that platform limitations drive model design.

In lieu of message passing, Myriad is based on uniform memory access (UMA) architecture. Specifically, every mechanism reads all parameters of interest from shared memory, and writes its output to shared memory, at every fixed timestep. Shared memory access, and a global clock that regulates barrier synchronization among all compute units (thereby coordinating all timesteps), are GPU hardware features. For parallel CPU simulations, the OpenMP 3.1+ API for shared-memory multiprocessing has implicit barrier and reduction intrinsics that provide equivalent, platform-independent functionality. Importantly, while this shared-memory design enables analog interactions to be parallelized efficiently, to take proper advantage of this capacity on GPUs, the simulation must execute on the GPU independently rather than being continuously controlled by the host system. To accomplish this, Myriad uses a code generation strategy embedded in its three-layer architecture. The lowest (solver) layer is written in C99 for both CPUs and NVIDIA GPUs (CUDA). The solver requires as input a list of isometric nodes and a list of coupling mechanisms that connect pairs of nodes, all with fully explicit parameters defined prior to compilation (i.e., execution of a Myriad model requires just-in-time compilation of the solver). To facilitate code reuse and inheritance from the higher (Python) layers, a custom-designed minimal object framework implemented in C supports on-device virtual functions; to our knowledge this is the first of its kind to execute on CUDA GPUs. The second, or interface, layer is written in Python; this layer defines top-level objects, instantiates the node and mechanism dichotomy, converts the Python objects defined at the top level into the two fully-specified lists that are passed to the solver, and manages communication with the simulation binaries. The top, or application layer, will comprise an expandable library of application-specific modules, also written in Python. These modules specify the relevant implementations of Myriad objects in terms familiar to the end user. For neuronal modeling, this could include neurite lengths, diameters, and branching, permeant ions (mass and charge), distributed mechanisms (e.g., membrane channels), point processes (e.g., synapses), and cable equations, among other concepts common to compartmental simulators. Additional top-layer modules can be written by end users for different purposes, or to support different code syntaxes.

Execution of a Myriad simulation begins with a transformation of the user-specified model definition into two Python lists of node and mechanism objects. Parameters are resolved, and the Python object lists are transferred to the solver layer via a custom-built Python-to-C pseudo-compiler (*pycast*; an AST-to-AST translator from Python's native abstract syntax tree (AST) to the AST of *pycparser* (a Myriad dependency), facilitated by Myriad's custom C object framework). These objects are thereby rendered into fully explicit C structs which are compiled as part of the simulation executable. The choice of CPU or GPU computation is specified at execution time via a compiler option. On CPUs and compliant GPUs, simulations execute using dynamic parallelism to maximize core utilization (via OpenMP 3.1+ for CPUs or CUDA 5.0+ on compute capability 3.5+ GPUs).

The limitation of Myriad's UMA strategy is scalability. Indeed, at its conception, Myriad was planned as a simulator on the intermediate scale between single neuron and large network simulations because its shared-memory, barrier synchronization-dependent architecture limited the scale of simulations to those that could fit within the memory of a single high-speed chassis (e.g., up to the memory capacity of a single motherboard or CUDA GPU card). However, current and projected hardware developments leveraging NVIDIA's NVLink interconnection bus are likely to ease this limitation.

Numerical Integration

For development purposes, Myriad supports the fourth-order Runge-Kutta method (RK4) and the backward Euler method. These and other methods will be benchmarked for speed, memory requirements, and stability prior to release.

NESTML

NESTML is a relatively new modeling language, which currently only targets the NEST simulator. It was developed to address the maintainability issues that followed from a rising number of models and model variants and ease the model development for neuroscientists without a strong background in computer science. NESTML is available unter the terms of the GNU General Public License v2.0 on GitHub and can serve as a well-defined and stable target platform for the generation of code from other model description languages such as NineML and NeuroML.

Main Modeling Focus

The current focus of NESTML is on integrate-and-fire neuron models described by a number of differential equations with the possibility to support compartmental neurons, synapse models, and also other targets in the future.

A neuron in NESTML is composed of multiple blocks. The whole model is contained in a neuron block, which can have three different blocks for defining model variables: initial_values, parameters, and internals. Variable declarations are composed of a non-empty list of variable names followed by their type. Optionally, initialization expressions can be used to set default values. The type can either be a plain data type such as integer and real, a physical unit (e.g., mV) or a composite physical unit (e.g., nS/ms).

Differential equations in the equations block can be used to describe the time evolution of variables in the initial_values block. Postsynaptic shapes and synonyms inside the *equations* block can be used to increase the expressiveness of the specification.

The type of incoming and outgoing events are defined in the input and output blocks. The neuron dynamics are specified inside the update block. This block contains an implementation of the propagation step and uses a simple embedded procedural language based on Python.

Code Generation Pipeline

In order to have full freedom for the design, the language is implemented as an external domain specific language with a syntax similar to that of Python. In contrast to an internal DSL an external DSL doesn't depend syntactically on a given host language, which allows a completely customized implementation of the syntax and results in a design that is tailored to the application domain.

Usually external DSLs require the manual implementation of the language and its processing tools. In order to avoid this task, the development of NESTML is backed by the language workbench MontiCore. MontiCore uses context-free grammars in order to define the abstract and concrete syntax of a DSL. Based on this grammar, MontiCore creates classes for the abstract syntax (metamodel) of the DSL and parsers to read the model description files and instantiate the metamodel.

NESTML is composed of several specialized sublanguages. These are composed through language embedding and a language inheritance mechanism: UnitsDSL provides all data types and physical units, ExpressionsDSL defines the style of Python compatible expressions and takes care of semantic checks for type correctness of expressions, EquationsDSL provides all means to define differential equations and postsynaptic shapes and ProceduralDSL enables users to specify parts of the model in the form of ordinary program code. In situations where a modeling intent cannot be expressed through language constructs this allows a more fine-grained control than a purely declarative description could.

The decomposition of NESTML into sublanguages enables an agile and modular development of the DSL and its processing infrastructure and independent testing of the sublanguages, which speeds up the development of the language itself. Through the language composition capabilities of the MontiCore workbench the sublanguages are composed into the unified DSL NESTML.

NESTML neurons are stored in simple text files. These are read by a parser, which instantiates a corresponding abstract syntax tree (AST). The AST is an instance of the metamodel and stores the essence of the model in a form which is easily processed by a computer. It completely abstracts the details of the user-visible model representation in the form of its concrete syntax. The symbol table and the AST together provide a semantic model.

Figure shows an excerpt of the NESTML grammar and explains the derivation of the metamodel. A grammar is composed of a non-empty set of productions. For every production a corresponding class in the metamodel is created. Based on the right hand side of the productions attributes are added to this class. Classes can be specified by means of specifications of explicit names in the production names of attributes in the metamodel.

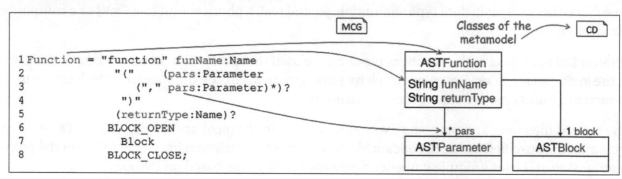

Example definition of a NESTML concept and generation of the AST: (Left) A production for a function in NESTML. The lefthandside defines the name of the production, the righthandside defines the production using terminals, other productions and special operators (*, ?). A function starts with the keyword function followed by the function's name and an optional list of parameters enclosed in parentheses followed by the optional return value. Optional parts are marked with ?. The function body is specified by the production (Block) between two keywords. (Right) The corresponding automatically derived meta-model as a class diagram. Every production is mapped to an AST class, which is used in the further language processing steps. NEST expects a model in the form of C++ code, using an internal programming interface providing hooks for parameter handling, recording of state variables, receiving and sending events, and updating instances of the model to the next simulation time step. The NESTML model thus needs to be transformed to this format.

For generating the C++ code for NEST, NESTML uses the code generation facilities provided by the MontiCore workbench, which are based on the template engine Freemarker. This approach enables a tight coupling of the model AST and the symbol table, from which the code is generated, with the text based templates for the generation of code.

Before the actual code generation phase, the AST undergoes several model to model transformations. First, equations and shapes are extracted from the NESTML AST and passed to an analysis framework based on the symbolic math package SymPy. This framework analyses all equations and shapes and either generates explicit code for the update step or code that can be handled by a solver from the GNU Scientific Library. The output of the analysis framework is a set of model fragments which can again be instantiated as NESTML ASTs and integrated into the AST of the original neuron and replace the original equations and shapes they were generated from.

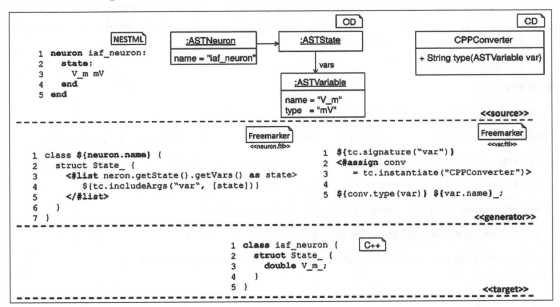

Figure explains Components for the code generation in NESTML: (Top) Source model, corresponding AST, and helper classes. (Middle) Templates for the generation of C++ code. The left template creates a C++ class body with an embedded C++ struct, the right template maps variable name and variable type using a helper class. The template on the left includes the template on the right once for each state variable defined in the source model. (Bottom) A C++ implementation as created from the source model using the generation templates. Before writing the C++ code, a *constant folding* optimization is performed, which uses the fact that internal variables in NESTML models do not change during the simulation. Thus, expressions involving only internal variables and constants can be factored out into dedicated expressions, which are computed only once in order to speed up the execution of the model.

NESTML differentiates between different types of ODEs. ODEs are categorized according to certain criteria and then assigned appropriate solvers. ODEs are solved either analytically if they are linear constant coefficient ODEs and are otherwise classified as stiff or non-stiff and then assigned either an implicit or an explicit numeric integration scheme.

Neuroml/LEMS

NeuroML version 1 was originally conceived as a simulator-agnostic domain specific language (DSL) for building biophysically inspired models of neuronal networks, focusing on separating model description from numerical implementation. As such, it provided a fixed set of components at three broad layers of abstraction: morphological, ion channel, and network, which allowed a number of pre-existing models to be described in a standardized, structured format. The role of code generation in *NeuroML1* pipelines was clear—the agnostic, abstract model definition needed to be eventually mapped into concrete implementations (e.g., code for NEURON) in order for the models to be simulated.

Nevertheless, the need for greater flexibility and extensibility beyond a predefined set of components and, more importantly, a demand for lower level model descriptions also described in a standardized format (contrarily to NeuroML1, where for example component dynamics were defined textually in the language reference, thus inaccessible from code) culminated in a major language redesign (referred to as NeuroML2), underpinned by a second, lower level language called Low Entropy Model Specification (LEMS).

References

- Computational-neuroscience: cnsorg.org, Retrieved 11, May 2020

- The-neuron, anatomy, brain-anatomy-and-function: brainfacts.org, Retrieved 24, January 2020

- Holonomic-brain-theory: scholarpedia.org, Retrieved 06, August 2020

- Neural-networks: ibm.com, Retrieved 13, March 2020

- Neurotransmission: human-memory.net, Retrieved 14, June 2020

- Neurotransmitter, science: britannica.com, Retrieved 25, April 2020

- Neural-coding, neuroscience: sciencedirect.com, Retrieved 10, February 2020

Diverse Models in Computational Neuroscience

There are various models which explain the concepts of computational neuroscience in a clear and concise manner. Some of the models explained in this chapter are single-neuron modeling, FitzHugh-Nagumo model, Hindmarsh-Rose model, Dehaene-Changeux model, Hodgkin-Huxley model, etc. This chapter has been carefully written to provide an easy understanding of these models of computational neuroscience.

Single-Neuron Modeling

Understanding the dynamics and computations of single neurons and their role within larger neural networks is therefore at the core of neuroscience: How do single-cell properties contribute to information processing and, ultimately, behavior? Quantitative models address these questions, summarize and organize the rapidly growing amount and sophistication of experimental data, and make testable predictions. As single-cell models and experiments become more closely interwoven, the development of data analysis tools for efficient parameter estimation and assessment of model performance constitutes a central element of computational studies.

All these tasks require a delicate balance between incorporating sufficient details to account for complex single-cell dynamics and reducing this complexity to the essential characteristics to make a model tractable. The appropriate level of description depends on the particular goal of the model. Indeed, finding the best abstraction level is often the key to success. We highlight these aspects for five main levels of single-cell modeling.

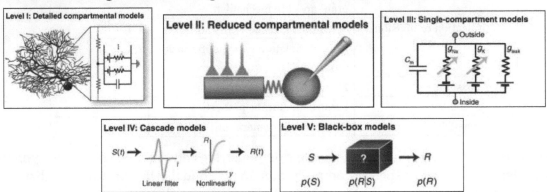

Examples for five levels of single-cell modeling are Level I: Detailed compartmental model of a Purkinje cell. The dendritic tree is segmented into electrically coupled Hodgkin-Huxley–type compartments (level III). Level II: Two-compartment model. The dendrite receives synaptic inputs and is coupled to the soma where the neuron's response is generated. Level III: Hodgkin-Huxley model, the prototype of single-compartment models. The cell's inside and outside are separated by a capacitance C_m and ionic conductances in series with batteries describing ionic reversal potentials.

Sodium and potassium conductances (g_{Na}, g_K) depend on voltage; the leak g_{leak} is fixed. Level IV: Linear-nonlinear cascade. Stimuli S(t) are convolved with a filter and then fed through a nonlinearity to generate responses R(t), typically time-dependent firing rates. Level V: Black-box model. Neglecting biophysical mechanisms, conditional probabilities p(R|S) describe responses R for given stimuli S.

Level I: Detailed Compartmental Models

Morphologically realistic models are based on anatomical reconstructions and focus on how the spatial structure of a neuron contributes to its dynamics and function. These models extend the cable theory of Rall, who showed mathematically that dendritic voltage attenuation spreads asymmetrically. This phenomenon allows dendrites to compute the direction of synaptic activation patterns, and thus provides a mechanism for motion detection. When voltage-dependent conductance are taken into account, numerical integration over the spatially discretized dendrite the "compartmental model"—is needed to solve the resulting high-dimensional system of equations.

For complex dendritic trees, more than 1000 compartments are required to capture the cell's specific electrotonic structure (e.g., to simulate spike back-propagation in pyramidal neurons). Such detailed models also generate testable mechanistic hypotheses. For instance, simulations of Purkinje cells predicted that a net inhibitory synaptic current underlies specific spike patterns in vivo, in accordance with later experimental findings. In turn, even established models such as the thalamocortical neuron are constantly improved by adding new biophysical details such as dendritic calcium currents responsible for fast oscillations.

Table: Information processing in single neurons: Basic computations that follow from generic neuronal properties.

Computation	Biophysical mechanism	Model level
Addition or subtraction	Dendritic summation of excitatory and/or inhibitory inputs	I, II
Subtraction	Shunting inhibition plus integrate-and-fire mechanism	I, II
Multiplication or division	Synaptic interaction	I, II
	Gain modulation via synaptic background noise	I, II
High-pass filter	Firing rate adaptation	III
Low-pass filter	Passive membrane properties	I, II, III
Toggle switch	Bistable spike generation	III

A large body of morphologically realistic models demonstrates how spatial aspects of synaptic integration in dendrites support specific computations. In pyramidal cells, for example, distal inputs are amplified via dendritic spikes or plateau potentials, supporting local coincidence detection and gain modulation. Dendritic inward currents play a major role in the control of spiking or the modulation of responses to synchronous inputs. Such interactions among synaptic inputs, voltage-gated conductances, and spiking output can be specifically affected by dendritic branching structures; axonal geometries, on the other hand, influence activity-dependent branch point failures and may thus implement filter and routing operations on the neuron's output side. Finally, detailed spatial representations help predict the effects of extracellular electrical stimulations. This is of great interest for deep-brain stimulation used in the treatment of Parkinson's disease and underscores the need for morphologically realistic models.

Table: Information processing in single neurons: Task-specific computations of direct behavioral relevance.

Biological goal	Computation	Biophysical mechanism	Model level	Experimental systems
Collision avoidance	Multiplication: object size x times angular velocity y	$xy = \exp(\log x + \log y)$ via input nonlinearity (log), dendritic summation (+), and output nonlinearity (exp)	III	Lobula giant movement detector in locusts
Sound localization	Logical AND: comparison of interaural time difference	Coincidence detection of two spikes, lagged by different axon delays	II	Binaural neurons in the auditory brainstem
Motion detection	Logical AND or AND-NOT: comparison of spatially adjacent but temporally shifted local light intensities	Coincidence detection of one lagged (axonal delay) and one nonlagged spike	IV	Peripheral neurons in the fly visual system
		Nonlinear dendritic processing	I, II	Retinal amacrine and ganglion cells
Motion anticipation	Linear filtering with negative feedback	Adaptation of neuronal gain	IV	Salamander and rabbit retinal ganglion cells
Intensity-invariant recognition of analog patterns	Separation of pattern identity and pattern intensity; subsequent comparison with stored template	Transformation: local stimulus intensity mapped to spike time using subthreshold membrane potential oscillations; readout: coincidence detection	III, IV	Insect and vertebrate olfactory neurons, in particular in antennal lobe and olfactory bulb, respectively
Short-term memory	Temporal integration or storage	Dendritic Ca waves	II	Layer V neurons in entorhinal cortex
		Transitions between two Ca-conductance tates	II	Layer V neurons in entorhinal cortex
Time interval prediction	Temporal integration or storage	Calcium dynamics with positive feedback	III	Climbing activity in prefrontal neurons
Redundancy reduction	Subtraction: local signal minus background signal	Dendritic summation	IV	Center-surround receptive fields in the visual system
Efficient coding in variable environment	Modification of tuning curve to track time-varying stimulus ensemble	Adaptation of single-cell input-output function	II, IV, V	Motion-sensitive H1 neuron in the fly visual system
		Consequence of Reichardt motion detector circuit	IV, V	

Level II: Reduced Compartmental Models

Although detailed compartmental models can approximate the dynamics of single neurons quite well, they suffer from several drawbacks. Their high dimensionality and intricate structure rule out any mathematical understanding of their emergent properties. Detailed models are also computationally expensive and are thus not well suited for large-scale network simulations. Reduced models with only one or few dendritic compartments overcome these problems and are often sufficient to understand somatodendritic interactions that govern spiking or bursting.

A well-matched task for such models is to relate behaviorally relevant computations on various time scales to salient features of neural structure and dynamics. For example, the detection of binaural time differences within Jeffress' time-delay framework has been explained in a three-compartment model of bipolar cells by local nonlinear input interactions and the fact that each of the two dendrites provides a sink for inputs received by the other dendrite. Computations involving short-term memory may rely in part on the existence of multiple stable firing rates in single neurons. Reduced compartmental models suggest that calcium currents are essential for this phenomenon, through dendritic calcium wavefronts or transitions between different conductance states. On longer time scales, neurons self-adjust their activity patterns, both during development and after external perturbations. Simulations with a two-compartment model show that such homeostatic plasticity can follow from cellular "learning" rules that recalibrate dendritic channel densities to yield optimal spike encoding of synaptic inputs. For large-scale network studies, reduced compartmental models offer a good compromise between realism and computational efficiency. For example, a simulation involving several classes of multi-compartmental cortical and thalamic neurons and a total of more than 3000 cells demonstrates that gap junctions are instrumental for cortical gamma oscillations. A slightly less complex network with two-compartment neurons reproduces slow-wave sleep oscillations. Clearly, the challenge for all such studies is to find the least complex neuron models with which the observed phenomena can still be recreated.

Level III: Single-Compartment

Models Single-compartment models such as the classic Hodgkin-Huxley model neglect the neuron's spatial structure and focus entirely on how it's various ionic currents contribute to subthreshold behavior and spike generation. These models have led to a quantitative understanding of many dynamical phenomena including phasic spiking, bursting, and spike-frequency adaptation.

Systematic mathematical reductions of Hodgkin-Huxley–type models and subsequent bifurcation and phase-plane analysis explain why, for example, some neurons resemble integrate-and-fire elements or why the membrane potential of others oscillates in response to current injections enabling a "resonate-and-fire" behavior. They also show which combination of dynamical variables governs the threshold operation and how adaptation and spike-generation mechanisms influence spike trains.

Diversity of neural response patterns: As illustrated in the top row, neurons can respond with rather different spiketrain patterns to identical step currents. For time-varying inputs (middle row), the computational power of even simple single-neuron models becomes apparent: A first current pulse might trigger a subthreshold oscillation. Only if a second pulse arrives at the right phase of this oscillation is a spike triggered through resonance. An integrator, on the other hand, is driven most effectively by quickly succeeding pulses. Finally, a bistable cell can realize a toggle-switch.

These phenomena are exhibited by the same point-neuron model: Its time evolution (bottom row, left) is derived from Hodgkin-Huxley–type dynamics; involves the membrane potential v and a slower auxiliary variable u; and generates the different responses for specific values (right) of the parameters c (reset of voltage v with peak p) and a, b, and d (decay rate, sensitivity, and reset of the auxiliary variable u).

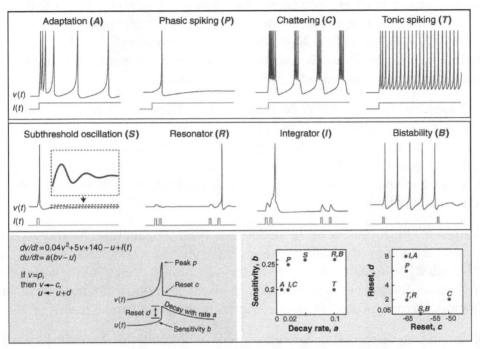

Spike generation is not a deterministic process. The stochastic dynamics of ion channels generate voltage noise that limits the reliability and precision of spikes. Background synaptic noise, on the other hand, can modulate the neural gain without changing spike variability or mean firing rates. But even without intrinsic noise, the all-or-none characteristics of spike generation amplify the input variability—perhaps this is the price of long-distance communication. More than 50 years after Hodgkin and Huxley analyzed the squid axon, simple neuron models still offer surprises, as these findings show. A recent study even indicates that the standard Hodgkin-Huxley formalism does not explain the sharp kink at the onset of cortical spikes. Its mechanistic origin and functional consequences require further investigation.

Level IV: Cascade Models

Whereas models incorporating specific ionic currents or morphological details are needed to investigate the biophysics of single neurons, modeling on a more conceptual level allows one to directly address their computations. To this end, cascade models based on a concatenation of mathematical primitives, such as linear filters, nonlinear transformations, and random processes, present an excellent framework for distilling key processing steps from measured data.

Consider, for example, a model that first convolves its time-varying input with a linear filter and then applies a rectifying nonlinearity. In studies of sensory systems, this simple structure is often considered as the canonical model for the receptive field of a neuron and the transformation of its internal activation state into a firing rate. The appeal of this linear-nonlinear (LN) cascade stems from its conceptual simplicity and the fact that, for white-noise stimulation, it can be easily fitted to experimental data by correlating response and stimulus. Recent studies even demonstrate that LN cascades can be obtained under far more naturalistic stimulation.

Cascade models have a long tradition in the investigation of the visual system. More recently, they have been used to assess neuronal sensitivity for different stimulus features and have helped to elucidate the simultaneous adaptation to mean light intensity and light contrast and the generic nature of adaptation in the retina. New analysis tools have opened up the possibility of using multiple parallel linear filters in an LN cascade to investigate, for example, complex cells in visual cortex and thus improve on classical energy-integration models.

Extending LN cascades allows one to capture additional neural characteristics while retaining the ability to fit these more complex models to experimental data. To reveal filter mechanisms that are otherwise hidden by spike-time jitter, one may append a noise process to the cascade or measure spike probabilities instead of spike times. For the latter method, temporal resolution is limited only by the precision of stimulus presentation so that parameters of more elaborate models (e.g., LNLN cascades) can be obtained.

The analog output of traditional cascade models describes a firing rate. An important conceptual extension is therefore achieved by adding an explicit spike generation stage. Using a fixed firing threshold and feedback mimicking neural refractoriness, this has led to a successful model of spike timing in early vision. Even when augmented with an integrate-and-fire mechanism and intrinsic bursting, this model structure still allows generic fits to measured spike trains.

Cascade models can also directly translate into specific computations: Experiments indicate that in locusts, an identified neuron multiplies the visual size x and angular velocity y of an object while tracking its approach. The nearly exponential shape of this neuron's output curve suggests that logarithmic transforms of x and y are summed on the dendrite and then passed through the output nonlinearity, implementing the multiplicative operation as an NLN cascade via the identity $\exp(\log x + \log y) = xy$.

Despite their success, simple model structures have their limitations—especially when applied to neurons far downstream from the sensory periphery and when aimed at generalizing over different stimulus types—because additional nonlinear dynamics, negligible within a specific stimulation context, affect the transition between different experimental conditions. In specific cases, however, LN models yield accurate information-theoretical descriptions of neuronal responses.

Level V: Black-Box Models

Last but not least, one may want to understand and quantify the signal-processing capabilities of a single neuron without considering its biophysical machinery. This approach may reveal general principles that explain, for example, where neurons place their operating points and how they alter their responses when the input statistics are modified.

For such questions about neural efficiency and adaptability, a neuron is best regarded as a black box that receives a set of time-dependent inputs—sensory stimuli or spike trains from other neurons—and responds with an output spike train. To account for cell-intrinsic noise, it is necessary to characterize the input-output relation by a probability distribution, $p(R|S)$, which measures the probability that response R occurs when stimulus S is presented.

Although models on levels I to IV make specific assumptions about neural processes and hence about the functional form of p(R|S), such assumptions can be overly restrictive at level V. Here, it is often advantageous to work with nonparametric estimates of p(R|S) that are directly taken from the measured data. Such models have, for example, been used to estimate the information that the spike train of a neuron conveys about its inputs and have revealed that sensory neurons operate highly efficiently, often close to their physical limits. Indeed, Barlow's "efficient coding hypothesis" suggests that neurons optimize the information about frequently occurring stimuli.

Theoretical studies have shown how individual neurons may shift their input-output curves to reach that goal. Moreover, recordings of a motion sensitive neuron in the fly visual system reveal that adaptation can modify a neuron's input-output function to maximize information about time-varying sensory stimuli. In this case, however, it is possible that the adaptive mechanism is not implemented on the single-cell level but instead results from the underlying multicellular Reichardt motion detection circuitry. Similar ambiguities between single-cell and network adaptation exist in the auditory midbrain. Evolutionary adaptations may not be guided to optimize the information about all natural stimuli. In acoustic communication systems, for example, neural responses are well matched to particular behaviorally relevant subensembles. Most likely, stimuli from those ensembles were selected as communication signals because they lead to efficient neural representations.

Challenges

"A good theoretical model of a complex system should be like a good caricature: it should emphasize those features which are most important and should downplay the inessential details. Now the only snag with this advice is that one does not really know which the inessential details are until one has understood the phenomena under study". This general dilemma, formulated by the physicist Frenkel almost a century ago, applies in particular to the single neuron. Which details of ionic conductances and morphology are relevant for particular aspects of its cell type–specific or individual dynamics? How do these dynamics contribute to the neuron's information processing? Identification of a fundamental computation performed by the neuron may help address these questions. Brain function, however, relies on the interplay of hundreds to billions of neurons that are arranged in specialized modules on multiple anatomical hierarchies. Even today, it remains unclear which level of single-cell modeling is appropriate to understand the dynamics and computations carried out by such large systems. However, only by understanding how single cells operate as part of a network can we assess their coding and thus the level of detail required for modeling. For example, most network models use point-neuron models, whereas several aspects of brain function require multi-compartmental models.

It has thus become increasingly clear that a thorough understanding of single-neuron function can be obtained only by relating different levels of abstraction. Trying to incorporate every biological detail of the investigated neuron is likely to obscure the focus on the essential dynamics, whereas limiting investigations to highly abstract processing schemes casts doubt on the biological relevance of specific findings. Help may come from analyzing the transition between different modeling levels. Interesting connections have been drawn, for example, by transforming a Hodgkin-Huxley–type model (level III) into a phenomenological firing rate description or a cascade on level IV. And the integrative properties of dendritic trees as evolved as those of pyramidal cells can be captured by a two layer feed-forward network (i.e., an NLN cascade) (level IV), at least for stationary stimuli. For non-stationary stimuli, however, the cascade fails. This underscores the need to alternate between different levels of single-neuron models in close connection with considerations about the neural codes of larger cell populations.

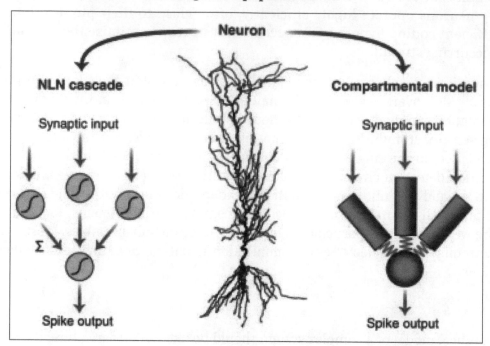

Figure above shows single-neuron computation: The neuron in the center can be approximated by an NLN cascade (left) for stationary inputs, or, more generally, by a compartmental model (right). The cascade (level IV) is equivalent to a two-layer feed-forward network and shows that under a firing-rate assumption, a single neuron may perform the function of an entire artificial neural net. Electrical couplings within compartmental models (levels I and II) are bidirectional. The right model therefore corresponds to a feedback network and can exhibit persistent activity, hysteresis, periodic oscillations, and even chaos. These phenomena are impossible in feed-forward systems and may support complex computations in the time domain. The relevance of either model depends on the statistics of synaptic inputs (i.e., on the neural code of the investigated brain area).

Deriving model parameters from experimental data brings about its own collection of problems: How should we deal with the cell-to-cell variability of parameter values? The common resort, population averaging, can be misleading because the dynamical behavior of single-cell models is, in general, not a monotone function of their parameters; the mean behavior within a class of models may strongly differ from that of a model with mean parameter values, and nearly identical dynamical characteristics may be implemented by rather different parameter combinations. With increasing model complexity, the number of parameters to be estimated increases to such an extent that they must be taken from different cells or even different preparations, further lowering the model's trustworthiness. Furthermore, models are often calibrated using in vitro data, yet they are designed to capture the neural dynamics and computations of behaving animals.

FitzHugh–Nagumo Model

Hodgkin-Huxley (HH), Hindmarsh-Rose (HR), and FitzHugh-Nagumo (FHN) models are among the most successful dynamical models in computational neuroscience for capturing neural firing behaviors. The HH model consists of four differential equations with a high number of coefficients. Although this model is capable of generating all the behaviors of neuron spiking, it is a highly nonlinear model. The HR model, on the other hand, consists of three differential equations, which are highly coupled, and it can exhibit all the firing modes obtained from the HH model except for biophysically meaningful behaviors. Finally, the FHN model consists of two differential equations, and is simpler than the HH and HR models, though it is unable to exhibit important firing behaviors such as bursting. In fact, it has been noted that without using a reset or adding noise, the FHN model cannot exhibit bursting.

The Fitzhugh-Nagumo Model with Time Varying Threshold

A simplified version of the HH model is the FHN model:

$$\frac{dv}{dt} = a\left(-v(v-1)(v-b)-w+I\right), \quad \frac{dw}{dt} = v - cw$$

where v is the membrane potential, w is the recovery variable, a and c are scaling parameters, and I is the stimulus current. Moreover, b is an unstable equilibrium that corresponds to the threshold between electrical silence and electrical firing. For appropriate constant parameters, it is possible to generate tonic firing using FHN, where tonic firing is referred to as a firing behavior in which the neuron spikes in a periodic manner.

Considering that conventionally the parameters in the FHN model are kept constant, certain firing behaviors such as bursting cannot be obtained using this model. Since I is an external input, it can externally control the firing mode observed in the output (v), and result in firing behaviors such as bursting; on the other hand, the parameters a, b, and c are governed by the mechanisms internal to the neuron, and their variations can be associated to some internal physiological system. We consider variations in b because b is the threshold between electrical silence and neural firing, and physiologically, it might be the case that this threshold is varying throughout the day, causing the neurons to switch on and off, and generate bursting.

Since b can control the firing frequency, we propose that by varying b in FHN, it is possible to obtain firing modes such as bursting. The following is our proposed extension to FHN model, which includes a time-varying threshold:

$$\frac{dv}{dt} = a\left(-v(v-1)(v-b)-w+I\right), \quad \frac{dw}{dt} = v - cw, \quad \frac{db}{dt} = g(t)$$

Tonic Bursting

Tonic bursting is a firing behavior in which a neuron fires a certain number of spikes and is silent for a certain amount of time. Then, it repeats this pattern in a periodic manner. To simulate tonic bursting using FHN, we keep a, I, and c at constant values 10^5, 1, and 0.2, respectively, and vary b using a sinusoidal function. This is one possible way of varying b in order to obtain tonic bursting.

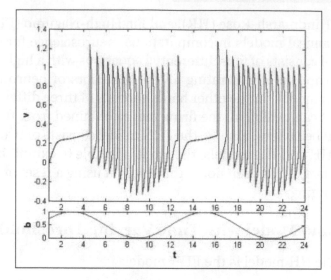

Varying Frequency Neural Firing

Neural firing with varying frequency can also be obtained using FHN. To simulate this firing mode, we keep the parameters a, I, and c fixed at constant values 10^5, 1, and 0.3, respectively, while slowly varying b using a two-harmonic function.

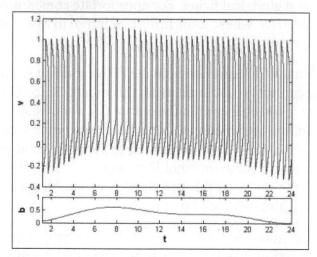

Parameter Estimation

Parameter estimation for the HH, HR and FHN models is usually done using standard methods such as Simulated Annealing, Genetic Algorithms, Differential Evolution, Adaptive Observer, or Extended Kalman Filter. However, in principle, if the model has a known structure, one could exploit it to formulate a parameter estimation method customized to that model and tune it to get better performance than the standard methods. In the following, we develop one such method for estimating the parameter b for the FHN model by exploiting the fast-slow dynamics of FHN. We will then compare the performance of this method with that of the EKF.

Estimating b using Fast-Slow Dynamics of the FitzHugh-Nagumo Model

Figure is a representation of the slow and fast manifolds of FHN on the wv-plane and its corresponding behavior with respect to the time-series plot of v. The phase portrait shows that, in case of tonic firing mode, the trajectories switch between slow scale dynamics and fast scale dynamics. Considering the dynamics of the FHN model, we propose to develop a novel estimation algorithm that exploits the multiple time-scale feature of FHN. To do so, we will start with a time-series plot of membrane potentials v that are firing in a tonic manner, and develop an algorithm to estimate b, which we refer to as the Fast-Slow Dynamics (FSD) estimation algorithm. Since v does not change much when the system is following the slow time scale dynamics of FHN, we will approximate its derivative as zero. $\dfrac{dv}{dt} = 0 \Rightarrow w = -v(v-1)(v-b)+I$. Then, define f as: $f(v,b,I) = -v(v-1)(v-b)+I$.

Let v_2 and v_0 be the values of v that maximize and minimize f:

$$v_0 = \frac{1}{3}\left(b+1-\sqrt{b^2-b+1}\right), \ v_2 = \frac{1}{3}\left(b+1+\sqrt{b^2-b+1}\right)$$

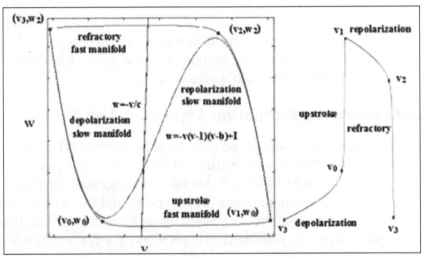

Phase Portrait (left) and Time-series Plot (right): a = 1369, b = 0.2, I = 1, c = 0.3.

As observed in figure, w_2 and w_0 do not exactly correspond to maximum and minimum values of f; however, we can approximate w_2 and w_0 by plugging in the values of v_2 and v_0 in f(v,b,I), as shown below:

$$w_0 \approx -\frac{2}{27}\sqrt{\left(b^2-b+1\right)^3} + \frac{2}{27}b^3 - \frac{1}{9}b^2 - \frac{1}{9}b + \frac{2}{27} + I$$

$$w_2 \approx \frac{2}{27}\sqrt{\left(b^2-b+1\right)^3} + \frac{2}{27}b^3 - \frac{1}{9}b^2 - \frac{1}{9}b + \frac{2}{27} + I$$

Let $h_0(b) = w_0 - I$ and $h_2(b) = w_2 - I$. From the time series data of membrane potentials, it is possible to obtain the maximum and minimum values of v, v_1 and v_3, respectively. As observed in figure, $f(v_1,b,I) \approx w_0$ and $f(v_3,b,I) \approx w_2$. Hence, we obtain:

$$-v_1(v_1-1)(v_1-b) \approx h_0(b), \ v_3(v_3-1)(v_3-b) \approx h_2(b).$$

Since there are two equations and one unknown, the system might not have a solution; in cases that the system has a solution, the solution can be obtained using equation below:

$$-v_1(v_1-1)(v_1-b)+ v_3(v_3-1)(v_3-b)=-\frac{4}{27}\sqrt{(b^2-b+1)^3}$$

For simplicity in the computation, one can approximate $-\frac{4}{27}\sqrt{(b^2-b+1)^3}$ by $-0.21b^2+0.21b-0.15$.

Let $h_b=-v_1(v_1-1)(v_1-b)+v_3(v_3-1)(v_3-b)+0.21b^2-0.21b+0.15$. Setting $h_b = 0$, two values for b are obtained, and considering that b takes on a value between zero and one, the value of b that satisfies this bound is the desired solution. In the cases that both solutions satisfy the bound, we plug both values of b into above equation, and the value that minimizes the absolute value of the difference between the two sides of equation above is the desired value of b. If a b value is not obtained using this approach, we will find the value of b that minimizes h_b. If this value still does not satisfy the bound, one could plug in values zero and one into above equation and the value that minimizes the absolute value of the difference between the two sides of above equation is the desired value of b.

Using parameters a = 10^5, I = 1, c = 0.3 for the FHN model, and starting with b = 0.05 and increasing the b value in 0.05 increments until the system does not have a tonic behavior (b = 0.75), we estimated b, and the error varied between 0.42% and 5.20%.

Comparison of Constant b Estimation Algorithm with Extended Kalman Filter

A novel approach for estimating b was proposed. Here, we compare the b estimates given by the Fast-Slow Dynamics (FSD) estimation algorithm and EKF. In order to compare our estimation method with EKF, process noise and sensor noise were incorporated into the simulations. Let σ_p and σ_s represent the standard deviation in the process noise and the sensor noise, respectively. In order to implement EKF, we discretized the system using Euler forward method with a sampling rate Δ. For this comparison, v was simulated using a = 10^5, I = 1, c = 0.3, b = 0.5 while adding a zero-mean normal process noise with a standard deviation of 0.1 (σ_p = 0.1), and the sampling rate and sensor noise were varied as discussed in the following three examples. Moreover, we averaged the data for 24 tonic firings to run FSD and implemented EKF while using the actual initial condition values as the initial guess, and an initial covariance estimate of zero.

A zero-mean sensor noise with σ_s = 0.001 was added to the simulated membrane potentials for Δ = 10^{-5}. Using our method, a b estimate of 0.5079 (1.58% error) was obtained. Then, EKF was implemented on the data, and the estimated value of b after one limit cycle was 0.5001 (0.02% error). In this simulation, the sampling rate was very high and the sensor noise was very low, putting EKF in an advantage. However, by increasing the sensor noise or decreasing the sampling rate, our method performed better than EKF.

By adding zero-mean sensor noise with σ_s = 0.01 to the simulated action potentials, and using Δ = 10^{-5}, a b estimate of 0.5253 (5.06% error) was obtained using our method while b estimates for EKF did not converge and varied between 0.1358 and 1.47. For Δ = 10^{-3}, and a zero-mean sensor noise with σ_s = 0.001, we implemented both FSD and EKF. Using FSD a b estimate of 0.5175 (3.5% error) was obtained, while EKF diverged. Hence, comparing the two methods, EKF is more sensitive to sampling rate than our method. Moreover, EKF does not converge if the sensor noise covariance is large.

Comparison of Time-varying b Estimation Algorithm with Extended Kalman Filter

Here, using examples, we will illustrate that FastSlow Dynamics (FSD) estimation algorithm for constant b can be employed on neural firing data that is generated by time-varying b. We will compare FSD estimation algorithm with EKF for tonic bursting, which can be obtained using a sinusoidal b. For this comparison, process noise and sensor noise were incorporated into the simulations. For this comparison, v was simulated using a = 10^5, I = 1, c = 0.3, b = 0.5 while adding a zero-mean normal process noise with σ_p = 0.1, and the sampling rate and sensor noise were varied as discussed in the following three examples.

We simulated five datasets using this method for each of the following examples, and used the average of these datasets in order to estimate the parameters. In order to run FSD for time-varying b, we found the membrane potential peaks, and broke the data into smaller data sets, in a way that each smaller dataset started at one peak and ended at the following peak (in other words, we break the data points in a way that each of these smaller datasets goes through the limit cycle once). Then, using our algorithm for estimating constant b, we estimated b for each of these smaller datasets. Then, we associated each of these estimates with the time that the second peak was observed. Let $\lambda = \dfrac{2\pi}{T}$. Knowing that b was a sinusoid of the form $\alpha \sin\left(\dfrac{2\pi}{T}t + \beta\right) + \gamma$, we found the period by looking at the time series plot of the b estimates, and then using the trigonometric identity, we rewrote this problem as $\alpha \sin\left(\dfrac{2\pi}{T}t\right)\cos(\beta) + \alpha \cos\left(\dfrac{2\pi}{T}t\right)\sin(\beta) + \gamma$, and implemented multiple regression to find the coefficients α, β, and γ. In order to implement EKF, we used the actual initial condition values as the initial guess, and an initial covariance estimate of zero.

After adding a zero-mean sensor noise with σ_s = 0.001 to data with $\Delta = 10^{-5}$, we implemented FSD and EKF. The parameter estimates and the corresponding percent error for each of the parameters is reported in Table. In reporting the EKF estimate, we ignored the estimates for which the error covariance matrix becomes very high.

Table: Comparison of parameter estimates obtained by FSD and EKF for example for time-varying b.

	FSD estimate	FSD error	EKF's estimate	EKF's error
$\alpha = 0.5$	0.4926	1.48%	0.5	0%
T = 12	11.933	0.5583%	12	0%
$\cos(\beta) = 1$	0.9804	1.9558%	1	0%
$\gamma = 0.5$	0.4937	1.26%	0.5	0%

By adding a zero-mean sensor noise with $\sigma_s^2 = 0.1$, and using $\Delta = 10^{-5}$, we implemented FSD and EKF. The EKF parameter estimates became very noisy; however, the average value of the noisy parameter estimates obtained by EKF had a small error, and here we are reporting the average value of the noisy estimates as the EKF parameter estimate. The parameter estimates and the corresponding percent error for each of the parameters are reported in table. For $\Delta = 10^{-3}$, and a zero-mean sensor noise with $\sigma_s = 0.001$, using our method parameter estimates reported in Table III were obtained, while EKF diverged.

Table: Comparison of parameter estimates obtained by FSD and EKF for example for time-varying b.

	FSD estimate	FSD error	EKF's estimate	EKF's error
$\alpha = 0.5$	0.5708	4.72%	0.5045	0.9%
$T = 12$	11.933	0.5583%	12.1461	1.2176%
$\cos(\beta) = 1$	0.9944	0.56%	1	0%
$\gamma = 0.5$	0.5602	12.04%	0.5062	1.24%

	FSD estimate	FSD error	EKF's estimate	EKF's error
$\alpha = 0.5$	0.4638	7.24%	Diverged	NA
$T = 12$	12.029	0.2417%	Diverged	NA
$\cos(\beta) = 1$	0.9215	7.8511%	Diverged	NA
$\gamma = 0.5$	0.4996	0.08%	Diverged	NA

Our proposed method could be implemented on other firing patterns such as the varying frequency neural firing pattern by again fitting the estimated values of b using multiple regressions. In the cases that b follows two or more different functions as a function of time, one could break the data into two parts at the point that the variations in the function occurs, and depending on the kind of function b is following linear or multiple regression could be used to fit the b estimates.

Hindmarsh–Rose Model

The Hodgkin-Huxley model is a mathematical model of current flow through ion-selective channels in neural membrane. Hodgkin and Huxley were able to describe the time behavior of the intracellular membrane potential and the currents through potassium (K) and sodium (Na) channels with simple first-order ordinary differential equations. This was done using parameters fitted from their voltage clamp Technique measurements on the giant axon of the squid. With this model, they quantitatively described the generation of action potentials by current injection and observable behavior such as the refractory period and the anode break phenomenon. With other sets of parameters, the Hodgkin-Huxley model has been used to describe many other types of voltage-dependent ion channels and has become a standard technique in compartmental modeling of neurons.

The mathematical model is based upon the equivalent circuit for a patch of cell membrane. The two variable conductances G_K and G_{Na} shown in the diagram represent the average effect of the binary gating of many potasssium and sodium channels, and the constant "leakage conductance" G_L represents the effect of other channels (primarily chloride) which are always open. Each of these is associated with an equilbrium potential, represented by a battery in series with the conductance.

The net current which flows into the cell through these channels has the effect of charging the membrane capacitance, giving the interior of the cell a membrane potential V_m relative to the exterior. From basic circuit theory, we know that the current which charges a capacitor is equal to the capacitance times the rate of change of the voltage across the capacitor. Ohm's law gives the current through each of the conductances, resulting in the equation,

$$C_m \frac{dV_m}{dt} = G_{Na}(E_{Na} - V_m) + G_K(E_K - V_m) + G_L(E_L - V_m) + I_{inject}.$$

Here, an additional term I_{inject} has been added to describe any currents which are externally applied during the course of an experiment. In principle, all that is needed in order to find the time course of the membrane potential is to solve this simple differential equation.

The hard part was to model the time and voltage dependence of the Na and K conductances. Their solution was to perform a series of voltage clamp experiments measuring both the total current and the current when the Na conductance was disabled. This enabled them to calculate the K current and, from these currents and the known voltages, calculate the values of the two conductances. By performing the experiments with different values of the clamp voltage, they were able to determine the time dependence and equilibrium value of the conductances at different voltages. Some typical results for the behavior of the K and Na conductances when the clamping voltage is stepped to several different values and then released. From these measurements they were able to fit the the K conductance to an equation of the form,

$$G_K = \bar{g}K^{n^4},$$

where n is called the "activation state variable" and has a simple exponential dependence governed by a single time constant, τ_n:

$$n(t) = n_\infty(V) - (n_\infty(V) - n_\infty(0))e^{-t/\tau_n}.$$

$n_\infty(V)$ is called the "steady state activation", i.e. the value reached by n when it is held at the potential V for a long period of time. Hodgkin and Huxley were able to fit the voltage dependence of n_∞ and τ_n to an analytic function of voltage involving exponentials. In the interest of brevity, we will not give these equations here. However, the plot of $n_\infty(V)$ shown further below, reveals that it is a monotonically increasing function of V, reaching a maximum value of 1.

If we are describing the time course of action potentials rather than the behavior during a voltage clamp, n_∞ and τ_n are changing along with the changing membrane potential, so we can't use this equation for n. Instead, we use a differential equation which has this solution when V is constant,

$$dn(V)/dt = (n_\infty(V) - n(V))/\tau_n(V)$$

Their fit for the Na conductance was a little different, because they found that at a fixed voltage, the conductance rose with time and then decreased, so they had to fit it to a product,

$$G_{Na} = \bar{g}_{Na}m^3h.$$

Here, m is the activation variable for Na, and h is called the "inactivation state variable", since it becomes smaller when m (and the membrane potential) becomes larger. m and h obey equations just like the ones for n, but with different voltage dependences for their steady state values and time constants. These voltage dependences are shown in the following plot, derived from Hodgkin and Huxley's fit to their experimental results:

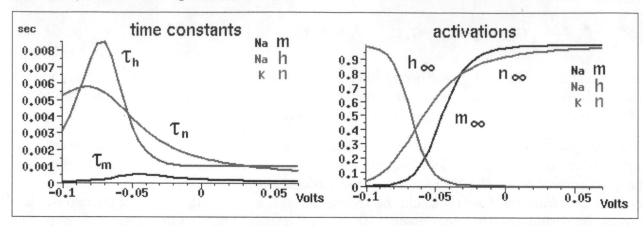

We now have all that was needed by Hodgkin and Huxley to reconstruct the action potential. For a given injection current I_{inject}, equation $C_m \dfrac{dV_m}{dt} = G_{Na}\left(E_{Na} - V_m\right) + G_K\left(E_K - V_m\right) + G_L\left(E_L - V_m\right) + I_{inject}$ is solved for V_m, using equations $G_K = \overline{g}K^{n^4}$ and $G_{Na} = \overline{g}_{Na} m^3 h$ for the conductances. These two equations must be solved simultaneously with Equation $dn(V)/dt = \left(n_\infty(V) - n(V)\right)/\tau_n(V)$ and the two analogous equations for m and h. These last equations make use of the voltage dependent quantities shown in the plot.

This plot shows that although the time constants vary with voltage, the time constant for the Na activation variable m is about an order of magnitude less than that for the Na inactivation and the K activation throughout the entire range. This means that during an action potential, when the voltage is high and m is large, and h is supposed to be small, it will take a while for h to decrease. Also, it will take n a while to become large and contribute to the opposing K current.

Building Equations to Produce an Action Potential

We will first describe how a very simple set of basic assumptions about the gates leads to a series of equations that describe the active properties of the nerve membrane. We will then describe how experimental data is used to provide numerical parameters to plug into these equations, so that the equations can reconstruct an action potential.

Voltage Dependency of Gate Position

In the HH model the individual gates act like a first order chemical reaction with two states. This can be written thus:

$$\text{shut} \underset{\beta}{\overset{\alpha}{\rightleftarrows}} \text{open}$$

The factors α and β are called the transition rate constants. α is the number of times per second that a gate which is in the shut state opens, while β is the number of times per second that a gate which is in the open state shuts. All the gates within a particular class have the same value of α and the same value of β (which is likely to be different from the value of α) at any instant in time, but gates which belong to different classes may have different values of α and β. This gives the different classes their different properties. The key factor in the HH model which allows action potentials to be generated is that α and β are voltage dependent.

So how does the open probability of a gate depend upon α and β? For a whole population of gates, let us say a proportion P are in the open state, where P varies between 0 and 1. This means that a proportion 1-P will be in the closed state. The fraction of the total population which opens in a given time is dependent on the proportion of gates which are shut, and the rate at which shut gates open:

$$\text{Fraction of gates opening} = \alpha(1-P)$$

and similarly,

$$\text{Fraction of gates shutting} = \beta P$$

If a system is in equilibrium, where the proportion of gates in the open state is not changing, then the fraction of gates opening must equal the fraction of gates closing in any given period of time,

$$\alpha(1-P) = \beta P$$

which rearranges as,

$$P_\omega = \frac{\alpha}{\alpha+\beta}$$

Thus if α is high and β is low, the gate has a high probability of being open, and vice versa. (The infinity subscript is used for P because the system only achieves equilibrium if α and β remain stable for a relatively long period of time).

The voltage dependency of P arises because the fundamental transition rate constants α and β are themselves voltage dependent. Clearly, if the membrane potential changes, and consequently the values of α and β for a particular class of gate change, then the open probability P for that class of gate must also change. For activation gates the voltage dependency of α and β is such that a depolarising shift in membrane potential causes P to increase, while for inactivation gates the change in α and β causes P to decrease.

The HH model assumes that α and β change instantly with a change in voltage. However, this does not lead to an instantaneous change in the value of P. The rate at which P achieves its new value following a change in α and/or β is equal to the difference in the rate of shutting and the rate of opening:

$$\frac{dP}{dt} = \alpha(1-P) - \beta P$$

If we substitute the steady-state value of P in terms of α and β from equation $P_\infty = \dfrac{\alpha}{\alpha+\beta}$ into the right hand side of this equation, dP/dt becomes 0, as of course it should in steady state conditions. Thus, following a change in voltage, the rate of change of P, as well as the direction and size of change, is dependent on the values of α and β. Depending on the values of α and β, some classes of gates will respond more rapidly to changes in voltage than others.

The differential equation above has a solution,

$$P = P_\infty - \left(P_\infty - P_{start}\right)e^{-t/r}$$

where,

$$\tau = \frac{1}{\alpha+\beta}$$

These equations can be understood as follows. We start with assuming that the system has been at a fixed constant voltage for a long period of time, and therefore P is at a starting equilibrium value P_{start} defined in equation $P_\infty = \dfrac{\alpha}{\alpha+\beta}$. The voltage is then changed suddenly, and α and β immediately switch to new values appropriate to the new voltage. P then starts to change, and approaches its new equilibrium value P_∞ (also defined in equation $P_\infty = \dfrac{\alpha}{\alpha+\beta}$ but with the new values for α and β) with an exponential time course with a time constant of τ. If either α or β are large, then the time constant is short and P arrives at its new value rapidly. If both are small, then the time constant is long and it takes longer for P to reach equilibrium.

By combining equations $P_\infty = \dfrac{\alpha}{\alpha+\beta}$ and $\tau = \dfrac{1}{\alpha+\beta}$ it is possible to express α and β in terms of P_∞ and τ:

$$\alpha = \frac{P_\infty}{\tau}$$

and

$$\beta = \frac{1-P_\infty}{\tau}$$

There is thus a simple relationship between α and β, and the equilibrium value of P and the time constant with which P attains this equilibrium value.

Voltage Dependency of Channel Conductance

Let us start the next stage of analysis by considering the situation when the voltage is stable, as it is when the membrane is sitting at the resting potential. For each class of gate in each type of channel, α and β have values appropriate for the voltage, and P (the probability of a gate being open) is at its steady-state equilibrium value given in equation $P_\infty = \dfrac{\alpha}{\alpha+\beta}$. If a channel contains several (say x) gates of that class within it, the probability of the whole channel being open is P raised to the power of the number of gates within the channel (i.e. P^x). This is because all the gates have to be open for the channel to be open.

HH proposed that each K channel has 4 identical activation gates (x = 4). We can replace the general probability value P with the specific probability of a K-channel n-gate being open, n, so the probability of a whole K channel being open is n^4. Thus, to make this concrete, if at a particular voltage the probability of an n-gate being open is one half (n = 0.5), then the probability of an individual K channel being open is 0.5*0.5*0.5*0.5, or 1 in 16. By scaling up, we can say that 1 out of every 16 in the whole population of K channels will be open, and thus the actual K conductance (gK) will be 1/16 of the maximum possible K conductance, i.e.

$$gK = n^4 gK_{max}$$

where gK_{max} is the membrane K conductance when all the K channels are open.

The HH model proposes that the Na channel has 3 activation m-gates, and one inactivation h-gate, and so by the same reasoning, the Na conductance is,

$$gNa = m^3 h gNa_{max}$$

Current Flow through Channels

Once the conductance of a population of ion channels is known, the ionic current that flows through the channels can be calculated. This is because there is usually a fairly simple relationship between current (I), conductance (g), membrane potential (E_m) and the reversal (equilibrium) potential (E_{eq}) of an ion, when the current is carried by that single ion species:

$$I = g\left(E_m - E_{eq}\right)$$

This equation is a variant of Ohm's law. The factor $E_m - E_{eq}$, which is a measure of how far the membrane potential is from the equilibrium potential of the ion in question, is called the driving force on the ion, and is equivalent to straight voltage in Ohm's law. We can make this equation specific for K ions,

$$I_K = gK\left(E_m - E_K\right)$$

where I_K is the K current and E_K is the K equilibrium potential. A similar equation gives the Na current,

$$I_{Na} = gNa\left(E_m - E_{Na}\right)$$

There is a third current we have to consider; the leakage current. As well as the voltage-dependent channels, the membrane has a small, non-voltage-dependent conductance to both Na and K. This is known as the leakage conductance, and it is always present and remains constant whatever the voltage. The K leakage conductance is much higher than the Na leakage conductance (although both are small compared to the voltage-dependent conductances when they are activated), and so the leakage conductance acts as if it had an equilibrium potential close to resting potential.

$$I_{leak} = gLeak(E_m - E_{Leak})$$

Equations for the Membrane Potential

It is intuitively obvious that if there is an imbalance in current across the membrane such that more positive charge enters the cell than leaves it, this will change the membrane potential and cause it to depolarise (and vice versa). The change in membrane potential occurs because the unbalanced current alters the charge on the membrane capacitor. This leads to the following relationship:

$$C_m \frac{dV}{dt} = I_{ionic} + I_{stim}$$

In this equation the expression $C_m(dV/dt)$ is the capacity current, and it derives simply from the property of capacitance, which says that the current into a capacitor is proportional to the size of the capacitance and the rate of change of voltage (dV/dt) across it. The equation states that the capacity current is equal to the arithmetic sum of all the currents across the membrane this follows from the fact that if there is an imbalance between positive and negative membrane current, the "spare" current has nowhere else to go except into the membrane capacitor. The membrane current consists of the ionic current I_{ionic}, which is the sum of the Na, K and leakage currents calculated from the modified Ohm's law given above in equations $I_K = gK(E_m - E_K)$, $I_{Na} = gNa(E_m - E_{Na})$ and $I_{leak} = g_{Leak}(E_m - E_{Leak})$ plus any stimulating current I_{stim} that is injected.

Equation above strictly applies only to a space-clamped neuron, or a single-compartment model. In other words, it assumes that there is no lateral flow of current within the neuron. If there were such flow, it would have to be added in to the right-hand side of the equation. We can re-write equation above thus,

$$\frac{dV}{dt} = \frac{-(I_{stim} + I_{ionic})}{C_m}$$

In the resting neuron by definition the membrane potential is not changing, i.e. dV/dt (the rate of change of voltage) is 0. There is no stimulus applied, so I_{stim} is 0, and therefore I_{ionic} must also be 0. If I_{ionic} is 0, this means that the inward and outward currents flowing through the ionic channels exactly balance to cancel each other, which, of course, is what you would expect for a resting neuron.

Now imagine what happens if a stimulus is applied to the neuron, so I_{stim} is not 0. Initially I_{ionic} does not change (because none of the right hand sides of equations $I_K = gK(E_m - E_K)$, $I_{Na} = gNa(E_m - E_{Na})$ and $I_{leak} = gLeak(E_m - E_{Leak})$ change), and therefore the stimulus current flows into the membrane capacitor and dV/dt becomes non-zero. Thus at the next instant in time, the membrane potential V has a new value. This will instantly change the values of α and β for the channel gates, which will start to change the value of P for each of the gate classes (equation $\frac{dP}{dt} = \alpha(1-P) - \beta P$). If P (i.e. m, n and h) changes, then the channel conductance g will change (equations $gK = n^4 gK_{max}$ and $gNa = m^3 hgNa_{max}$). A change in both conductance and voltage is likely to result in a change in ionic current and this in turn is likely to lead to a further change in voltage (equation below). In this way an iterative feedback process is initiated. The triumph of the HH model is that when you put all these equations together with the appropriate parameters, the voltage changes have the waveform of an action potential.

Works of Hodgkin and Huxley

The original work of Hodgkin and Huxley (and some others) consisted of a three-stage process:

First: The Model Assumptions

They proposed the basic model, consisting of independent channels containing gates following first order kinetics, and with currents carried entirely by ions moving down electrochemical gradients. This is simple to state, but since there are very many alternative models that could have been proposed this was a very insightful step.

Second: Obtaining Parameters for the Model

In order to make use of the equations, appropriate numerical values had to be found to fill in the unknown parameters. There were 3 levels of detail required. First, the macro characteristics of the channel types (ionic specificity, maximum conductances, equilibrium potentials), had to be determined. Second, the number of activation and inactivation gates in each channel type had to be determined. Third, equations had to be found to describe the quantitative voltage dependency of α and β for each gate type in each channel type.

Ionic Properties

The fact that Na and K are the major ions involved in generating the squid action potential had been established in earlier work, as had the equilibrium potentials for those ions. HH used ion substitutions to treat Na and K currents separately, since TTX and TEA were not available in those days. They then used the voltage clamp technique to measure the steady-state current at various voltages, and the rate of change of current following a change in voltage. Since the equilibrium potentials were known, the Na and K conductances could be determined from the current records using equations $I_K = gK(E_m - E_K)$ and $I_{Na} = gNa(E_m - E_{Na})$. These conductance data provided the information needed to determine the remaining parameters.

Number of Gates

HH observed that during the depolarising step of a voltage clamp experiment the conductance change had a sigmoid shape, but during the repolarising step the conductance change had an exponential shape. HH knew that single first-order reactions of the type proposed for the individual channel gates should produce exponential curves, but that sigmoid curves would result from co-operative processes in which several first order reactions had to occur simultaneously. This fitted with the notion that the channels contained several gates, all of which had to be open at once in order for the channel itself to be open, hence the sigmoid shape of the rising curve. On the other hand, only one gate had to shut for the channel to shut, hence the exponential shape of the falling curve. In co-operative processes, the shape of the sigmoid part of the curve depends on the number of events involved; the greater the number of events, the more pronounced the inflexions on the curve. It was the exact shape of the experimentally-measured sigmoid curve that suggested that 4 would be the best estimate of independent gates within the K channel. Similar analysis of conductance curve shapes for Na suggested that 3 activation gates and one inactivation gate would best fit the data.

Voltage Dependency of Alpha and Beta

For any gate type there is a simple relation between the values of the transition rate constants α and β, the fraction of gates in the open state P, and the time constant with which that fraction approaches its equilibrium value τ. This means that if P and τ can be measured at a particular voltage, then α and β can easily be calculated. This was the approach taken by HH. It will be illustrated in detail for the K channel, but a similar approach was taken for the Na channel.

Equation $P = P_{\infty} - (P_{\infty} - P_{start})e^{-t/r}$ shows how the n-variable (the open probability of a single n gate in a K channel) changes with time upon a change of the transition rate constants α and β. Equation $gK = n^4 gK_{max}$ shows how the K conductance varies as the n-variable changes. Combining these equations yields the following:

$$gK(t) = \left\{ gK_{\infty}^{0.25} - \left(gK_{\infty}^{0.25} - gK_{start}^{0.25} \right) e^{\frac{-t}{\tau_n}} \right\}^4$$

Note that this equation (given as equation $gK = n^4 gK_{max}$ in the HH paper) is very similar to equation $P = P_{\infty} - (P_{\infty} - P_{start})e^{-t/r}$ except that the K conductance g_K replaces the general probability P, and that several factors are either raised to the fourth power, or the fourth root (this takes care of the fact that there are 4 n-gates per K channel). The equation describes a voltage clamp experiment in which gK_{start} is the stable K conductance at the holding potential before the clamp pulse, gK_{∞} is the final K conductance attained during a sustained clamp pulse of a particular voltage, gK(t) is the K conductance at time t after the switch from holding potential to clamp potential, and τ_n is the time constant of the change in the K activation variable n at the clamp potential. All the values except the last (τ_n) can be read directly from the results of a voltage clamp experiment. HH performed experiments using a wide range of different clamp potentials, and then found which values of τ_n gave the best fit of this above equation to the data at each clamp potential. In this way they determined the voltage dependency of τ.

The next task was to determine the values of n at each clamp potential. The K conductance when all channels are fully open (gK_{max}) was measured as the maximum conductance achieved with a very depolarised clamp potential. The stable K conductance (gK_{∞}) measured at other clamp potentials could then be expressed as a fraction of this maximum. The activation variable n was then taken as the fourth root of this fraction (equation $gK = n^4 gK_{max}$). Similar experiments gave the voltage dependency of the activation and inactivation variables for the gates in the Na channels.

The α and β values were then calculated from the P and τ values for each gate type (n, m and h) and plotted against voltage. The plots followed a series of smooth curves that could be fitted by the following equations (where V is the membrane potential in mV).

K activation:

$$\alpha_m = \frac{-0.01V(V+60)}{e^{\left(\frac{V+60}{-10}\right)} - 1}$$

$$\beta_m = 0.125e^{\frac{V+70}{-80}}$$

Na activation:

$$\alpha_m = \frac{-0.1(V+45)}{e^{\left(\frac{V+45}{-10}\right)} - 1}$$

$$\beta_m = 4e^{\frac{V+70}{-18}}$$

Na inactivation:

$$\alpha_k = 0.07e^{\frac{V+70}{-20}}$$

$$\beta_k = \frac{1}{1 + e^{\frac{V+40}{-10}}}$$

These equations are essentially empirical, but are based upon equations that describe the movement of a charged particle in an electric field. Since that is the physical model of a gate moving within a channel to open and close, this seems reasonable.

Third: Reconstructing the Spike

Having derived the model and its equations, and having determined the appropriate numerical parameters by experiment, HH then worked forwards and "reconstructed" the effects of applying a depolarising stimulus to an axon. This was done by numerical integration of the equations, starting with equation $\frac{dV}{dt} = \frac{-(I_{stim} + I_{ionic})}{C_m}$. When this was done with the appropriate stimulus parameters, they found that there was a truly excellent correspondence between the predicted values of the membrane potential, and the actual shape of an action potential in a space clamped axon.

Perspective

The HH model has been amazingly successful in both describing and predicting a large number of neuronal properties. Extensions of this model, incorporating a variety of voltage-dependent channel types beyond the original HH pair, have been very widely used in research throughout the world. However, as HH were they well aware, the success of the model does not in itself constitute convincing evidence that the "pictorial" interpretation of the HH equations is a true reflection of the real molecular events. It is therefore very gratifying, although perhaps surprising, the extent to which modern investigations into the molecular structure of the various channels have confirmed the physical reality, or approximate reality, of many aspects of the model.

Dehaene–Changeux Model

Global Neuronal Workspace Model (GNW) also called Dehaene–Changeux Model. In its original formulation relies upon a few simple assumptions. Its main postulate is that conscious access is global information availability: what we subjectively experience as conscious access is the selection, amplification and global broadcasting, to many distant areas, of a single piece of information selected for its salience or relevance to current goals.

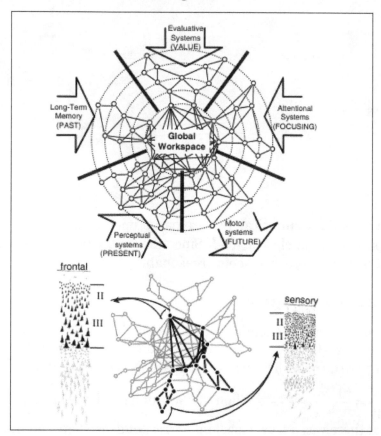

Figure shows schema of the global neuronal workspace (GNW) model: The GNW model proposes that associative perceptual, motor, attention, memory and value areas interconnect to form a higher-level unified space where information is broadly shared and broadcasted back to lower-level processors. The GNW is characterized by its massive connectivity, made possible by thick layers II/III with large pyramidal cells sending long-distance cortico-cortical axons, particularly dense in PFC.

From a neuronal architecture standpoint, two main computational spaces are distinguished within the brain, each characterized by a distinct pattern of connectivity: (1) a processing network, composed of a set of parallel, distributed and functionally specialized processors or modular subsystems subsumed by topologically distinct cortical domains with highly specific local or medium-range connections that "encapsulate" information relevant to its function. Processors typically operate non-consciously and in a bottom-up manner, although local top-down projections may also contribute to their operation by providing local predictions and prediction errors; and (2) a global neuronal workspace (GNW), consisting of a distributed set of cortical neurons characterized by their ability to receive from and send back to homologous neurons in other cortical areas horizontal projections through long-range excitatory axons. Such long-range cortico-cortical connections include callosal connections and mostly originate from the pyramidal cells of layers 2 and 3 that are particularly elevated in prefrontal, parieto-temporal and cingulate associative cortices, together with their thalamo-cortical relationships.

GNW neurons typically accumulate information through recurrent top–down/bottom–up loops, in a competitive manner such that a single representation eventually achieves a global conscious status. Because GNW neurons are broadly distributed, there is no single brain center where conscious information is gathered and dispatched but rather a brain-scale process of conscious synthesis achieved when multiple processors converge to a coherent metastable state.

According to the GNW hypothesis, conscious access proceeds in two successive phases. In a first phase, lasting from ~100 to ~300 ms, the stimulus climbs up the cortical hierarchy of processors in a primarily bottom–up and non-conscious manner. In a second phase, if the stimulus is selected for its adequacy to current goals and attention state, it is amplified in a top–down manner and becomes maintained by sustained activity of a fraction of GNW neurons, the rest being inhibited. The entire workspace is globally interconnected in such a way that only one such conscious representation can be active at any given time. This all-or-none invasive property distinguishes it from peripheral processors in which, due to local patterns of connections, several representations with different formats may coexist. Simulations, further detailed below, indicate that the late global phase is characterized by several unique features. These predicted "signatures" of conscious access include a sudden, late and sustained firing in GNW neurons, a late sensory amplification in relevant processor neurons, and an increase in high-frequency oscillations and long-distance phase synchrony.

The state of activation of GNW neurons is assumed to be globally regulated by vigilance signals from the ascending reticular activating system that are powerful enough to control major transitions between the awake state (GNW active) and slow-wave sleep (GNW inactive) states. In the resting awake state, the brain is the seat of an important ongoing metabolic activity. An important statement of the GNW model is that the GNW network is the seat of a particular kind of brain-scale activity state characterized by spontaneous "ignitions" similar to those that can be elicited by external stimuli, but occurring endogenously. A representation that has invaded the workspace may remain active in an autonomous manner and resist changes in peripheral activity. If it is negatively evaluated, or if attention fails, it may, however, be spontaneously and randomly replaced by another discrete combination of workspace neurons, thus implementing an active "generator of diversity" that constantly projects and tests hypotheses on the outside world. The dynamics of workspace neuron activity is thus characterized by a constant flow of individual coherent episodes of variable duration, selected by specialized reward processors.

Structure

General Structure

The Dehaene–Changeux model is a meta neural network (i.e. a network of neural networks) composed of a very large number of integrate-and-fire neurons programmed in either a stochastic or deterministic way. The neurons are organised in complex thalamo-cortical columns with long-range connexions and a critical role played by the interaction between von Economo's areas. Each thalamo-cortical column is composed of pyramidal cells and inhibitory interneurons receiving a long-distance excitatory neuromodulation which could represent noradrenergic input.

A Swarm and a Multi-Agent System Composed of Neural Networks

Among others Cohen and Hudson had already used "Meta neural networks as intelligent agents for diagnosis" Similarly to Cohen and Hudson, Dehaene and Changeux have established their model as an interaction of meta-neural networks (thalamocortical columns) themselves programmed in the manner of a "hierarchy of neural networks that together act as an intelligent agent", in order to use them as a system composed of a large scale of inter-connected intelligent agents for predicting the self-organized behaviour of the neural correlates of consciousness. It may also be noted that Jain et al. had already clearly identified spiking neurons as intelligent agents since the lower bound for computational power of networks of spiking neurons is the capacity to simulate in real-time for boolean-valued inputs any Turing machine. The DCM being composed of a very large number of interacting sub-networks which are themselves intelligent agents, it is formally a Multi-agent system programmed as a Swarm or neural networks and a fortiori of spiking neurons.

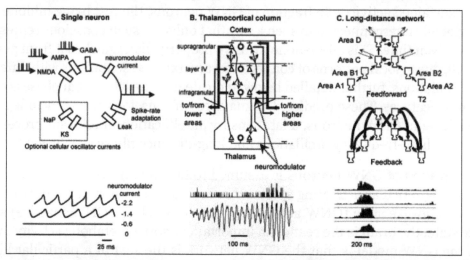

The three levels of complexity of the global workspace model: the integrate-and-fire neuron, the thalamo-cortical bundle and the long-range connexion. The authors provide the legend: "Shown are the constituents of the simulation (upper diagrams) and typical patterns of spontaneous activity that they can produce (lower tracings). We simulated a nested architecture in which spiking neurons (A) are incorporated within thalamocortical columns (B), which are themselves interconnected hierarchically by local and long-distance cortical connections (C). While single neurons may generate sustained oscillations of membrane potentials (A), only the column and network levels generate complex waxing-and-waning EEG-like oscillations (B) and metastable global states of sustained firing (C)."

Behavior

The DCM exhibits several surcritical emergent behaviors such as multistability and a Hopf bifurcation between two very different regimes which may represent either sleep or arousal with a various all-or-none behaviors which Dehaene et al. use to determine a testable taxonomy between different states of consciousness.

Scholarly Reception

Self-Organized Criticality

The Dehaene-Changeux Model contributed to the study of nonlinearity and self-organized criticality in particular as an explanatory model of the brain's emergent behaviors, including consciousness. Studying the brain's phase-locking and large-scale synchronization, Kitzbichler et al. confirmed that criticality is a property of human brain functional network organization at all frequency intervals in the brain's physiological bandwidth.

Furthermore, exploring the neural dynamics of cognitive efforts after, inter alia, the Dehaene-Changeux Model, researchers demonstrated how cognitive effort breaks the modularity of mind to make human brain functional networks transiently adopt a more efficient but less economical configuration. Werner used the Dehaene-Changeux Global Neuronal Workspace to defend the use of statistical physics approaches for exploring phase transitions, scaling and universality properties of the so-called "Dynamic Core" of the brain, with relevance to the macroscopic electrical activity in EEG and EMG. Furthermore, building from the Dehaene-Changeux Model, Werner proposed that the application of the twin concepts of scaling and universality of the theory of non-equilibrium phase transitions can serve as an informative approach for elucidating the nature of underlying neural-mechanisms, with emphasis on the dynamics of recursively reentrant activity flow in intracortical and cortico-subcortical neuronal loops. Friston also claimed that "the nonlinear nature of asynchronous coupling enables the rich, context-sensitive interactions that characterize real brain dynamics, suggesting that it plays a role in functional integration that may be as important as synchronous interactions".

States of Consciousness and Phenomenology

It contributed to the study of phase transition in the brain under sedation, and notably GABA-ergic sedation such as that induced by propofol. The Dehaene-Changeux Model was contrasted and cited in the study of collective consciousness and its pathologies. Boly et al. used the model for a reverse somatotopic study, demonstrating a correlation between baseline brain activity and somatosensory perception in humans. Boly et al. also used the DCM in a study of the baseline state of consciousness of the human brain's default network.

Hodgkin–Huxley Model

Hodgkin and Huxley developed a series of equations that could accurately predict and depict action potentials. Their work is a cornerstone for computational modeling as computer modeling can now be used to mimic the biological properties of a neuron that we are unable to directly observe. Really the Hodgkin-Huxley Model is just an elaboration on the Integrate and Fire Model. The Integrate and Fire model was generated by French neuroscientist Louis Lapicque, who in 1907 sought to generate a mathematical model that could be used to predict and graph an action potential. In his efforts to understand action potentials, Lapicque chose to model the flow of ions as a single leak current.

Hodgkin and Huxley took the single conductance term from the Integrate and Fire Model is broken up into three separate conductance terms, each relating to a different ion channel. These conductance terms are known as gating variables and are labeled m, n, and h. Voltage-gated sodium channel activation is modeled by the letter ms. Voltage-gated sodium channels have three subunits, as these three subunits are involved in the channels activation, m is raised to the third power. Voltage-gated sodium channel also inactivate at the peak of the action potential and this variable is modeled by the letter h. The combination of m and h gives rise to the conductance of Voltage-gated sodium channel which is modeled below:

$$\overline{g}_{Na} m^3 h \left(V(t) - E_{Na} \right)$$

Voltage-gated potassium channels are modeled by the letter n. Voltage-gated potassium channels have four subunits, and thus the gating variable, n, is raised to the fourth power. The conductance of Voltage-gated potassium channels is modeled below:

$$\overline{g}_K n^4 \left(V(t) - E_K \right)$$

The final conductance taken into account by Hodgkin and Huxley is the leak potential of all the ions. The Leak conductance is taken into account for the instance when all ion channels are open. This conductance is represented below:

$$\overline{g}_L \left(V(t) - E_L \right)$$

These three conductance variables are combined together to form the Hodgkin-Huxley equation which is written as follows:

$$C \frac{dV}{dt} = I_e(t) - \left[\left(\overline{g}_{Na} m^3 h \left(V(t) - E_{Na} \right) \right) + \left(\overline{g}_K n^4 \left(V(t) - E_K \right) \right) + \left(\overline{g}_L \left(V(t) - E_L \right) \right) \right]$$

Expression	Meaning
n	Potassium gating variable.
m	Sodium activation gating variable.
h	Sodium inactivation gating variable.
C_m	Specific membrane capacitance.
I_e	Injected current.
$\overline{g}_{Na}$	Maximum Na+ conductance.
$\overline{g}_K$	Maximum K+ conductance.
$\overline{g}_L$	Maximum leak conductance.
V_m	Membrane potential.

F_{Na}	Sodium Nernst potential.
E_K	Potassium Nernst potential.
E_L	Leak Nernst potential.

Additionally, we can calculate the value of each gating variable over different voltages and times:

$$m\frac{dV}{dt} = \alpha_m(V)(1-m) - \beta_m(V)m$$

Both n and h can be substituted for m in the above equation in order to calculate values for each gating variable. Additionally, note the α and β in the equation are rate constants that govern the opening and closing (respectively), of their channels. Here are their values:

$$\alpha_n(V_m) = \frac{0.01(V_m + 55)}{1 - \exp(-0.1(V_m + 55))}$$

$$\alpha_m(V_m) = \frac{0.1(V_m + 40)}{1 - \exp(-0.1(V_m + 40))}$$

$$\alpha_h(V_m) = 0.07\exp(-0.05(V_m + 65))$$

$$\beta_n(V_m) = 0.125\exp(-0.0125(V_m + 65))$$

$$\beta_m(V_m) = 4\exp(-0.0556(V_m + 65))$$

$$\beta_h(V_m) = \frac{1}{1 + \exp(-0.1(V_m + 35))}$$

Expression	Meaning
α_n	Rate constant for K+ channel opening.
α_m	Rate constant for Na+ activation gate opening.
α_h	Rate constant for Na+ inactivation gate opening.
β_n	Rate constant for K+ channel closing.
β_m	Rate constant for Na+ activation gate closing.
β_h	Rate constant for Na+ inactivation gate closing.

Example: Have you ever wondered how anesthesia makes a tooth extraction painless? It's because anesthesia works by blocking the activation of voltage-dependent Na+ channels. This prevents the propagation of the action potentials that carry that awful pain sensation. Using the equations below, calculate the maximum conductances of each ion in the resting state.

Useful parameters:

- V_m = -68 mV

- $C_m = -20.1 \text{ nF}$

- $E_L = -54 \text{ mV}$

- $E_{Na} = 50 \text{ mV}$

- $E_K = -77 \text{ mV}$

- $R_L = 1/3 \text{M}\Omega$

- $g_{Na} = 1200 \text{mS/mm}^2$

Equations:

$$I_{ion} = g_{Na} \cdot m^3 h \left(V_m - E_{Na}\right) + g_K \cdot n^4 \left(V_m - E_K\right) + g_L \cdot \left(V_m - E_L\right)$$

$$\frac{dn}{dt} = \alpha_n(V) \cdot (1-n) - \beta_n(V) \cdot (n)$$

$$\frac{dm}{dt} = \alpha_m(V) \cdot (1-m) - \beta_m(V) \cdot (m)$$

$$\frac{dh}{dt} = \alpha_h(V) \cdot (1-h) - \beta_h(V) \cdot (h)$$

Step 1: Understand the question, the resting potential can be considered to be a steady state because the voltage is not changing. Therefore, $\frac{dp}{dt} = 0$ for p = {n, m, h} and therefore the last three equations will not be used.

Step 2: Calculate n, m, and h we need to now use the resting potential to solve for the steady state values of the gating variables.

$$p_\infty = \frac{\alpha_p}{\alpha_p + \beta_p}$$

for p = {n, m, h}

Therefore, the very first step is to calculate each α and β.

$$\alpha_n(V_m) = \frac{0.01(V_m + 55)}{1 - \exp\left(-0.1(V_m + 55)\right)}$$

$$\alpha_n(V_{rest}) = \frac{0.01(-68 + 55)}{1 - \exp\left(-0.1(-68 + 55)\right)}$$

$$\alpha_n = 0.049$$

$$\alpha_m(V_m) = \frac{0.1(V_m + 40)}{1 - \exp\left(-0.1(V_m + 40)\right)}$$

$$\alpha_m(V_{rest}) = \frac{0.1(-68 + 40)}{1 - \exp\left(-0.1(-68 + 40)\right)}$$

$$\alpha_m\left(V_{rest}\right) = 0.18$$

$$\alpha_h\left(V_m\right) = 0.07\exp\left(-0.05\left(V_m + 65\right)\right)$$

$$\alpha_h\left(V_{rest}\right) = 0.07 \cdot \exp\left(-0.05 \cdot \left(-68 + 65\right)\right)$$

$$\alpha_h\left(V_{rest}\right) = 0.08$$

$$\beta_n\left(V_m\right) = 0.125\exp\left(-0.0125\left(V_m + 65\right)\right)$$

$$\beta_n\left(V_{rest}\right) = 0.125 \cdot \exp\left(-0.0125 \cdot \left(-68 + 65\right)\right)$$

$$\beta_n\left(V_{rest}\right) = 0.13$$

$$\beta_m\left(V_m\right) = 4\exp\left(-0.0556\left(V_m + 65\right)\right)$$

$$\beta_m\left(V_{rest}\right) = 4 \cdot \exp\left(-0.0556 \cdot \left(-68 + 65\right)\right)$$

$$\beta_m\left(V_{rest}\right) = 4.73$$

$$\beta_h\left(V_m\right) = \frac{1}{1 + \exp\left(-0.1\left(V_m + 35\right)\right)}$$

$$\beta_h\left(V_{rest}\right) = \frac{1}{1 + \exp\left(-0.1\left(-68 + 35\right)\right)}$$

$$\beta_h\left(V_{rest}\right) = 0.036$$

Now, with each of our α and β values, we can calculate our gating variables:

$$n_\infty = \frac{\alpha_n}{\alpha_n + \beta_n}$$

$$n_\infty = \frac{0.049}{0.049 + 0.13} = 0.274$$

$$m_\infty = \frac{\alpha_m}{\alpha_m + \beta_m}$$

$$m_\infty = \frac{0.18}{0.18 + 4.73} = 0.037$$

$$h_\infty = \frac{\alpha_h}{\alpha_h + \beta_h}$$

$$h_\infty = \frac{0.08}{0.08 + 0.036} = 0.690$$

Step 3: Calculate g_L *from resistance units*. Remember that $g = \frac{1}{R}$!

$$g_L = (1/R) = (1/(1/3)) = 3mS/mm^2$$

Step 4: Solve for g_K Remember that from Kirchhoff's Law that the algebraic sum of all the currents entering and leaving a junction must be equal to 0. Therefore:

$$0 = g_{Na} \cdot m^3 h (V_m - E_{Na}) + g_K \cdot n^4 (V_m - E_K) + g_L \cdot (V_m - E_L)$$

and we may plug in the values that we already have:

$$0 = 1200 \cdot 0.037^3 0.69 \cdot (-68 - 50) + g_K \cdot 0.274^4 \cdot (-68 - 77) + 3 \cdot (-68 - 54.387)$$
$$0 = 4.956 + g_K \cdot 0.051 + (-40.84)$$
$$g_K = 703.6$$

Example: The voltage of a neuron is clamped at -20 mV, depolarized from its resting potential of -65 mV. The steady-state values of the gating variables in the two conditions are shown below. Comment on what these changes mean for the neuron's behavior.

V = -65 mV	V = -20mV
m = 0.0529	m = 0.875
n = 0.3177	n = 0.820
h = 0.5961	h = 0.009

Solution: The value of m represents the probability of voltage-gated Na^+ channels to be open. This probability increases as the cell depolarizes. The n value represents the probability that the voltage-gated K^+ channel is open. Like the Na^+ channels, this probability increases with depolarization, but not to the same extent. The h values represent the probability of Na^+ channel inactivation. This decreases significantly with depolarization because we have not hit the peak of the action potential. It is fair to assume that the h value will increase as we near the peak.

Spike Response Model

The Spike Response Model is a generalization of the leaky integrate-and-fire model and gives a simple description of action potential generation in neurons. Just as in the integrate-and-fire model, action potentials are generated when the voltage passes a threshold from below. In contrast to the leaky integrate-and-fire model, the spike response model includes refractoriness. A notational difference is that integrate-and-fire models are formulated using differential equations for the voltage, whereas the Spike Response Model is formulated using filters.

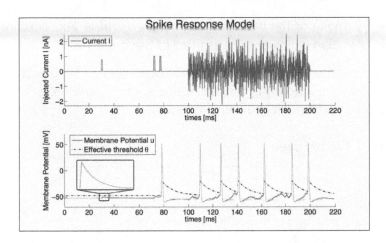

The Spike Response Model contains a filter κ which describes the voltage response (red, zoomed region) to an incoming pulse (input current shown in blue), a function η which describes the form of an action potential (green), and a dynamic threshold which increases after a spike has been triggered (dashed line).

Mathematical Formulation

The membrane potential in the spike response model is given by,

$$u(t) = \eta\left(t - \hat{t}\right) + \int_0^\infty \kappa\left(t - \hat{t}, s\right) I(t - s) \, ds$$

where $\hat{t}$ is the firing time of the last spike of the neuron, η describes the form of the action potential and its spike after-potential, κ the linear response to an input pulse and $I(t)$ a stimulating current. The next spike occurs if the membrane potential u hits a threshold $\theta(t - \hat{t})$ from below in which case $\hat{t}$ is updated.

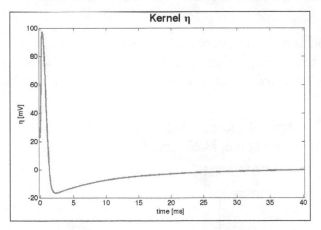

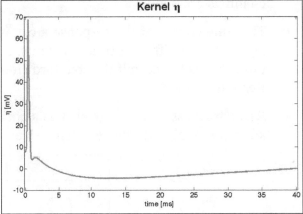

Example of a spike shape η with rapid reset, followed by a hyperpolarizing action potential, extracted from data.

Example of a spike shape η with depolarizing after potential, extracted from data.

- The name spike response model stems from the fact that κ describes the response of the neuron to an incoming short pulse (such as a spike arriving from another neuron) and η describes the response of the membrane to its own spike. The functions η and κ are also called kernels, κ is also called the linear filter of the membrane.

- From the mathematical point of view it is not necessary to keep both a dynamic threshold and the spike shape η, since only the difference x = u − θ between the membrane potential and the threshold matters for the spike dynamics.

Main Features and Examples

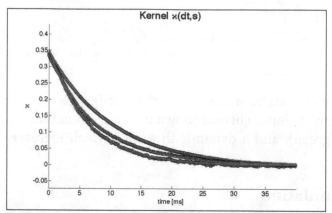

Example of an impulse response current κ(dt, s) as a function of s, extracted from data for three different values of the time dt that has passed since the last spike.

- The threshold θ is not fixed but depends on the time since the last spike. Typically the threshold is higher immediately after a spike and decays then back to its resting value.

- The spike shape η is a function of the time since the last spike. It can describe a depolarizing, hyperpolarizing, or resonating spike-after potential.

- The responsiveness κ to an input pulse depends on the time since the last spike, because typically the effective membrane time constant after a spike is shorter, since many ion channels are open.

- The time course of the response κ can include single exponential, combinations of exponentials with different time constants, or resonating behavior in form of a delayed oscillation. This is the case if the standard Hodgkin-Huxley model is approximated by the Spike Response Model.

- Refractoriness can be modeled as a combination of increased threshold, hyperpolarizing after potential and reduced responsiveness after a spike, as observed in real neurons.

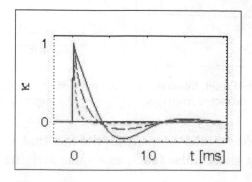

Example of an impulse response current κ with damped oscillations, extracted from the Hodgkin-Huxley model. The graph shows κ(dt, s) as a function of s for different choices of the time dt that has passed between the last postsynaptic spike and presynaptic spike arrival.

Fits to Experimental Data

The Spike Response Model can be fitted to experimental data where a neuron is stimulated by a rapidly varying time dependent current or conductance. To do so, use the following steps:

- Subtract from the experimental data the resting potential. This gives a normalized voltage trace u(t).

- Align spikes and determine the mean shape of the spike and spike-afterpotential. This gives $\eta(t-\hat{t})$.

- Remove spikes and calculate the subthreshold membrane potential $y(t) = u(t) - \eta(t-\hat{t})$.

- Determine the best linear filter to approximate the subthreshold potential y(t) by $\int_0^\infty \kappa(t-\hat{t},s) I^{ext}(t-s) ds$.

- Optimize the threshold θ so as to get the correct mean firing rate of the neuron.

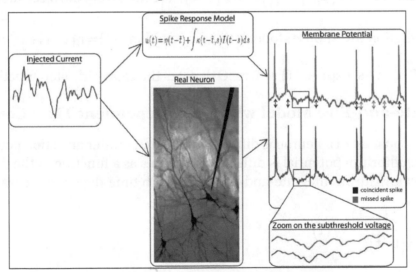

The same time-dependent input (left) is given to the Spike Response Model (top) and a real neuron (bottom). Comparison of the voltage (right) shows that the Spike Response Model follows the subthreshold membrane potential and predicts spike times.

The above parameter extraction procedure yields a Spike Response Model that fits experimental data to a high degree of accuracy and predicts a large fraction of spikes with a precision of +/- 2ms. The same procedure has also been used to approximate detailed neuron models of the Hodgkin-Huxley type by the Spike Response Model.

In a public competition of spike-time prediction under random conductance injection, the Spike Response Model was in the group of winning models whereas a standard leaky integrate-and-fire model performed significantly worse. These and other results show that inclusion of refractory properties is important. Refractory properties can be measured directly and manifest themselves in the time course of the spike afterpotential $\eta(t-\hat{t})$, by a reduction in the effective membrane time constant influencing $\kappa(t-\hat{t})$, and by an increase of the threshold θ after a spike.

Special Cases and Variants of the Spike Response Model

Leaky Integrate-and-Fire Model

The leaky integrate and fire model is a special case of the Spike Response Model. To see this, take the differential equation of the leaky integrate-and-fire model,

$$\frac{dv}{dt} = -\frac{v - v_{eq}}{\tau} + I(t)$$

where v is the membrane potential, v_{eq} is the equilibrium potential and $\tau = RC$ is the membrane time constant. Integration of the differential equation for arbitrary input $I(t)$, yields,

$$u(t) = \eta(t-\hat{t}) + \int_0^\infty \Theta(t-\hat{t}-s)\exp(-s/\tau)I(t-s)ds$$

where $u = v - v_{eq}$ and $\eta(t-\hat{t}) = (v_{reset} - v_{eq})\exp\left[-(t-\hat{t})/\tau\right]$ comes from the reset after each spike. This

is a special case of the Spike Response Model defined in equation $u(t) = \eta(t-\hat{t}) + \int_0^\infty \kappa(t-\hat{t},s)I(t-s)ds$

with $\kappa(t-\hat{t},s) = \Theta(t-\hat{t}-s)\exp(-s/\tau)$ where Θ denotes the Heaviside step function.

Leaky Integrate-and-Fire Model with Time-Dependent Time Constant

The effective time constant of a neuron is different immediately after an action potential. Similarly, the momentary equilibrium potential is different and varies as a function of the time since the last spike. Hence we can write an integrate-and-fire model with time-dependent parameters,

$$\frac{dv}{dt} = -\frac{v - v_{eq}(t-\hat{t})}{\tau(t-\hat{t})} + I(t)$$

Integration of this equation gives a special case of the Spike Response Model,

$$u(t) = \eta(t-\hat{t}) + \int_0^\infty \kappa(t-\hat{t},s)I(t-s)ds.$$

Spike Input and Synaptic Response Kernel ϵ

In the case of input generated by synaptic current pulses caused by presynaptic spike arrival, the Spike Response Model can be written as,

$$u(t) = \eta(t-\hat{t}) + \sum_j \sum_f w_j \epsilon(t-\hat{t}, t-t_j^f)$$

where w_j is the weight of synapse j, t_j^f the arrival time of the f th spike at synapse j, and ϵ the time course of a postsynaptic potential caused by spike arrival.

To see the connection with equation $u(t) = \eta(t-\hat{t}) + \int_0^\infty \kappa(t-\hat{t},s)I(t-s)ds$ suppose that the input to the Spike Response Model consists not of an imposed current, but of synaptic input currents of amplitude w_j and time course $\alpha(t-t_j^f)$ where t_j^f is the spike arrival time at synapse j, that is, $I(t) = \sum_j \sum_f w_j \alpha(t-t_j)$ Convolution of the kernel κ with the current α yields the postsynaptic potential ϵ.

Spike Response Model SRM$_0$

SRM$_0$ is a simplified version of the Spike Response Model. It does not include a dependence of the response kernel κ upon the time since the last spike. Hence we have,

$$u(t) = \eta(t-\hat{t}) + \int \kappa(s)I^{ext}(t-s)ds$$

instead of equation $u(t) = \eta(t-\hat{t}) + \int_0^\infty \kappa(t-\hat{t},s)I(t-s)ds$. The threshold can be dynamic as before.

The variant SRM$_0$ is easier to fit to experimental data than the full Spike Response Model, since it needs less data.

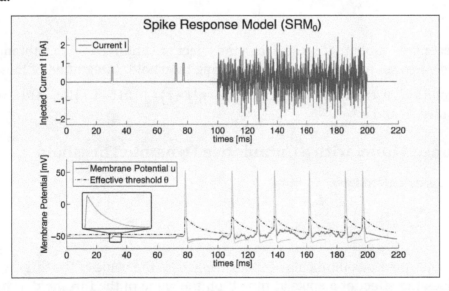

The Spike Response Model SRM$_0$ has a filter κ which describes the voltage response (red, zoomed region) to an incoming pulse (input current shown in blue). In contrast to the full Spike Response Model, this filter does not depend on the time since the last spike. As before, the function η describes the form of an action potential (green), and a dynamic threshold increases after a spike has been triggered (dashed line).

Cumulative Spike Response Model: Bursting and Adaptation

The term Spike Response Model was used for a model where refractoriness and adaptation were modeled by the combined effects of the spike after potentials of several previous spikes, rather than only the most recent spike. Hence equation $u(t) = \eta(t - \hat{t}) + \int_0^\infty \kappa(t - \hat{t}, s) I(t - s) ds$ is replaced by,

$$u(t) = \sum_{t^k} \eta(t - t^k) + \int \kappa(t - \hat{t}, s) I^{ext}(t - s) ds$$

where $t^k < t$ denotes previous moments of spike firing. Similarly, the threshold increases.

The reason for keeping in the normal Spike Response Model only the effect of the most recent spike is that a closed-form mathematical analysis of large networks in the form of mean-field equations is much easier in the standard Spike Response Model than in the cumulative Spike Response Model. The advantage of the cumulative model is that it accounts for adaptation and bursting.

Resonate-and-Fire Model

The resonate-and-fire model is a special case of the Cumulative Spike Response Model. The resonate and fire model consists of two linear equations:

$$\frac{du}{dt} = -\frac{v - v_{eq}}{\tau} - cw + I(t)$$

$$\tau_w \frac{dw}{dt} = a(v - v_{eq}) - w$$

where w is a second variable that summarizes the effect of subthreshold membrane current. The voltage variable v is reset whenever it reaches a firing threshold. Integration of these linear equations gives a solution of the form equation $u(t) = \eta(t - \hat{t}) + \int_0^\infty \kappa(t - \hat{t}, s) I(t - s) ds$ with a specific choice for the filters η and κ.

Spike Response Model with a Cumulative Dynamic Threshold

The threshold θ is calculated as,

$$\theta(t) = \theta_0 + \sum_{t^k} \vartheta(t - t^k)$$

where $t^k < t$ denotes previous moments of spike firing, θ_0 is the value of the threshold at rest, and $\vartheta(t - t^k)$ describes the effect of a spike at time t^k on the value of the threshold at time t. The difference to the standard form of the spike response model is that now the value of the threshold depends on all previous spikes, not only the most recent one. Having a cumulative threshold is one possible way to incorporate adaptation. Furthermore, a spike response model with cumulative threshold makes it possible to have a single model with a fixed set of parameters that fits experimental data across a broad range of firing rates.

In the Spike Response Model with cumulative threshold, the dynamic threshold increases after each spike by a fixed amount so that the effects of several spikes accumulate (dashed line). This is in contrast to the normal spike response model where the threshold always restarts at the same value.

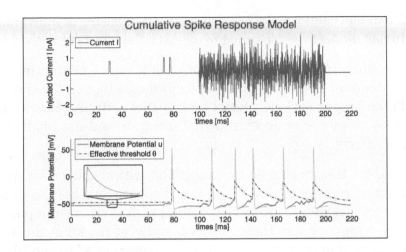

Noise in the Spike Response Model

Noise can be included into the Spike Response Model by replacing the strict threshold criterion $u(t) = \theta$ by a stochastic process. The probability P of firing a spike within a very short time Δt is $P = \rho(t)\,\Delta t$ where the instantaneous firing rate or firing intensity $\rho(t)$ is a function of the momentary difference between the membrane potential $u(t)$ and the threshold $\theta(t)$,

$$\rho = f(u - \theta).$$

This noise model has been called stochastic threshold or escape noise. Typical functional forms for f could be an exponential function or a rectified linear function. A saturating form for f is not a good choice, because it introduces a finite response time even for strong input well above threshold.

The advantage of the escape noise model in combination with a Spike Response Model is that interspike interval distributions can be expressed analytically for arbitrary time-dependent input. Given a spike at time $\hat{t}$ and an input I(t), the next spike will occur at time t with probability density,

$$P\left(t\,|\,\hat{t}\right) = \rho(t)\exp\left[\int_{\hat{t}}^{t} -\rho(t')dt'\right]$$

From the point of view of stochastic processes, this is a time-dependent (inhomogeneous) version of a renewal model. Because stochastic spike arrival with time-dependent input rates can be well represented by an equivalent escape noise model, one can calculate interspike interval distributions even for cases where the first-passage time problem of the leaky integrate-and-fire model with diffusive noise cannot be solved analytically. The Spike Response Model with escape noise has turned out to be useful for description of experimental data.

Effects not Captured by a Spike Response Model

The Spike Response Model is not suited to describe the following effects:

- Pharmacological blocking of ion channels: The biophysics of the neuronal membrane is not described explicitly in the Spike Response Model. Instead, the combined effects of several ion channel are captured phenomenological in the spike shape function η and the filter κ.

Therefore the model cannot make predictions about blocking of individual ion channels. A Hodgkin-Huxley model is better suited to describe the effects of individual channels.

- Delayed spike initiation: For isolated input pulses, type I neuron models exhibit action potentials of standard shape, but different delay depending on the amplitude of the input pulse. The Spike Response Model cannot capture these effects, because of the strict threshold criterion. A quadratic or an exponential integrate-and-fire model is better suited to describe these effects.

- Dependence of the threshold upon the input: The critical voltage for spike initiation with very slow ramp currents or constant currents (rheobase threshold) is different in real neurons from the critical voltage for spike initiation with short current pulses. The Spike Response Model cannot capture these effects because of the strict threshold criterion. An adaptive exponential integrate-and-fire model is better suited to describe these effects.

Galves–Löcherbach Model

The Galves–Löcherbach model is a model with intrinsic stochasticity for biological neural nets, in which the probability of a future spike depends on the evolution of the complete system since the last spike. This model of spiking neurons was developed by mathematicians Antonio Galves and Eva Löcherbach. In the first article on the model, in 2013, they called it a model of a "system with interacting stochastic chains with memory of variable length."

Some inspirations of the Galves–Löcherbach model are the Frank Spitzer's interacting particle system and Jorma Rissanen's notion of stochastic chain with memory of variable length. Another work that influenced this model was Bruno Cessac's study on the leaky integrate-and-fire model, who himself was influenced by Hédi Soula. Galves and Löcherbach referred to the process that Cessac described as "a version in a finite dimension" of their own probabilistic model.

Prior integrate-and-fire models with stochastic characteristics relied on including a noise to simulate stochasticity. The Galves–Löcherbach model distinguishes itself because it is inherently stochastic, incorporating probabilistic measures directly in the calculation of spikes. It is also a model that may be applied relatively easily, from a computational standpoint, with a good ratio between cost and efficiency. It remains a non-Markovian model, since the probability of a given neuronal spike depends on the accumulated activity of the system since the last spike.

Contributions to the model were made, considering the hydrodynamic limit of the interacting neuronal system, the long-range behavior and aspects pertaining to the process in the sense of predicting and classifying behaviors according to a function of parameters, and the generalization of the model to the continuous time. The Galves–Löcherbach model was a cornerstone to the Research, Innocation and Dissemination Center for Neuromathematics.

The model considers a countable set of neurons I and models its evolution in discrete-time periods $t \in \mathbb{Z}$ with a stochastic chain $(X_t)_{t \in \mathbb{Z}}$, considering values in $\{0,1\}^I$. More precisely, for each neuron $i \in I$ and time period $t \in \mathbb{Z}$ we define $X_t(i) = 1$ if neuron i spikes in period t, and conversely

$X_t(i) = 0$. The configuration of the set of neurons, in the time period $t \subset \mathbb{Z}$ is therefore defined as $X_t = (X_t(i), i \in I)$. For each time period $t \in \mathbb{Z}$ we define a sigma-algebra $\mathcal{F}_t = \sigma(X_s(j), j \in I, s \leq t)$ representing the history of the evolution of the activity of this set of neurons until the relevant time period t. The dynamics of the activity of this set of neurons is defined as follows. Once the history $\mathcal{F}_{t-1}$ is given, neurons spike or not in the next time period t independently from one another, that is, for each finite subset $F \subset I$ and any configuration $a_i \in \{0,1\}, i \in F$, we have,

$$\mathrm{Prob}\left(X_t(i) = a_i, i \in I \mid \mathcal{F}_{t-1}\right) = \prod_{i \in I} \mathrm{Prob}\left(X_t(i) = a_i \mid \mathcal{F}_{t-1}\right).$$

Furthermore, the probability that a given neuron i spikes in a time period t, according to the probabilistic model, is described by the formula,

$$\mathrm{Prob}\left(X_t(i) = 1 \mid \mathcal{F}_{t-1}\right) = \phi_i\left(\sum_{j \in I} W_{j \to i} \sum_{s=L_t^i}^{t-1} g_j(t-s) X_s(j), t - L_t^i\right)$$

where $W_{j \to i}$ is synaptic weight that expresses the increase of membrane potential of neuron i because of neuron j's spike, g_j is a function that models the leak of potential and L_t^i is the most recent period of neuron i's spike before the given time period t, considering the formula,

$$L_t^i = \sup\left\{s < t : X_s(i) = 1\right\}.$$

At time s before t, neuron i spikes, restoring the membrane potential to its initial value.

Ermentrout-Kopell Canonical Model

The Ermentrout-Kopell canonical model is better known as the "theta model" and is a simple one-dimensional model for the spiking of a neuron. It is closely related to the quadratic integrate and fire neuron. The model takes the following form:

$$\frac{d\theta}{dt} = 1 - \cos\theta + (1 + \cos\theta)I(t)$$

where I(t) are the inputs to the model. The variable θ lies on the unit circle and ranges between 0 and 2π. When $\theta = \pi$ the neuron "spikes", that is, it produces an action potential.

Derivation

The theta model is the normal form for the saddle-node on a limit cycle bifurcation (SNIC). (Do not confuse this with a saddle-node of limit cycles in which a pair of limit cycles collide and annihilate). Figure shows a schematic of the bifurcation as a parameter varies through the critical value of I = 0. When I < 0 there is a pair of equilibria. One of the equilibria is a saddle point with a one-dimensional unstable manifold. The two branches of the unstable manifold form an invariant circle with the stable equilibrium point. In neurophysiological terms, the stable manifold of the saddle point forms a true threshold for the neuron. In Figure, the stable manifold is shown in green. Any initial conditions to the left of the manifold will be attracted to the stable equilibrium (in blue), while initial data to the right of the manifold will make a large excursion around the circle before returning to the rest state.

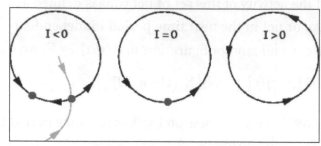

Saddle node on limit cycle.

Near the transition, the local dynamics is like a saddle-node bifurcation and has the form:

$$\frac{dx}{dt} = x^2 + I$$

For $I < 0$ (resp $I > 0$) there are two (resp no) equilibria. In the case where $I > 0$ solutions to this differential equation "blow up" in finite time,

$$T_{blow} = 1/2\left(-2\arctan\left(\frac{x(0)}{\sqrt{I}}\right) + \pi\right)\frac{1}{\sqrt{I}}$$

Here $x(0)$ is the initial condition. In particular, suppose we reset $x(t)$ to $-\infty$ when it blows up to $+\infty$. Then the total transit time is,

$$T_{per} = \frac{\pi}{\sqrt{I}}$$

Thus the frequency (the reciprocal of the period) goes to zero as the parameter approaches criticality from the right. This observation led Rinzel & Ermentrout to remark that this bifurcation corresponded to Hodgkin's Class I excitable membranes while the more familiar Andronov-Hopf bifurcation corresponded to Class II excitability. The latter is best exemplified by the classical Hodgkin-Huxley model for the squid axon. Neural models undergoing a SNIC bifurcation include the Connor-Stevens model for crab leg axons, the Wang-Buzsaki model for inhibitory interneurons, the Hindmarsh-Rose model, and the Morris-Lecar model under some circumstances.

The quadratic integrate and fire model is essentially equation $\frac{dx}{dt} = x^2 + I$ with a finite value for the blow up and a finite reset. It is closely related to the Izhikevich neuron, which has an additional linear variable modeling the dynamics of a recovery variable.

To derive the theta model $\frac{d\theta}{dt} = 1 - \cos\theta + (1 + \cos\theta)I(t)$ from the saddle-node $\frac{dx}{dt} = x^2 + I$ we make a simple change of variables, $x = \tan(\theta/2)$ from which it is simple calculus to obtain the theta model. We note that as θ approaches π from the left, x goes to $+\infty$. The theta model collapses the real line to the circle. The SNIC is a global bifurcation, so that to rigorously prove the equivalence of the SNIC and the theta model requires quite a bit more work than is shown in this formal derivation. The advantage of the theta model over the quadratic integrate and fire model is that there is no reset to deal with and the resulting dynamics are smooth and stay bounded. However, as the Izhikevich neuron demonstrates, it is sometimes useful to have the freedom to reset the dynamics anywhere.

Noisy Theta Models

To obtain the noisy theta model, we start with the original quadratic model with additive white noise:

$$dx = \left(x^2 + I(t)\right)dt + \sigma dW$$

and make the change of variables, $x = \tan(\theta/2)$, where we are careful to account for the fact that we must use Ito Calculus. The resulting noisy theta model takes the form:

$$d\theta = \left(1 - \cos\theta + [1 + \cos\theta]\left(I(t) - \frac{\sigma^2}{2}\sin\theta\right)\right)dt + \sigma(1 + \cos\theta)dW.$$

Note that the sine term in the equation comes from the Ito change of variables. For small noise, that is, $\sigma \ll 1$, this term can be neglected and one gets the equation analyzed in Gutkin and Ermentrout.

The Phase Resetting Curve for the Theta Model

In the oscillatory regime, the phase resetting curve (PRC) can be computed. Izhikevich computed the PRC for finite size stimuli by adding an instantaneous pulse of size a to the quadratic version of the model. From this, he obtained a map from the old phase to the new phase:

$$\theta \rightarrow 2\arctan\left(\tan\frac{\theta}{2} + a\right)$$

The PRC is set in phase coordinates rather than in time coordinates. The adjoint or infinitesimal PRC is very easy to compute using the quadratic version of the model. For any scalar oscillator model, $du/dt = f(u)$, the adjoint is $u_a(t) = 1/du/dt$. Since the "periodic" solution to the quadratic model is,

$$u(t) = -\sqrt{I}\cot\left(\sqrt{I}t\right)$$

the PRC is,

$$PRC(t) = \frac{1}{du/dt} = \frac{1}{2\sqrt{I}}\left(1 - \cos\left(2\sqrt{I}t\right)\right).$$

This is non-negative and has been suggested as the signature of neurons undergoing a SNIC bifurcation.

Relation to other Models

The canonical model described here is closely related to other phase models arising in applications. For example, the classical description of forced oscillations in a damped pendulum is given by the differential equation,

$$\mu\ddot{\theta} + f\dot{\theta} + \ddot{H}(t)\cos\theta + \ddot{V}(t)\sin\theta = \omega$$

where θ is the angle between the down direction and the radius through the center of mass, μ is the mass, f is the coefficient of friction (damping), $\ddot{H}$ and $\ddot{V}$ are the horizontal and vertical accelerations of the support point, and $\omega(t)$ is the torque applied to the support point. This model has been applied to describe mechanical systems (e.g. pendulums), micro-electromechanical systems, rotating electrical machinery, power systems, electronic circuits, such as phase-locked loops and parametric amplifiers, quantum mechanical devices and neurons.

The model $\dfrac{d\theta}{dt} = 1 - \cos\theta + (1 + \cos\theta)I(t)$ is equivalent to above equation when $\mu \to 0$ and H(t), V(t), and ω are chosen appropriately. Although $\dfrac{d\theta}{dt} = 1 - \cos\theta + (1 + \cos\theta)I(t)$ may have been referred to as being the theta-equation, this causes confusion when working with theta rhythms in the brain, and so is not preferred. Hoppensteadt and Izhikevich suggested calling it the Ermentrout-Kopell canonical model.

Wilson–Cowan Model

The Wilson-Cowan model describes the evolution of excitatory and inhibitory activity in a synaptically coupled neuronal network. As opposed to being a detailed biophysical model, the system is a coarse-grained description of the overall activity of a large-scale neuronal network, employing just two differential equations. Key parameters in the model are the strength of connectivity between each subtype of population (excitatory and inhibitory) and the strength of input to each subpopulation. Varying these generates a diversity of dynamical behaviors that are representative of observed activity in the brain, like multi-stability, oscillations, traveling waves, and spatial patterns.

Many regions of the brain process large-scale spatiotemporally structured inputs. Understanding the resulting neural activity requires macroscopic models that can track the average firing rate across many areas of a neuronal network. This was the approach in the seminal work of Wilson and Cowan, who derived effective equations for the macroscopic behavior of a large network of neurons. The approach is analogous to using statistical thermodynamics to relate the Brownian motion of particles to a mean ensemble motion of a whole fluid or gas. Thus, Wilson and Cowan derive an effective system for the mean field of an underlying statistical process.

Space-Clamped Model

Starting with a large population of densely coupled neurons, Wilson and Cowan derived effective equations for the proportion of cells in a population that are active per unit time. Crucially, the effective behavior of the population relies on interactions between excitatory and inhibitory cells, where $a_e(t)$ and $a_i(t)$ are the proportion of excitatory and inhibitory cells firing per unit time at instant t. Thus, $a_{e,i}(t) = 0$ corresponds to a low-activity resting state. Excitatory (inhibitory) neurons make their neighbors more (less) likely to become active, and activation is a nonlinear function $F_e(F_i)$ of the presently active proportion of cells. These assumptions yield the system,

$$\tau_e \frac{da_e}{dt} = -a_e(t) + \left[1 - r_e a_e(t)\right] F_e\left(w_{ee} a_e(t) - w_{ei} a_i(t) + I_e(t)\right),$$

$$\tau_i \frac{da_i}{dt} = -a_i(t) + \left[1 - r_i a_i(t)\right] F_i\left(w_{ie} a_e(t) - w_{ii} a_i(t) + I_i(t)\right).$$

Thus, the activity variables $a_{e,i}(t)$ obey first-order kinetics with timescales $\tau_{e,i}$, tracking the response of each subpopulation. The nonlinearities are typically chosen to be sigmoidal,

$$F_j(x) = \frac{1}{1 + e^{-\gamma_j(x - \theta_j)}}, \quad j = e, i$$

where the gain γ_j and threshold θ_j can depend on the population type $j = e,i$. The argument x is a weighted sum of the proportion of active excitatory and inhibitory cells, where $w_{jk} \geq 0$ describes the strength of connection from cell type k to j.

The system equation,

$$\tau_e \frac{da_e}{dt} = -a_e(t) + \left[1 - r_e a_e(t)\right] F_e\left(w_{ee} a_e(t) - w_{ei} a_i(t) + I_e(t)\right),$$

$$\tau_i \frac{da_i}{dt} = -a_i(t) + \left[1 - r_i a_i(t)\right] F_i\left(w_{ie} a_e(t) - w_{ii} a_i(t) + I_i(t)\right)$$

also captures the refractory dynamics of both populations, defined by the pre-factors $[1 - r_j a_j(t)]$, tracking the period of time during which cells are incapable of stimulation following an activation. This term has often been neglected in subsequent considerations of the model, and Pinto et al. showed that it effectively rescales the parameters of the nonlinearities $F_{e,i}$. The inputs $I_j(t)$ represent the sum of currents arriving to population j from external sources (e.g., other brain areas or an implanted electrode). The derivation of above equation also presumes important characteristics of time-dependent rates $a_{e,i}$ for large-scale computation that are captured by temporally coarse-grained traces.

By performing a phase plane analysis on above equation to find the stability of fixed points $(a_e(t))$, $a_i(t) = (\bar{a}_e, \bar{a}_i)$, Wilson and Cowan observed two typical modes of behavior. First, when the strength of synapses between excitatory cells is sufficiently strong, multiple stable fixed points can exist: a high excitation and a low excitation state. Alternatively, when the strength of connections between inhibitory subpopulation is sufficiently weak, the system above equation supports limit cycle solutions. In these limit cycles, a small proportion of active excitatory cells kindle other cells' activation, eventually recruiting inhibitory cells that turn all cells off, starting the cycle over. Thus, Wilson and Cowan presented a simple mechanism for oscillations in firing rate activity, an ubiquitous neural phenomenon. Notably, mutually inhibitory models were adapted from above equation by considering an arbitrary number N of neural populations coupled together solely by inhibition. Each population is then conceived of as representing a separate stimulus or percept, making such models ideal for studying the neural mechanisms of decision making and perceptual rivalry.

Spatially Structured Model

The model equation $\tau_e \dfrac{da_e}{dt} = -a_e(t) + [1 - r_e a_e(t)] F_e(w_{ee} a_e(t) - w_{ei} a_i(t) + I_e(t))$, $\tau_i \dfrac{da_i}{dt} = -a_i(t) +$

$[1 - r_i a_i(t)] F_i(w_{ie} a_e(t) - w_{ii} a_i(t) + I_i(t))$ ignores potential spatial structure in the network of synaptic connections or the external inputs to the network. Upon considering a spatially organized network of neurons, Wilson and Cowan described the connectivity between different regions of the network using functions that depend on the position of the origin y and target x of a synaptic connection. In doing so, this yields a set of partial integral equations,

$$\tau_e \frac{\partial a_e(x,t)}{\partial t} = -a_e(x,t) + [1 - r_e a_e(x,t)] F_e(w_{ee}^* a_e - w_{ei}^* a_i + I_e(x,t)),$$

$$\tau_i \frac{\partial a_i(x,t)}{\partial t} = -a_i(x,t) + [1 - r_i a_i(x,t)] F_i(w_{ei}^* a_e - w_{ii}^* a_i + I_i(x,t)),$$

where $w_{jk}^* a_k$ is a convolution operator,

$$w_{jk}^* a_k = \int_\Omega w_{jk}(x-y) a_k(y,t) dy$$

representing the effective drive to population j at location x received from population k. Writing the network of synaptic interactions as a spatial convolution gives a more general definition of the geometry of the network than discrete neural network models that use matrices to describe connectivity. Typical weight functions are the Gaussians,

$$w_{jk}(x-y) = k_{jk} e^{-(x-y)^2/\sigma_k^2}$$

which represent a distance-dependent decay in cortical connectivity. The spatial domain Ω can be of arbitrary dimension and size, but it is usually taken to be one or two dimensional as we describe below. The nonlinearities $F_{e,i}$ are often sigmoids equation $F_j(x) = \dfrac{1}{1 + e^{-\gamma_j(x-\theta_j)}}$, $j = e,i$ and refractoriness is modeled by the term $[1 - r_j a_j]$ as before.

We note that in equation,

$$\tau_e \frac{\partial a_e(x,t)}{\partial t} = -a_e(x,t) + [1 - r_e a_e(x,t)] F_e(w_{ee}^* a_e - w_{ei}^* a_i + I_e(x,t)),$$

$$\tau_i \frac{\partial a_i(x,t)}{\partial t} = -a_i(x,t) + \left[1 - r_i a_i(x,t)\right] F_i\left(w_{ei}{}^* a_e - w_{ii}{}^* a_i + I_i(x,t)\right),$$

it is possible to track the spatiotemporal evolution of inputs, not just the temporal evolution. A key assumption in deriving above equation is that the intricacies in firing rate variation that occur on very fine spatiotemporal scales can be coarse-grained. This results in a system of partial integro differential equations that are amenable to mathematical analysis.

Applications and Extensions

Originally, Wilson and Cowan developed the spatial model above equation to analyze neural hysteresis phenomena related to binocular vision. Since then, the system above equation has been used as a canonical model of visual cortical activity, since higher mammals' visual systems possess spatially organized feature maps. For instance, a mathematical theory of geometric visual hallucination patterns was developed by using symmetric bifurcation theory to analyze the emergence of Turing patterns when above equation evolved in $\Omega = \mathbb{R}^2$. Aside from spontaneous visual experience, the model above equation was also modified with an additional equation for Hebbian plasticity in the weights w_{jk} to understand the spontaneous organization of the cortical feature maps that underlie the processing of spatiotemporally structured inputs. All the periodically ordered maps for certain features like ocular dominance and orientation selectivity can be incorporated into above equation by employing the appropriate spatial domain Ω.

Since its inception, the system above equation has also been used to model a variety of other sensory, memory, and motor processes. Early on, work in a related model to above equation showed the combination of short-range excitation and long-range inhibition ($\sigma_e < \sigma_i$ in equation $w_{jk}(x-y) = k_{jk} e^{-(x-y)^2/\sigma_k^2}$) could stabilize persistent activity into the shape of a bump. Thus, even in the absence of inputs $I_j(x, t)$, the system above equation can support a nontrivial profile of spatiotemporal activity due to the activity sustained by recurrent excitation w_{ee}. This mechanism has now been used extensively as a model of visuospatial working memory, since the spatial position of a transient stimulus is known to be stored in cortex as persistent activity that can last for up to several seconds. Related to this, lateral inhibitory networks have also been employed as idealized models of spatial navigation and movement preparation, whose neural correlates are also known to be spatially localized, tuned, persistent activity.

The Wilson-Cowan model above equation has been extended in many ways to account for the rich diversity of currents, synaptic processes, and fluctuations present in the brain. Spike rate adaptation was considered by Hansel and Sompolinsky, who showed that this resulted in traveling waves of neural activity. Similar phenomena arise upon considering the effects of short-term plasticity, which dynamically modulates the strength of the synaptic weight functions w_{jk}. Finally, there has been a lot of interest recently in capturing the effects of fluctuations on spatially extended rate models like above equation. Early efforts have simply considered additive spatiotemporal noise processes, but a great deal of progress has been made in deriving effective langevin equation from stochastic neural networks using path integral methods or a system size expansion.

References

- Modeling_Single-Neuron-Dynamics-and-Computations-A-Balance-of-Detail-and-Abstraction-6770709: researchgate.net, Retrieved 03, March 2020

- Dehaene-Global-Neuronal-Workspace: cs.helsinki.fi, Retrieved 15, July 2020

- Computational-neuroscience-textbook: github.io, Retrieved 12, April 2020

- Ermentrout-Kopell-canonical-model: scholarpedia.org, Retrieved 08, August 2020

- Kilpatrick: colorado.edu, Retrieved 17, February 2020

Techniques used in Computational Neuroscience

There are several tools and technologies used in computational neuroscience. Some of the topics discussed in this chapter are brain-computer interface, single-unit recording, Bayesian approaches to brain function, mind uploading, neurocomputational speech processing and brain-reading. All these tools and technologies used in computational neuroscience have been carefully analyzed in this chapter.

Brain–Computer Interface

A brain–computer interface (BCI), sometimes called a mind-machine interface (MMI), direct neural interface (DNI), or brain–machine interface (BMI), is a direct communication pathway between an enhanced or wired brain and an external device. BCIs are often directed at researching, mapping, assisting, augmenting, or repairing human cognitive or sensory-motor functions.

Research on BCIs began in the 1970s at the University of California, Los Angeles (UCLA) under a grant from the National Science Foundation, followed by a contract from DARPA. The papers published after this research also mark the first appearance of the expression *brain–computer interface* in scientific literature.

The field of BCI research and development has since focused primarily on neuro-prosthetics applications that aim at restoring damaged hearing, sight and movement. Thanks to the remarkable cortical plasticity of the brain, signals from implanted prostheses can, after adaptation, be handled by the brain like natural sensor or effector channels. Following years of animal experimentation, the first neuroprosthetic devices implanted in humans appeared in the mid-1990s.

History

The history of brain–computer interfaces (BCIs) starts with Hans Berger's discovery of the electrical activity of the human brain and the development of electroencephalography (EEG). In 1924 Berger was the first to record human brain activity by means of

EEG. Berger was able to identify oscillatory activity, such as Berger's wave or the alpha wave (8–13 Hz), by analyzing EEG traces.

Berger's first recording device was very rudimentary. He inserted silver wires under the scalps of his patients. These were later replaced by silver foils attached to the patients' head by rubber bandages. Berger connected these sensors to a Lippmann capillary electrometer, with disappointing results. However, more sophisticated measuring devices, such as the Siemens double-coil recording galvanometer, which displayed electric voltages as small as one ten thousandth of a volt, led to success.

Berger analyzed the interrelation of alternations in his EEG wave diagrams with brain diseases. EEGs permitted completely new possibilities for the research of human brain activities.

Jacques Vidal coined the term "BCI" and produced the first peer-reviewed publications on this topic. Vidal is widely recognized as the inventor of BCIs in the BCI community, as reflected in numerous peer-reviewed articles reviewing and discussing the field (e.g.,).

Vidal's first BCI relied on visual evoked potentials to allow users to control cursor direction, and visual evoked potentials are still widely used in BCIs (Allison et al., 2010, 2012; Bin et al., 2011; Guger et al., 2012; Kaufmann et al., 2012; Jin et al., 2014; Kapeller et al., 2015).

After his early contributions, Vidal was not active in BCI research, nor BCI events such as conferences, for many years. In 2011, however, he gave a lecture in Graz, Austria, supported by the Future BNCI project, presenting the first BCI, which earned a standing ovation. Vidal was joined by his wife, Laryce Vidal, who previously worked with him at UCLA on his first BCI project. Prof. Vidal will also present a lecture on his early BCI work at the Sixth Annual BCI Meeting, scheduled for May–June 2016 at Asilomar, California.

Versus Neuroprosthetics

Neuroprosthetics is an area of neuroscience concerned with neural prostheses, that is, using artificial devices to replace the function of impaired nervous systems and brain related problems, or of sensory organs. The most widely used neuroprosthetic device is the cochlear implant which, as of December 2010, had been implanted in approximately 220,000 people worldwide. There are also several neuroprosthetic devices that aim to restore vision, including retinal implants.

The difference between BCIs and neuroprosthetics is mostly in how the terms are used: neuroprosthetics typically connect the nervous system to a device, whereas BCIs usually connect the brain (or nervous system) with a computer system. Practical neuroprosthetics can be linked to any part of the nervous system—for example, peripheral nerves—while the term "BCI" usually designates a narrower class of systems which interface with the central nervous system.

The terms are sometimes, however, used interchangeably. Neuroprosthetics and DCIs seek to achieve the same aims, such as restoring sight, hearing, movement, ability to communicate, and even cognitive function. Both use similar experimental methods and surgical techniques.

Animal BCI Research

Several laboratories have managed to record signals from monkey and rat cerebral cortices to operate BCIs to produce movement. Monkeys have navigated computer cursors on screen and commanded robotic arms to perform simple tasks simply by thinking about the task and seeing the visual feedback, but without any motor output. In May 2008 photographs that showed a monkey at the University of Pittsburgh Medical Center operating a robotic arm by thinking were published in a number of well known science journals and magazines. Other research on cats has decoded their neural visual signals.

Early Work

Monkey operating a robotic arm with brain–computer interfacing
(Schwartz lab, University of Pittsburgh).

In 1969 the operant conditioning studies of Fetz and colleagues, at the Regional Primate Research Center and Department of Physiology and Biophysics, University of Washington School of Medicine in Seattle, showed for the first time that monkeys could learn to control the deflection of a biofeedback meter arm with neural activity. Similar work in the 1970s established that monkeys could quickly learn to voluntarily control the firing rates of individual and multiple neurons in the primary motor cortex if they were rewarded for generating appropriate patterns of neural activity.

Studies that developed algorithms to reconstruct movements from motor cortex neurons, which control movement, date back to the 1970s. In the 1980s, Apostolos Georgopoulos at Johns Hopkins University found a mathematical relationship between the electrical responses of single motor cortex neurons in rhesus macaque monkeys and the direction in which they moved their arms (based on a cosine function). He also found that dispersed groups of neurons, in different areas of the monkey's brains, collectively controlled motor commands, but was able to record the firings of neurons in only one area at a time, because of the technical limitations imposed by his equipment.

There has been rapid development in BCIs since the mid-1990s. Several groups have been able to capture complex brain motor cortex signals by recording from neural ensembles (groups of neurons) and using these to control external devices.

Prominent Research Successes

Kennedy and Yang Dan

Phillip Kennedy (who later founded Neural Signals in 1987) and colleagues built the first intracortical brain–computer interface by implanting neurotrophic-cone electrodes into monkeys.

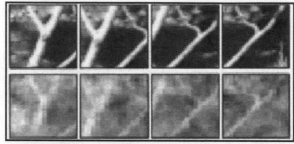

Yang Dan and colleagues' recordings of cat vision using a BCI implanted in the lateral geniculate nucleus (top row: original image; bottom row: recording).

In 1999, researchers led by Yang Dan at the University of California, Berkeley decoded neuronal firings to reproduce images seen by cats. The team used an array of electrodes embedded in the thalamus (which integrates all of the brain's sensory input) of sharp-eyed cats. Researchers targeted 177 brain cells in the thalamus lateral geniculate nucleus area, which decodes signals from the retina. The cats were shown eight short movies, and their neuron firings were recorded. Using mathematical filters, the researchers decoded the signals to generate movies of what the cats saw and were able to reconstruct recognizable scenes and moving objects. Similar results in humans have since been achieved by researchers in Japan.

Nicolelis

Miguel Nicolelis, a professor at Duke University, in Durham, North Carolina, has been a prominent proponent of using multiple electrodes spread over a greater area of the brain to obtain neuronal signals to drive a BCI.

After conducting initial studies in rats during the 1990s, Nicolelis and his colleagues developed BCIs that decoded brain activity in owl monkeys and used the devices to reproduce monkey movements in robotic arms. Monkeys have advanced reaching and grasping abilities and good hand manipulation skills, making them ideal test subjects for this kind of work.

By 2000 the group succeeded in building a BCI that reproduced owl monkey movements while the monkey operated a joystick or reached for food. The BCI operated in real time and could also control a separate robot remotely over Internet protocol. But the monkeys could not see the arm moving and did not receive any feedback, a so called open-loop BCI.

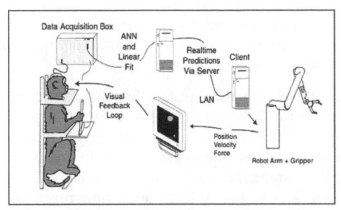

Diagram of the BCI developed by Miguel Nicolelis and colleagues for use on rhesus monkeys.

Later experiments by Nicolelis using rhesus monkeys succeeded in closing the feedback loop and reproduced monkey reaching and grasping movements in a robot arm. With their deeply cleft and furrowed brains, rhesus monkeys are considered to be better models for human neurophysiology than owl monkeys. The monkeys were trained to reach and grasp objects on a computer screen by manipulating a joystick while corresponding movements by a robot arm were hidden. The monkeys were later shown the robot directly and learned to control it by viewing its movements. The BCI used velocity predictions to control reaching movements and simultaneously predicted handgripping force. In 2011 O'Doherty and colleagues showed a BCI with sensory feedback with rhesus monkeys. The monkey was brain controlling the position of an avatar arm while receiving sensory feedback through direct intracortical stimulation (ICMS) in the arm representation area of the sensory cortex.

Donoghue, Schwartz and Andersen

Other laboratories which have developed BCIs and algorithms that decode neuron signals include those run by John Donoghue at Brown University, Andrew Schwartz at the University of Pittsburgh and Richard Andersen at Caltech. These researchers have been able to produce working BCIs, even using recorded signals from far fewer neurons than did Nicolelis (15–30 neurons versus 50–200 neurons).

Donoghue's group reported training rhesus monkeys to use a BCI to track visual targets on a computer screen (closed-loop BCI) with or without assistance of a joystick. Schwartz's group created a BCI for three-dimensional tracking in virtual reality and also reproduced BCI control in a robotic arm. The same group also created headlines when they demonstrated that a monkey could feed itself pieces of fruit and marshmallows using a robotic arm controlled by the animal's own brain signals.

Andersen's group used recordings of premovement activity from the posterior parietal cortex in their BCI, including signals created when experimental animals anticipated receiving a reward.

Other Research

In addition to predicting kinematic and kinetic parameters of limb movements, BCIs that predict electromyographic or electrical activity of the muscles of primates are being developed. Such BCIs could be used to restore mobility in paralyzed limbs by electrically stimulating muscles.

Miguel Nicolelis and colleagues demonstrated that the activity of large neural ensembles can predict arm position. This work made possible creation of BCIs that read arm movement intentions and translate them into movements of artificial actuators. Carmena and colleagues programmed the neural coding in a BCI that allowed a monkey to control reaching and grasping movements by a robotic arm. Lebedev and colleagues argued that brain networks reorganize to create a new representation of the robotic appendage in addition to the representation of the animal's own limbs.

The biggest impediment to BCI technology at present is the lack of a sensor modality that provides safe, accurate and robust access to brain signals. It is conceivable or even likely, however, that such a sensor will be developed within the next twenty years. The use of such a sensor should greatly expand the range of communication functions that can be provided using a BCI.

Development and implementation of a BCI system is complex and time consuming. In response to this problem, Gerwin Schalk has been developing a general-purpose system for BCI research, called BCI2000. BCI2000 has been in development since 2000 in a project led by the Brain–Computer Interface R&D Program at the Wadsworth Center of the New York State Department of Health in Albany, New York, United States.

A new 'wireless' approach uses light-gated ion channels such as Channelrhodopsin to control the activity of genetically defined subsets of neurons in vivo. In the context of a simple learning task, illumination of transfected cells in the somatosensory cortex influenced the decision making process of freely moving mice.

The use of BMIs has also led to a deeper understanding of neural networks and the central nervous system. Research has shown that despite the inclination of neuroscientists to believe that neurons have the most effect when working together, single neurons can be conditioned through the use of BMIs to fire at a pattern that allows primates to control motor outputs. The use of BMIs has led to development of the single neuron insufficiency principle which states that even with a well tuned firing rate single neurons can only carry a narrow amount of information and therefore the highest level of accuracy is achieved by recording firings of the collective ensemble. Other principles discovered with the use of BMIs include the neuronal multitasking principle, the neuronal mass principle, the neural degeneracy principle, and the plasticity principle.

BCIs are also proposed to be applied by users without disabilities. A user-centered categorization of BCI approaches by Thorsten O. Zander and Christian Kothe introduces the term passive BCI. Next to active an reactive BCI that are used for directed control, passive BCIs allow for assessing and interpreting changes in the user state during Human-Computer Interaction (HCI). In a secondary, implicit control loop the computer system adapts to its user improving its usability in general.

The BCI Award

The Annual BCI Research Award, endowed with 3,000 USD, is awarded in recognition of outstanding and innovative research in the field of Brain-Computer Interfaces. Each year, a renowned research laboratory is asked to judge the submitted projects and to award the prize. The jury consists of world-leading BCI experts recruited by the awarding laboratory. Following list consists the winners of the BCI Award:

- 2010: Cuntai Guan, Kai Keng Ang, Karen Sui Geok Chua and Beng Ti Ang, (A*STAR, Singapore).

  Motor imagery-based Brain-Computer Interface robotic rehabilitation for stroke.

- 2011: Moritz Grosse-Wentrup and Bernhard Schölkopf, (Max Planck Institute for Intelligent Systems, Germany).

  What are the neuro-physiological causes of performance variations in brain-computer interfacing?

- 2012: Surjo R. Soekadar and Niels Birbaumer, (Applied Neurotechnology Lab, University Hospital Tübingen and Institute of Medical Psychology and Behavioral Neurobiology, Eberhard Karls University, Tübingen, Germany).

  Improving Efficacy of Ipsilesional Brain-Computer Interface Training in Neurorehabilitation of Chronic Stroke.

- 2013: M. C. Dadarlat[a,b], J. E. O'Doherty[a], P. N. Sabes[a,b] ([a]Department of Physiology, Center for Integrative Neuroscience, San Francisco, CA, US, [b]UC Berkeley-UCSF Bioengineering Graduate Program, University of California, San Francisco, CA, US).

  A learning-based approach to artificial sensory feedback: intracortical microstimulation replaces and augments vision.

- 2014: Katsuhiko Hamada, Hiromu Mori, Hiroyuki Shinoda, Tomasz M. Rutkowski, (The University of Tokyo, JP, Life Science Center of TARA, University of Tsukuba, JP, RIKEN Brain Science Institute, JP).

  Airborne Ultrasonic Tactile Display BCI.

Human BCI Research

Invasive BCIs

Invasive BCI research has targeted repairing damaged sight and providing new functionality for people with paralysis. Invasive BCIs are implanted directly into the grey matter of the brain during neurosurgery. Because they lie in the grey matter, invasive devices produce the highest quality signals of BCI devices but are prone to scar-tissue build-up, causing the signal to become weaker, or even non-existent, as the body reacts to a foreign object in the brain.

Jens Naumann, a man with acquired blindness, being interviewed
about his vision BCI on CBS's The Early Show.

In *vision science*, direct brain implants have been used to treat non-congenital (acquired) blindness. One of the first scientists to produce a working brain interface to restore sight was private researcher William Dobelle.

Dobelle's first prototype was implanted into "Jerry", a man blinded in adulthood, in 1978. A single-array BCI containing 68 electrodes was implanted onto Jerry's visual cortex and succeeded in producing phosphenes, the sensation of seeing light. The system included cameras mounted on glasses to send signals to the implant. Initially, the implant allowed Jerry to see shades of grey in a limited field of vision at a low framerate. This also required him to be hooked up to a mainframe computer, but shrinking electronics and faster computers made his artificial eye more portable and now enable him to perform simple tasks unassisted.

In 2002, Jens Naumann, also blinded in adulthood, became the first in a series of 16 paying patients to receive Dobelle's second generation implant, marking one of the earliest commercial uses of BCIs. The second generation device used a more sophisticated implant enabling better mapping of phosphenes into coherent vision. Phosphenes are spread out across the visual field in what researchers call "the starry-night effect". Immediately after his implant, Jens was able to use his imperfectly restored vision to drive an automobile slowly around the parking area of the research institute. Unfortunately,

Dobelle died in 2004 before his processes and developments were documented. Subsequently, when Mr. Naumann and the other patients in the program began having problems with their vision, there was no relief and they eventually lost their "sight" again. Naumann wrote about his experience with Dobelle's work in *Search for Paradise: A Patient's Account of the Artificial Vision Experiment* and has returned to his farm in Southeast Ontario, Canada, to resume his normal activities.

Dummy unit illustrating the design of a BrainGate interface.

Movement

BCIs focusing on *motor neuroprosthetics* aim to either restore movement in individuals with paralysis or provide devices to assist them, such as interfaces with computers or robot arms.

Researchers at Emory University in Atlanta, led by Philip Kennedy and Roy Bakay, were first to install a brain implant in a human that produced signals of high enough quality to simulate movement. Their patient, Johnny Ray (1944–2002), suffered from 'locked-in syndrome' after suffering a brain-stem stroke in 1997. Ray's implant was installed in 1998 and he lived long enough to start working with the implant, eventually learning to control a computer cursor; he died in 2002 of a brain aneurysm.

Tetraplegic Matt Nagle became the first person to control an artificial hand using a BCI in 2005 as part of the first nine-month human trial of Cyberkinetics's BrainGate chip-implant. Implanted in Nagle's right precentral gyrus (area of the motor cortex for arm movement), the 96-electrode BrainGate implant allowed Nagle to control a robotic arm by thinking about moving his hand as well as a computer cursor, lights and TV. One year later, professor Jonathan Wolpaw received the prize of the Altran Foundation for Innovation to develop a Brain Computer Interface with electrodes located on the surface of the skull, instead of directly in the brain.

More recently, research teams led by the Braingate group at Brown University and a group led by University of Pittsburgh Medical Center, both in collaborations with the United States Department of Veterans Affairs, have demonstrated further success in direct control of robotic prosthetic limbs with many degrees of freedom using direct connections to arrays of neurons in the motor cortex of patients with tetraplegia.

Partially Invasive BCIs

Partially invasive BCI devices are implanted inside the skull but rest outside the brain rather than within the grey matter. They produce better resolution signals than non-invasive BCIs where the bone tissue of the cranium deflects and deforms signals and have a lower risk of forming scar-tissue in the brain than fully invasive BCIs. There has been preclinical demonstration of intracortical BCIs from the stroke perilesional cortex.

Electrocorticography (ECoG) measures the electrical activity of the brain taken from beneath the skull in a similar way to non-invasive electroencephalography, but the electrodes are embedded in a thin plastic pad that is placed above the cortex, beneath the dura mater. ECoG technologies were first trialled in humans in 2004 by Eric Leuthardt and Daniel Moran from Washington University in St Louis. In a later trial, the researchers enabled a teenage boy to play Space Invaders using his ECoG implant. This research indicates that control is rapid, requires minimal training, and may be an ideal tradeoff with regards to signal fidelity and level of invasiveness.

(Note: these electrodes had not been implanted in the patient with the intention of developing a BCI. The patient had been suffering from severe epilepsy and the electrodes were temporarily implanted to help his physicians localize seizure foci; the BCI researchers simply took advantage of this.)

Signals can be either subdural or epidural, but are not taken from within the brain parenchyma itself. It has not been studied extensively until recently due to the limited access of subjects. Currently, the only manner to acquire the signal for study is through the use of patients requiring invasive monitoring for localization and resection of an epileptogenic focus.

ECoG is a very promising intermediate BCI modality because it has higher spatial resolution, better signal-to-noise ratio, wider frequency range, and less training requirements than scalp-recorded EEG, and at the same time has lower technical difficulty, lower clinical risk, and probably superior long-term stability than intracortical single-neuron recording. This feature profile and recent evidence of the high level of control with minimal training requirements shows potential for real world application for people with motor disabilities.

Light reactive imaging BCI devices are still in the realm of theory. These would involve implanting a laser inside the skull. The laser would be trained on a single neuron and the neuron's reflectance measured by a separate sensor. When the neuron fires, the laser light pattern and wavelengths it reflects would change slightly. This would allow researchers to monitor single neurons but require less contact with tissue and reduce the risk of scar-tissue build-up.

In 2014, a BCI study using near-infrared spectroscopy for "locked-in" patients with amyotrophic lateral sclerosis (ALS) was able to restore some basic ability of the patients to communicate with other people.

Non-invasive BCIs

There have also been experiments in humans using non-invasive neuroimaging technologies as interfaces. The substantial majority of published BCI work involves non-invasive EEG-based BCIs. Noninvasive EEG-based technologies and interfaces have been used for a much broader variety of applications. Although EEG-based interfaces are easy to wear and do not require surgery, they have relatively poor spatial resolution and cannot effectively use higher-frequency signals because the skull dampens signals, dispersing and blurring the electromagnetic waves created by the neurons. EEG-based interfaces also require some time and effort prior to each usage session, whereas non-EEG-based ones, as well as invasive ones require no prior-usage training. Overall, the best BCI for each user depends on numerous factors.

Non EEG-based

Pupil-size Oscillation

In a recent 2016 article, an entirely new communication device and non EEG-based BCI was developed, requiring no visual fixation or ability to move eyes at all, that is based on covert interest in (i.e. without fixing eyes on) chosen letter on a virtual keyboard with letters each having its own (background) circle that is micro-oscillating in brightness in different time transitions, where the letter selection is based on best fit between, on one hand, unintentional pupil-size oscillation pattern, and, on the other hand, the circle-in-background's brightness oscillation pattern. Accuracy is additionally improved by user's mental rehearsing the words 'bright' and 'dark' in synchrony with the brightness transitions of the circle/letter.

EEG-based

Overview

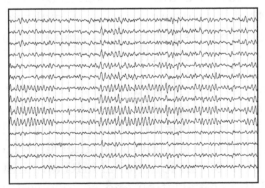

Recordings of brainwaves produced by an electroencephalogram.

Electroencephalography (EEG) is the most studied non-invasive interface, mainly due to its fine temporal resolution, ease of use, portability and low set-up cost. The technology is somewhat susceptible to noise however. In the early days of BCI research, another substantial barrier to using EEG as a brain–computer interface was the extensive training required before users can work the technology. For example, in experiments beginning in the mid-1990s, Niels Birbaumer at the University of Tübingen in Germany trained severely paralysed people to self-regulate the *slow cortical potentials* in their EEG to such an extent that these signals could be used as a binary signal to control a computer cursor. (Birbaumer had earlier trained epileptics to prevent impending fits by controlling this low voltage wave.) The experiment saw ten patients trained to move a computer cursor by controlling their brainwaves. The process was slow, requiring more than an hour for patients to write 100 characters with the cursor, while training often took many months. However, the slow cortical potential approach to BCIs has not been used in several years, since other approaches require little or no training, are faster and more accurate, and work for a greater proportion of users.

Another research parameter is the type of oscillatory activity that is measured. Birbaumer's later research with Jonathan Wolpaw at New York State University has focused on developing technology that would allow users to choose the brain signals they found easiest to operate a BCI, including *mu* and *beta* rhythms.

A further parameter is the method of feedback used and this is shown in studies of P300 signals. Patterns of P300 waves are generated involuntarily (stimulus-feedback) when people see something they recognize and may allow BCIs to decode categories of thoughts without training patients first. By contrast, the biofeedback methods described above require learning to control brainwaves so the resulting brain activity can be detected.

Lawrence Farwell and Emanuel Donchin developed an EEG-based brain–computer interface in the 1980s. Their "mental prosthesis" used the P300 brainwave response to allow subjects, including one paralyzed Locked-In syndrome patient, to communicate words, letters and simple commands to a computer and thereby to speak through a speech synthesizer driven by the computer. A number of similar devices have been developed since then. In 2000, for example, research by Jessica Bayliss at the University of Rochester showed that volunteers wearing virtual reality helmets could control elements in a virtual world using their P300 EEG readings, including turning lights on and off and bringing a mock-up car to a stop.

While an EEG based brain-computer interface has been pursued extensively by a number of research labs, recent advancements made by Bin He and his team at the University of Minnesota suggest the potential of an EEG based brain-computer interface to accomplish tasks close to invasive brain-computer interface. Using advanced functional neuroimaging including BOLD functional MRI and EEG source imaging, Bin He and co-workers identified the co-variation and co-localization of electrophysiological and hemodynamic signals induced by motor imagination. Refined by a neuroimaging approach and by a training protocol, Bin He and co-workers demonstrated the ability of a non-invasive EEG based brain-computer interface to control the flight of a virtual helicopter in 3-dimensional space, based upon motor imagination. In June 2013 it was announced that Bin He had developed the technique to enable a remote-control helicopter to be guided through an obstacle course.

In addition to a brain-computer interface based on brain waves, as recorded from scalp EEG electrodes, Bin He and co-workers explored a virtual EEG signal-based brain-computer interface by first solving the EEG inverse problem and then used the resulting virtual EEG for brain-computer interface tasks. Well-controlled studies suggested the merits of such a source analysis based brain-computer interface.

A 2014 study found that severely motor-impaired patients could communicate faster and more reliably with non-invasive EEG BCI, than with any muscle-based communication channel.

Dry Active Electrode Arrays

In the early 1990s Babak Taheri, at University of California, Davis demonstrated the first single and also multichannel dry active electrode arrays using micro-machining. The single channel dry EEG electrode construction and results were published in 1994. The arrayed electrode was also demonstrated to perform well compared to silver/silver chloride electrodes. The device consisted of four sites of sensors with integrated electronics to reduce noise by impedance matching. The advantages of such electrodes are: (1) no electrolyte used, (2) no skin preparation, (3) significantly reduced sensor size, and (4) compatibility with EEG monitoring systems. The active electrode array is an integrated system made of an array of capacitive sensors with local integrated circuitry housed in a package with batteries to power the circuitry. This level of integration was required to achieve the functional performance obtained by the electrode.

The electrode was tested on an electrical test bench and on human subjects in four modalities of EEG activity, namely: (1) spontaneous EEG, (2) sensory event-related potentials, (3) brain stem potentials, and (4) cognitive event-related potentials. The performance of the dry electrode compared favorably with that of the standard wet electrodes in terms of skin preparation, no gel requirements (dry), and higher signal-to-noise ratio.

In 1999 researchers at Case Western Reserve University, in Cleveland, Ohio, led by Hunter Peckham, used 64-electrode EEG skullcap to return limited hand movements to quadriplegic Jim Jatich. As Jatich concentrated on simple but opposite concepts like up and down, his beta-rhythm EEG output was analysed using software to identify patterns in the noise. A basic pattern was identified and used to control a switch: Above average activity was set to on, below average off. As well as enabling Jatich to control a computer cursor the signals were also used to drive the nerve controllers embedded in his hands, restoring some movement.

Prosthesis and Environment Control

Non-invasive BCIs have also been applied to enable brain-control of prosthetic upper and lower extremity devices in people with paralysis. For example, Gert Pfurtscheller of Graz University of Technology and colleagues demonstrated a BCI-controlled functional electrical stimulation system to restore upper extremity movements in a person with tetraplegia due to spinal cord injury. Between 2012 and 2013, researchers at the University of California, Irvine demonstrated for the first time that it is possible to use BCI technology to restore brain-controlled walking after spinal cord injury. In their spinal cord injury research study, a person with paraplegia was able to operate a BCI-robotic gait orthosis to regain basic brain-controlled ambulation. In 2009 Alex Blainey, an independent researcher based in the UK, successfully used the Emotiv EPOC to control a 5 axis robot arm. He then went on to make several demonstration mind controlled wheelchairs and home automation that could be operated by people with limited or no motor control such as those with paraplegia and cerebral palsy.

Other Research

Electronic neural networks have been deployed which shift the learning phase from the user to the computer. Experiments by scientists at the Fraunhofer Society in 2004 using neural networks led to noticeable improvements within 30 minutes of training.

Experiments by Eduardo Miranda, at the University of Plymouth in the UK, has aimed to use EEG recordings of mental activity associated with music to allow the disabled to express themselves musically through an encephalophone. Ramaswamy Palaniappan has pioneered the development of BCI for use in biometrics to identify/authenticate a person. The method has also been suggested for use as PIN generation device (for example in ATM and internet banking transactions. The group which is now at University of Wolverhampton has previously developed analogue cursor control using thoughts.

Researchers at the University of Twente in the Netherlands have been conducting research on using BCIs for non-disabled individuals, proposing that BCIs could improve error handling, task performance, and user experience and that they could broaden the user spectrum. They particularly focused on BCI games, suggesting that BCI games could provide challenge, fantasy and sociality to game players and could, thus, improve player experience.

The first BCI session with 100% accuracy (based on 80 right-hand and 80 left-hand movement imaginations) was recorded in 1998 by Christoph Guger. The BCI system used 27 electrodes overlaying the sensorimotor cortex, weighted the electrodes with Common Spatial Patterns, calculated the running variance and used a linear discriminant analysis.

Research is ongoing into military use of BCIs and since the 1970s DARPA has been funding research on this topic. The current focus of research is user-to-user communication through analysis of neural signals. The project "Silent Talk" aims to detect and analyze the word-specific neural signals, using EEG, which occur before speech is vocalized, and to see if the patterns are generalizable.

DIY and Open Source BCI

In 2001, The OpenEEG Project was initiated by a group of DIY neuroscientists and engineers. The ModularEEG was the primary device created the OpenEEG community; it was a 6-channel signal capture board that cost between $200 and $400 to make at home. The OpenEEG Project marked a significant moment in the emergence of DIY brain-computer interfacing.

In 2010, the Frontier Nerds of NYU's ITP program published a thorough tutorial titled How To Hack Toy EEGs. The tutorial, which stirred the minds of many budding DIY BCI enthusiasts, demonstrated how to create a single channel at-home EEG with an Arduino and a Mattel Mindflex at a very reasonable price. This tutorial amplified the DIY BCI movement.

In 2013, OpenBCI emerged from a DARPA solicitation and subsequent Kickstarter campaign. They created a high-quality, open-source 8-channel EEG acquisition board, known as the 32bit Board, that retailed for under $500. Two years later they created the first 3D-printed EEG Headset, known as the Ultracortex, as well as, a 4-channel EEG acquisition board, known as the Ganglion Board, that retailed for under $100.

In 2015, NeuroTechX was created with the mission of building an international network for neurotechnology. They bring hackers, researchers and enthusiasts all together in many different cities around the world. According to their rapid growth, the DIY neurotech / BCI community was already waiting for such initiative to see light.

MEG and MRI

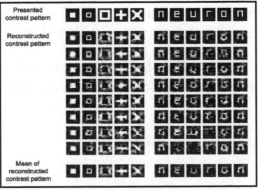

ATR Labs' reconstruction of human vision using fMRI (top row: original image; bottom row: reconstruction from mean of combined readings).

Magnetoencephalography (MEG) and functional magnetic resonance imaging (fMRI) have both been used successfully as non-invasive BCIs. In a widely reported experiment, fMRI allowed two users being scanned to play Pong in real-time by altering their haemodynamic response or brain blood flow through biofeedback techniques.

fMRI measurements of haemodynamic responses in real time have also been used to control robot arms with a seven-second delay between thought and movement.

In 2008 research developed in the Advanced Telecommunications Research (ATR) Computational Neuroscience Laboratories in Kyoto, Japan, allowed the scientists to reconstruct images directly from the brain and display them on a computer in black and white at a resolution of 10x10 pixels. The article announcing these achievements was the cover story of the journal Neuron of 10 December 2008.

In 2011 researchers from UC Berkeley published a study reporting second-by-second reconstruction of videos watched by the study's subjects, from fMRI data. This was achieved by creating a statistical model relating visual patterns in videos shown to the subjects, to the brain activity caused by watching the videos. This model was then used to look up the 100 one-second video segments, in a database of 18 million seconds of random YouTube videos, whose visual patterns most closely matched the brain activity recorded when subjects watched a new video. These 100 one-second video extracts were then combined into a mashed-up image that resembled the video being watched.

Neurogaming

Currently, there is a new field of gaming called Neurogaming, which uses non-invasive BCI in order to improve gameplay so that users can interact with a console without the use of a traditional controller. Some Neurogaming software use a player's brain waves, heart rate, expressions, pupil dilation, and even emotions to complete tasks or affect the mood of the game. For example, game developers at Emotiv have created non-invasive BCI that will determine the mood of a player and adjust music or scenery accordingly. This new form of interaction between player and software will enable a player to have a more realistic gaming experience. Because there will be less disconnect between a player and console, Neurogaming will allow individuals to utilize their "psychological state" and have their reactions transfer to games in real-time.

However, since Neurogaming is still in its first stages, not much is written about the new industry. The first NeuroGaming Conference was held in San Francisco on May 1–2, 2013.

BCI Control Strategies in Neurogaming
Motor Imagery

Motor imagery involves the imagination of the movement of various body parts resulting in sensorimotor cortex activation,which modulates sensorimotor oscillations in the

EEG. This can be detected by the BCI to infer a user's intent. Motor imagery typically requires a number of sessions of training before acceptable control of the BCI is acquired. These training sessions may take a number of hours over several days before users can consistently employ the technique with acceptable levels of precision. Regardless of the duration of the training session, users are unable to master the control scheme. This results in very slow pace of the gameplay. Advance machine learning methods were recently developed to compute a subject-specific model for detecting the performance of motor imagery. The top performing algorithm from BCI Competition IV (http://www.bbci.de/competition/iv/) dataset 2 for motor imagery is the Filter Bank Common Spatial Pattern, developed by Ang et al. from A*STAR, Singapore).

Bio/Neurofeedback for Passive BCI Designs

Biofeedback is used to monitor a subject's mental relaxation. In some cases, biofeedback does not monitor electroencephalography (EEG), but instead bodily parameters such as electromyography(EMG), galvanic skin resistance (GSR), and heart rate variability (HRV).Many biofeedback systems are used to treat certain disorders such as attention deficit hyperactivity disorder (ADHD), sleep problems in children, teeth grinding, and chronic pain. EEG biofeedback systems typically monitor four different bands (theta: 4–7 Hz, alpha:8–12 Hz, SMR: 12–15 Hz, beta: 15–18 Hz) and challenge the subject to control them. Passive BCI involves using BCI to enrich human–machine interaction with implicit information on the actual user's state, for example, simulations to detect when users intend to push brakes during an emergency car stopping procedure. Game developers using passive BCIs need to acknowledge that through repetition of game levels the user's cognitive state will change or adapt. Within the first play of a level, the user will react to things differently from during the second play: for example, the user will be less surprised at an event in the game if he/she is expecting it.

Visual Evoked Potential (VEP)

A VEP is an electrical potential recorded after a subject is presented with a type of visual stimuli. There are several types of VEPs.

Steady-state visually evoked potentials (SSVEPs) use potentials generated by exciting the retina, using visual stimuli modulated at certain frequencies. SSVEP's stimuli are often formed from alternating checkerboard patterns and at times simply use flashing images . The frequency of the phase reversal of the stimulus used can be clearly distinguished in the spectrum of an EEG; this makes detection of SSVEP stimuli relatively easy . SSVEP has proved to be successful within many BCI systems . This is due to several factors, the signal elicited is measurable in as large a population as the transient VEP and blink movement and electro cardiographic artefacts do not affect the frequencies monitored. In addition, the SSVEP signal is exceptionally robust; the topographic organization of the primary visual cortex is such that a broader area obtains afferents from the central or fovial region of the visual field .SSVEP does have several problems however. As SSVEPs use flashing stimuli to infer a user's intent, the user must gaze at one of the flashing or iterating symbols in order to interact with the system. It is, therefore, likely that the symbols could become irritating and uncomfortable to use during longer play sessions, which can often last more than an hour which may not be an ideal gameplay.

Another type of VEP used with applications is the P300 potential. The P300 event-related potential is a positive peak in the EEG that occurs at roughly 300 ms after the appearance of a target stimulus (a stimulus for which the user is waiting or seeking) or oddball stimuli . The P300 amplitude decreases as the target stimuli and the ignored stimuli grow more similar.The P300 is thought to be related to a higher level attention process or an orienting response Using P300 as a control scheme has the advantage of the participant only having to attend limited training sessions. The first application to use the P300 model was the P300 matrix . Within this system, a subject would choose a letter from a grid of 6 by 6 letters and numbers. The rows and columns of the grid flashed sequentially and every time the selected "choice letter" was illuminated the user's P300 was (potentially) elicited. However, the communication process, at approximately 17 characters per minute, was quite slow. The P300 is a BCI that offers a discrete selection rather than a continuous control mechanism. The advantage of P300 use within games is that the player does not have to teach himself/herself how to use a completely new control system and so only has to undertake short training instances, to learn the gameplay mechanics and basic use of the BCI paradigm.

Synthetic Telepathy/Silent Communication

In a $6.3 million Army initiative to invent devices for telepathic communication, Gerwin Schalk, underwritten in a $2.2 million grant, found that it is possible to use ECoG signals to discriminate the vowels and consonants embedded in spoken and in imagined words. The results shed light on the distinct mechanisms associated with production of vowels and consonants, and could provide the basis for brain-based communication using imagined speech.

Research into synthetic telepathy using subvocalization is taking place at the University of California, Irvine under lead scientist Mike D'Zmura. The first such communication took place in the 1960s using EEG to create Morse code using brain alpha waves. Using EEG to communicate imagined speech is less accurate than the invasive method of placing an electrode between the skull and the brain. On February 27, 2013 the group of Miguel Nicolelis at Duke University and IINN-ELS successfully connected the brains of two rats with electronic interfaces that allowed them to directly share information, in the first-ever direct brain-to-brain interface.

On 3 September 2014, scientists reported that direct communication between human brains was possible over extended distances through Internet transmission of EEG signals.

In March and in May 2014 a study conducted by Dipartimento di Psicologia Generale - Università di Padova, EVANLAB - Firenze, LiquidWeb s.r.l. company and Dipartimento di Ingegneria e Architettura - Università di Trieste, reports confirmatory results analyzing the EEG activity of two human partners spatially separated approximately 190 km apart when one member of the pair receives the stimulation and the second one is connected only mentally with the first.

Cell-culture BCIs

Researchers have built devices to interface with neural cells and entire neural networks in cultures outside animals. As well as furthering research on animal implantable devices, experiments on cultured neural tissue have focused on building problem-solving networks, constructing basic computers and manipulating robotic devices. Research into techniques for stimulating and recording from individual neurons grown on semiconductor chips is sometimes referred to as neuroelectronics or neurochips.

The world's first Neurochip, developed by Caltech researchers Jerome Pine and Michael Maher.

Development of the first working neurochip was claimed by a Caltech team led by Jerome Pine and Michael Maher in 1997. The Caltech chip had room for 16 neurons.

In 2003 a team led by Theodore Berger, at the University of Southern California, started work on a neurochip designed to function as an artificial or prosthetic hippocampus. The neurochip was designed to function in rat brains and was intended as a prototype for the eventual development of higher-brain prosthesis. The hippocampus was chosen because it is thought to be the most ordered and structured part of the brain and is the most studied area. Its function is to encode experiences for storage as long-term memories elsewhere in the brain.

In 2004 Thomas DeMarse at the University of Florida used a culture of 25,000 neurons taken from a rat's brain to fly a F-22 fighter jet aircraft simulator. After collection, the cortical neurons were cultured in a petri dish and rapidly began to reconnect themselves to form a living neural network. The cells were arranged over a grid of 60 electrodes and used to control the pitch and yaw functions of the simulator. The study's focus was on understanding how the human brain performs and learns computational tasks at a cellular level.

Ethical Considerations

Important ethical, legal and societal issues related to brain-computer interfacing are:

- Conceptual issues (researchers disagree over what is and what is not a brain-computer interface).

- Obtaining informed consent from people who have difficulty communicating.

- Risk/benefit analysis.

- Shared responsibility of BCI teams (e.g. how to ensure that responsible group decisions can be made).

- The consequences of BCI technology for the quality of life of patients and their families.

- Side-effects (e.g. neurofeedback of sensorimotor rhythm training is reported to affect sleep quality).

- Personal responsibility and its possible constraints (e.g. who is responsible for erroneous actions with a neuroprosthesis).

- Issues concerning personality and personhood and its possible alteration.

- Therapeutic applications and their possible exceedance.

- Questions of research ethics that arise when progressing from animal experimentation to application in human subjects.

- Mind-reading and privacy.

- Mind-control.

- Use of the technology in advanced interrogation techniques by governmental authorities.

- Selective enhancement and social stratification.

- Communication to the media.

Clausen stated in 2009 that "BCIs pose ethical challenges, but these are conceptually similar to those that bioethicists have addressed for other realms of therapy". Moreover, he suggests that bioethics is well-prepared to deal with the issues that arise with BCI technologies. Haselager and colleagues pointed out that expectations of BCI efficacy and value play a great role in ethical analysis and the way BCI scientists should approach media. Furthermore, standard protocols can be implemented to ensure ethically sound informed-consent procedures with locked-in patients.

Researchers are well aware that sound ethical guidelines, appropriately moderated enthusiasm in media coverage and education about BCI systems will be of utmost importance for the societal acceptance of this technology. Thus, recently more effort is made inside the BCI community to create consensus on ethical guidelines for BCI research, development and dissemination.

Clinical and Research-grade BCI-based Interfaces

Some companies have been producing high-end systems that have been widely used in established BCI labs for several years. These systems typically entail more channels than the low-cost systems below, with much higher signal quality and robustness in real-world settings. Some systems from new companies have been gaining attention for new BCI applications for new user groups, such as persons with stroke or coma.

- In 2011, Nuamps EEG from www.neuroscan.com was used to study the extent of detectable brain signals from stroke patients who performed motor imagery using BCI in a large clinical trial, and the results showed that majority of the patients (87%) could use the BCI.

- In March 2012 g.tec introduced the intendiX-SPELLER, the first commercially available BCI system for home use which can be used to control computer games and apps. It can detect different brain signals with an accuracy of 99%. has hosted several workshop tours to demonstrate the intendiX system and other hardware and software to the public, such as a workshop tour of the US West Coast during September 2012.

- A German-based company called BrainProducts makes systems that are widely used within established BCI labs.

- In 2012 an Italian startup company, Liquidweb s.r.l., released "Braincontrol", a first prototype of an AAC BCI-based, designed for patients in locked-in state. It was validated from 2012 and 2014 with the involvement of LIS and CLIS patients. In 2014 the company introduced the commercial version of the product, with the CE mark class I as medical device.

Low-cost BCI-based Interfaces

Recently a number of companies have scaled back medical grade EEG technology (and in one case, NeuroSky, rebuilt the technology from the ground up to create inexpensive BCIs. This technology has been built into toys and gaming devices; some of these toys have been extremely commercially successful like the NeuroSky and Mattel MindFlex.

- In 2006 Sony patented a neural interface system allowing radio waves to affect signals in the neural cortex.

- In 2007 NeuroSky released the first affordable consumer based EEG along with the game NeuroBoy. This was also the first large scale EEG device to use dry sensor technology.

- In 2008 OCZ Technology developed a device for use in video games relying primarily on electromyography.

- In 2008 the Final Fantasy developer Square Enix announced that it was partnering with NeuroSky to create a game, Judecca.

- In 2009 Mattel partnered with NeuroSky to release the Mindflex, a game that used an EEG to steer a ball through an obstacle course. By far the best selling consumer based EEG to date.

- In 2009 Uncle Milton Industries partnered with NeuroSky to release the Star Wars Force Trainer, a game designed to create the illusion of possessing The Force.

- In 2009 Emotiv released the EPOC, a 14 channel EEG device that can read 4 mental states, 13 conscious states, facial expressions, and head movements. The EPOC is the first commercial BCI to use dry sensor technology, which can be dampened with a saline solution for a better connection.

- In November 2011 Time Magazine selected "necomimi" produced by Neurowear as one of the best inventions of the year. The company announced that it expected to launch a consumer version of the garment, consisting of cat-like ears controlled by a brain-wave reader produced by NeuroSky, in spring 2012.

- In February 2014 They Shall Walk (a nonprofit organization fixed on constructing exoskeletons, dubbed LIFESUITs, for paraplegics and quadriplegics) began a partnership with James W. Shakarji on the development of a wireless BCI.

Future Directions for BCIs

A consortium consisting of 12 European partners has completed a roadmap to support the European Commission in their funding decisions for the new framework program Horizon 2020. The project, which was funded by the European Commission, started in November 2013 and ended in April 2015. The roadmap is now complete, and can be downloaded on the project's webpage. A 2015 publication describes some of the analyses and achievements of this project, as well as the emerging Brain-Computer Interface Society. For example, this article reviewed work within this project that further defined BCIs and applications, explored recent trends, discussed ethical issues, and evaluated different directions for new BCIs. As the article notes, their new roadmap generally extends and supports the recommendations from the Future BNCI project, which conveys some enthusiasm for emerging BCI directions.

In addition to, other recent publications have explored the most promising future BCI directions for new groups of disabled users (e.g.,). Some prominent examples are summarized below.

Disorders of Consciousness (DOC)

Some persons have a disorder of consciousness (DOC). This state is defined to include persons with coma, as well as persons in a vegetative state (VS) or minimally conscious state (MCS). New BCI research seeks to help persons with DOC in different ways. A key initial goal is to identify patients who are able to perform basic cognitive tasks, which would of course lead to a change in their diagnosis. That is, some persons who are diagnosed with DOC may in fact be able to process information and make important life decisions (such as whether to seek therapy, where to live, and their views on end-of-life decisions regarding them). Very sadly, some persons who are diagnosed with DOC die as a result of end-of-life decisions, which may be made by family members who sincerely feel this is in the patient's best interests. Given the new prospect of allowing these patients to provide their views on this decision, there would seem to be a strong ethical pressure to develop this research direction to guarantee that DOC patients are given an opportunity to decide whether they want to live.

These and other articles describe new challenges and solutions to use BCI technology to help persons with DOC. One major challenge is that these patients cannot use BCIs based on vision. Hence, new tools rely on auditory and/or vibrotactile stimuli. Patients may wear headphones and/or vibrotactile stimulators placed on the wrists, neck, leg, and/or other locations. Another challenge is that patients may fade in and out of consciousness, and can only communicate at certain times. This may indeed be a cause of mistaken diagnosis. Some patients may only be able to respond to physicians' requests during a few hours per day (which might not be predictable ahead of time) and thus may have been unresponsive during diagnosis. Therefore, new methods rely on tools that are easy to use in field settings, even without expert help, so family members and other persons without any medical or technical background can still use them. This reduces the cost, time, need for expertise, and other burdens with DOC assessment. Automated tools can ask simple questions that patients can easily answer, such as "Is your father named George?" or "Were you born in the USA?" Automated instructions inform patients that they may convey yes or no by (for example) focusing their attention on stimuli on the right vs. left wrist. This focused attention produces reliable changes in EEG patterns that can help determine that the patient is able to communicate. The results could be presented to physicians and therapists, which could lead to a revised diagnosis and therapy. In addition, these patients could then be provided with BCI-based communication tools that could help them convey basic needs, adjust bed position and HVAC (heating, ventilation, and air conditioning), and otherwise empower them to make major life decisions and communicate.

This research effort was supported in part by different EU-funded projects, such as the DECODER project led by Prof. Andrea Kuebler at the University of Wuerzburg. This project contributed to the first BCI system developed for DOC assessment and communication, called mindBEAGLE. This system is designed to help non-expert users work with DOC patients, but is not intended to replace medical staff. An EU-funded project scheduled to begin in 2015 called ComAlert will conduct further research and development to improve DOC prediction, assessment, rehabilitation, and communication, called "PARC" in that project. Another project funded by the National Science Foundation is led by Profs. Dean Krusienski and Chang Nam. This project provides for improved vibrotactile systems, advanced signal analysis, and other improvements for DOC assessment and communication.

Functional Brain Mapping

Each year, about 400,000 people undergo brain mapping during neurosurgery. This procedure is often required for people with tumors or epilepsy that do not respond to medication. During this procedure, electrodes are placed on the brain to precisely identify the locations of structures and functional areas. Patients may be awake during neurosurgery and asked to perform certain tasks, such as moving fingers or repeating words. This is necessary so that surgeons can remove only the desired tissue while sparing other regions, such as critical movement or language regions. Removing too much brain tissue can cause permanent damage, while removing too little tissue can leave the underlying condition untreated and require additional neurosurgery. Thus, there is a strong need to improve both methods and systems to map the brain as effectively as possible.

In several recent publications, BCI research experts and medical doctors have collaborated to explore new ways to use BCI technology to improve neurosurgical mapping. This work focuses largely on high gamma activity, which is difficult to detect with non-invasive means. Results have led to improved methods for identifying key areas for movement, language, and other functions. A recent article addressed advances in functional brain mapping and summarizes a workshop.

BCI Society

Many people within the BCI community have been working toward an official Brain-Computer Interface Society over the last few years. At the Fifth International BCI Meeting in Asilomar, CA in 2013, a plenary session of the attendees unanimously voted in favor of forming this Society. Since then, several people have been active developing bylaws, articles of incorporation, official statements, a membership infrastructure, official website, and other details. The Board consists of many of the most established people in BCI research, including three officers: Prof. Jonathan Wolpaw (President), Prof. Nick Ramsey (Vice-President), and Dr. Christoph Guger (Treasurer).

Single-unit Recording

In neuroscience, single-unit recordings provide a method of measuring the electro-physiological responses of single neurons using a microelectrode system. When a neuron generates an action potential, the signal propagates down the neuron as a current which flows in and out of the cell through excitable membrane regions in the soma and axon. A microelectrode is inserted into the brain, where it can record the rate of change in voltage with respect to time. These microelectrodes must be fine-tipped, high-impedance conductors; they are primarily glass micro-pipettes or metal microelectrodes made of platinum or tungsten. Microelectrodes can be carefully placed within (or close to) the cell membrane, allowing the ability to record intracellularly or extracellularly.

Single-unit recordings are widely used in cognitive science, where it permits the analysis of human cognition and cortical mapping. This information can then be applied to brain machine interface (BMI) technologies for brain control of external devices.

Overview

There are many techniques available to record brain activity—including electroencephalography (EEG), magnetoencephalography (MEG), and functional magnetic resonance imaging (fMRI)—but these do not allow for single-neuron resolution. Neurons are the basic functional units in the brain; they transmit information through the body using electrical signals called action potentials. Currently, single-unit recordings provide the most precise recordings from single neurons. A single unit is defined as a single, firing neuron whose spike potentials are distinctly isolated by a recording microelectrode.

The ability to record signals from neurons is centered around the electric current flow through the neuron. As an action potential propagates through the cell, the electric current flows in and out of the soma and axons at excitable membrane regions. This current creates a measurable, changing voltage potential within (and outside) the cell. This allows for two basic types of single-unit recordings. Intracellular single-unit recordings occur within the neuron and measure the voltage change (with respect to time) across the membrane during action potentials. This outputs as a trace with information on membrane resting potential, postsynaptic potentials and spikes through the soma (or axon). Alternatively, when the microelectrode is close to the cell surface extracellular recordings measure the voltage change (with respect to time) outside the cell, giving only spike information. Different types of microelectrodes can be used for single-unit recordings; they are typically high-impedance, fine-tipped and conductive. Fine tips allow for easy penetration without extensive damage to the cell, but they also correlate with high impedance. Additionally, electrical and/or ionic conductivity allow for recordings from both non-polarizable and polarizable electrodes. The two primary classes of electrodes are glass micropipettes and metal electrodes. Electrolyte-filled glass micropipettes are mainly used for intracellular single-unit recordings; metal electrodes (commonly made of stainless steel, platinum, tungsten or iridium) and used for both types of recordings.

Single-unit recordings have provided tools to explore the brain and apply this knowledge to current technologies. Cognitive scientists have used single-unit recordings in the brains of animals and humans to study behaviors and functions. Electrodes can also be inserted into the brain of epileptic patients to determine the position of epileptic foci. More recently, single-unit recordings have been used in brain machine interfaces (BMI). BMIs record brain signals and decode an intended response, which then controls the movement of an external device (such as a computer cursor or prosthetic limb).

History

The ability to record from single units started with the discovery that the nervous system has electrical properties. Since then, single unit recordings have become an important method for understanding mechanisms and functions of the nervous system. Over the years, single unit recording continued to provide insight on topographical mapping of the cortex. Eventual development of microelectrode arrays allowed recording from multiple units at a time.

- 1790s: The first evidence of electrical activity in the nervous system was observed by Luigi Galvani in the 1790s with his studies on dissected frogs. He discovered that you can induce a dead frog leg to twitch with a spark.

- 1888: Santiago Ramón y Cajal, a Spanish neuroscientist, revolutionized neuroscience with his neuron theory, describing the structure of the nervous system and presence of basic functional units— neurons. He won the Nobel Prize in Physiology or Medicine for this work in 1906.

- 1928: The first account of being able to record from the nervous system was by Edgar Adrian in his 1928 publication "The Basis of Sensation". In this, he describes his recordings of electrical discharges in single nerve fibers using a Lippmann electrometer. He won the Nobel Prize in 1932 for his work revealing the function of neurons.

- 1940: Renshaw, Forbes & Morrison performed original studies recording discharge of pyramidal cells in the hippocampus using glass microelectrodes in cats.

- 1950: Woldring and Dirken report the ability to obtain spike activity from the surface of the cerebral cortex with platinum wires.

- 1952: Li and Jasper applied the Renshaw, Forbes, & Morrison method to study electrical activity in the cerebral cortex of a cat. Hodgkin–Huxley model was revealed, where they used a squid giant axon to determine the exact mechanism of action potentials.

- 1953: Iridium microelectrodes developed for recording.

- 1957: John Eccles used intracellular single-unit recording to study synaptic mechanisms in motoneurons (for which he won the Nobel Prize in 1963).

- 1958: Stainless steel microelectrodes developed for recording.

- 1959: Studies by David H. Hubel and Torsten Wiesel. They used single neuron recordings to map the visual cortex in unanesthetized, unrestrained cats using tungsten electrodes. This work won them the Nobel Prize in 1981 for information processing in the visual system.

- 1960: Glass-insulated platinum microelectrodes developed for recording.

- 1967: The first record of multi-electrode arrays for recording was published by Marg and Adams. They applied this method to record many units at a single time in a single patient for diagnostic and therapeutic brain surgery.

- 1978: Schmidt et al. implanted chronic recording micro-cortical electrodes into the cortex of monkeys and showed that they could teach them to control neuronal firing rates, a key step to the possibility of recording neuronal signals and using them for BMIs.

- 1981: Kruger and Bach assemble 30 individual microelectrodes in a 5x6 configuration and implant the electrodes for simultaneous recording of multiple units.

- 1992: Development of the "Utah Intracortical Electrode Array (UIEA), a multiple-electrode array which can access the columnar structure of the cerebral cortex for neurophysiological or neuroprosthetic applications".

- 1994: The Michigan array, a silicon planar electrode with multiple recording sites, was developed. NeuroNexus, a private neurotechnology company, is formed based on this technology.

- 1998: A key breakthrough for BMIs was achieved by Kennedy and Bakay with development of neurotrophic electrodes. In patients with amyotrophic lateral sclerosis (ALS), a neurological condition affecting the ability to control voluntary movement, they were able to successfully record action potentials using microelectrode arrays to control a computer cursor.

Electrophysiology

The basis of single-unit recordings relies on the ability to record electrical signals from neurons.

Neuronal Potentials and Electrodes

When a microelectrode is inserted into an aqueous ionic solution, there is a tendency for cations and anions to react with the electrode creating an electrode-electrolyte interface. The forming of this layer has been termed the Helmholtz layer. A charge distribution occurs across the electrode, which creates a potential which can be measured against a reference electrode. The method of neuronal potential recording is dependent on the type of electrode used. Non-polarizable electrodes are reversible (ions in the solution are charged and discharged). This creates a current flowing through the electrode, allowing for voltage measurement through the electrode with respect to time. Typically, non-polarizable electrodes are glass micropipettes filled with an ionic solution or metal. Alternatively, ideal polarized electrodes do not have the transformation of ions; these are typically metal electrodes. Instead, the ions and electrons at the surface of the metal become polarized with respect to the potential of the solution. The charges orient at the interface to create an electric double layer; the metal then acts like a capacitor. The change in capacitance with respect to time can be measured and converted to voltage using a bridge circuit. Using this technique, when neurons fire an action potential they create changes in potential fields that can be recorded using microelectrodes.

Intracellularly, the electrodes directly record the firing of action, resting and postsynaptic potentials. When a neuron fires, current flows in and out through excitable regions in the axons and cell body of the neuron. This creates potential fields around the neuron. An electrode near a neuron can detect these extracellular potential fields, creating a spike.

Experimental Setup

The basic equipment needed to record single units is microelectrodes, amplifiers, micromanipulators and recording devices. The type of microelectrode used will depend on the application. The high resistance of these electrodes creates a problem during signal amplification. If it were connected to a conventional amplifier with low input resistance, there would be a large potential drop across the microelectrode and the amplifier would only measure a small portion of the true potential. To solve this problem, a cathode follower amplifier must be used as an impedance matching device to collect the voltage and feed it to a conventional amplifier. To record from a single neuron, micromanipulators must be used to precisely insert an electrode into the brain. This is especially important for intracellular single-unit recording.

Finally, the signals must be exported to a recording device. After amplification, signals are filtered with various techniques. They can be recorded by an oscilloscope and camera, but more modern techniques convert the signal with an analog-to-digital converter and output to a computer to be saved. Data-processing techniques can allow for separation and analysis of single units.

Types of Microelectrodes

There are two main types of microelectrodes used for single-unit recordings: glass micropipettes and metal electrodes. Both are high-impedance electrodes, but glass micropipettes are highly resistive and metal electrodes have frequency-dependent impedance. Glass micropipettes are ideal for resting- and action-potential measurement, while metal electrodes are best used for extracellular spike measurements. Each type has different properties and limitations, which can be beneficial in specific applications.

Glass Micropipettes

Glass micropipettes are filled with an ionic solution to make them conductive; a silver-silver chloride (Ag-AgCl) electrode is dipped into the filling solution as an electrical terminal. Ideally, the ionic solutions should have ions similar to ionic species around the electrode; the concentration inside the electrode and surrounding fluid should be the same. Additionally, the diffusive characteristics of the different ions within the electrode should be similar. The ion must also be able to "provide current carrying capacity adequate for the needs of the experiment". And importantly, it must not cause biological changes in the cell it is recording from. Ag-AgCl electrodes are primarily used with a potassium chloride (KCl) solution. With Ag-AgCl electrodes, ions react with it to produce electrical gradients at the interface, creating a voltage change with respect to time. Electrically, glass microelectrode tips have high resistance and high capacitance. They have a tip size of approximately 0.5-1.5 μm with a resistance of about 10-50 MΩ. The small tips make it easy to penetrate the cell membrane with minimal damage for intracellular recordings. Micropipettes are ideal for measurement of resting membrane potentials and with some adjustments can record action potentials. There are some issues to consider when using glass micropipettes. To offset high resistance in glass micropipettes, a cathode follower must be used as the first-stage amplifier. Additionally, high capacitance develops across the glass and conducting solution which can attenuate high-frequency responses. There is also electrical interference inherent in these electrodes and amplifiers.

Metal

Metal electrodes are made of various types of metals, typically silicon, platinum, and tungsten. They "resemble a leaky electrolytic capacitor, having a very high low-frequency impedance and low high-frequency impedance". They are more suitable for measurement of extracellular action potentials, although glass micropipettes can also be used. Metal electrodes are beneficial in some cases because they have high signal-to-noise due to lower impedance for the frequency range of spike signals. They also have better mechanical stiffness for puncturing through brain tissue. Lastly, they are more easily fabricated into different tip shapes and sizes at large quantities. Platinum electrodes are platinum black plated and insulated with glass. "They normally give stable recordings, a high signal-to-noise ratio, good isolation, and they are quite rugged in the usual tip sizes". The only limitation is that the tips are very fine and fragile. Silicon electrodes are alloy electrodes doped with silicon and an insulating glass cover layer. Silicon technology provides better mechanical stiffness and is a good supporting carrier to allow for multiple recording sites on a single electrode. Tungsten electrodes are very rugged and provide very stable recordings. This allows manufacturing of tungsten electrodes with very small tips to isolate high-frequencies. Tungsten, however, is very noisy at low frequencies. In mammalian nervous system where there are fast signals, noise can be removed with a high-pass filter. Slow signals are lost if filtered so tungsten is not a good choice for recording these signals.

Types of Single-unit Recordings

Single unit recordings can be done either intracellularly or extracellularly. While extracellular recordings can only give spike information, intracellular single unit recordings can give information on resting potentials and postsynaptic potentials. The use of either technique depends on the specific application and what information is desired.

Intracellular

Intracellular single unit recordings require electrodes be inserted through the cell membrane to record from within the cell. Glass micropipettes or metal electrodes may be used for intracellular single unit recordings, but glass micropipettes are preferred because their high input resistance allows more precise recordings for measurement of resting potentials. Additionally, very fine glass tip micropipettes are much better at successfully penetrating and retaining neurons. Intracellular single unit recordings provide much more information on single neuron discharges. They can give information on steady and resting membrane voltage, postsynaptic potentials, and spikes (action potentials) from both the axon and cell body. Limitations of intracellular recording are that one can only record from cell bodies of, usually, the largest cells. There is little information obtained on neural information transfer from further dendrites or axons. Recordings from small neurons are quite difficult and usually must be supported with extracellular single unit recordings.

Extracellular

Extracellular single unit recordings are more suitable for measuring extracellular action potentials. They are measured using either glass micropipettes or metal electrodes that are placed close to the neuron. Extracellular recordings can easily measure spike discharge from a neuron with any suitably small electrode. Single neurons can also be isolated and recorded for longer periods of time with no worry of damage to the cells. This makes it much easier to obtain these signals in an awake and moving animal. Limitations of extracellular recordings are that signal detection is a primary concern and it is unable to give information on postsynaptic potentials or resting membrane potentials.

Combined Recordings

More recently, efforts have been made to obtain extracellular and intracellular recordings simultaneously. This involves careful placement of extracellular and intracellular electrodes in a single neuron. The primary use for this is to provide a better understanding of the relationship between intracellular action potentials and extracellular spike recordings.

Applications

Single-unit recordings have allowed the ability to monitor single-neuron activity. This has allowed researchers to discover the role of different parts of the brain in function and behavior. More recently, recording from single neurons can be used to engineer "mind-controlled" devices.

Cognitive Science

Noninvasive tools to study the CNS have been developed to provide structural and functional information, but they do not provide very high resolution. To offset this problem invasive recording methods have been used. Single unit recording methods give high spatial and temporal resolution to allow for information assessing the relationship between brain structure, function, and behavior. By looking at brain activity at the neuron level, researchers can link brain activity to behavior and create neuronal maps describing flow of information through the brain. For example, Boraud et al. report the use of single unit recordings to determine the structural organization of the basal ganglia in patients with Parkinson's disease. Evoked potentials provide a method to couple behavior to brain function. By stimulating different responses, one can visualize what portion of the brain is activated. This method has been used to explore cognitive functions such as perception, memory, language, emotions, and motor control.

Brain-machine Interfaces

Brain-machine interfaces (BMIs) have been developed within the last 20 years. By recording single unit potentials, these devices can decode signals through a computer and output this signal for control of an external device such as a computer cursor or prosthetic limb. BMIs have the potential to restore function in patients with paralysis or neurological disease. This technology has potential to reach a wide variety of patients but is not yet available clinically due to lack of reliability in recording signals over time. The primary hypothesis regarding this failure is that the chronic inflammatory response around the electrode causes neurodegeneration that reduces the number of neurons it is able to record from (Nicolelis, 2001). In 2004, the BrainGate pilot clinical trial was initiated to "test the safety and feasibility of a neural interface system based on an intracortical 100-electrode silicon recording array". This initiative has been successful in advancement of BCIs and in 2011, published data showing long term computer control in a patient with tetraplegia (Simeral, 2011).

Bayesian Approaches to Brain Function

Bayesian approaches to brain function investigate the capacity of the nervous system to operate in situations of uncertainty in a fashion that is close to the optimal prescribed by Bayesian statistics. This term is used in behavioural sciences and neuroscience and studies associated with this term often strive to explain the brain's cognitive abilities based on statistical principles. It is frequently assumed that the nervous system maintains internal probabilistic models that are updated by neural processing of sensory information using methods approximating those of Bayesian probability.

Origins

This field of study has its historical roots in numerous disciplines including machine learning, experimental psychology and Bayesian statistics. As early as the 1860s, with the work of Hermann Helmholtz in experimental psychology the brain's ability to extract perceptual information from sensory data was modeled in terms of probabilistic estimation. The basic idea is that the nervous system needs to organize sensory data into an accurate internal model of the outside world.

Bayesian probability has been developed by many important contributors. Pierre-Simon Laplace, Thomas Bayes, Harold Jeffreys, Richard Cox and Edwin Jaynes developed mathematical techniques and procedures for treating probability as the degree of plausibility that could be assigned to a given supposition or hypothesis based on the available evidence. In 1988 E.T. Jaynes presented a framework for using Bayesian Probability to model mental processes. It was thus realized early on that the Bayesian statistical framework holds the potential to lead to insights into the function of the nervous system.

This idea was taken up in research on unsupervised learning, in particular the Analysis by Synthesis approach, branches of machine learning. In 1983 Geoffrey Hinton and colleagues proposed the brain could be seen as a machine making decisions based on the uncertainties of the outside world. During the 1990s researchers including Peter Dayan, Geoffrey Hinton and Richard Zemel proposed that the brain represents knowledge of the world in terms of probabilities and made specific proposals for tractable neural processes that could manifest such a Helmholtz Machine.

Psychophysics

A wide range of studies interpret the results of psychophysical experiments in light of Bayesian perceptual models. Many aspects of human perceptual and motor behavior can be modeled with Bayesian statistics. This approach, with its emphasis on behavioral outcomes as the ultimate expressions of neural information processing, is also known for modeling sensory and motor decisions using Bayesian decision theory. Examples are the work of Landy, Jacobs, Jordan, Knill, Kording and Wolpert, and Goldreich.

Neural Coding

Many theoretical studies ask how the nervous system could implement Bayesian algorithms. Examples are the work of Pouget, Zemel, Deneve, Latham, Hinton and Dayan. George and Hawkins published a paper that establishes a model of cortical information processing called hierarchical temporal memory that is based on Bayesian network of Markov chains. They further map this mathematical model to the existing knowledge about the architecture of cortex and show how neurons could recognize patterns by hierarchical Bayesian inference.

Electrophysiology

A number of recent electrophysiological studies focus on the representation of probabilities in the nervous system. Examples are the work of Shadlen and Schultz.

Predictive Coding

Predictive coding is a neurobiologically plausible scheme for inferring the causes of sensory input based on minimizing prediction error. These schemes are related formally to Kalman filtering and other Bayesian update schemes.

Free Energy

During the 1990s some researchers such as Geoffrey Hinton and Karl Friston began examining the concept of free energy as a calculably tractable measure of the discrepancy between actual features of the world and representations of those features captured by neural network models. A synthesis has been attempted recently by Karl Friston, in which the Bayesian brain emerges from a general principle of free energy minimisation. In this framework, both action and perception are seen as a consequence of suppressing free-energy, leading to perceptual and active inference and a more embodied (enactive) view of the Bayesian brain. Using variational Bayesian methods, it can be shown how internal models of the world are updated by sensory information to minimize free energy or the discrepancy between sensory input and predictions of that input. This can be cast (in neurobiologically plausible terms) as predictive coding or, more generally, Bayesian filtering.

According to Friston:

"The free-energy considered here represents a bound on the surprise inherent in any exchange with the environment, under expectations encoded by its state or configuration. A system can minimise free energy by changing its configuration to change the way it samples the environment, or to change its expectations. These changes correspond to action and perception, respectively, and lead to an adaptive exchange with the environment that is characteristic of biological systems. This treatment implies that the system's state and structure encode an implicit and probabilistic model of the environment."

This area of research was summarized in terms understandable by the layperson in a 2008 article in New Scientist that offered a unifying theory of brain function. Friston makes the following claims about the explanatory power of the theory:

"This model of brain function can explain a wide range of anatomical and physiological aspects of brain systems; for example, the hierarchical deployment of cortical areas, recurrent architectures using forward and backward connections and functional asymmetries in these connections. In terms of synaptic physiology, it predicts associative plasticity and, for dynamic models, spike-timing-dependent plasticity. In terms of electrophysiology it accounts for classical and extra-classical receptive field effects and long-latency or endogenous components of evoked cortical responses. It predicts the attenuation of responses encoding prediction error with perceptual learning and explains many phenomena like repetition suppression, mismatch negativity and the P300 in electroencephalography. In psychophysical terms, it accounts for the behavioural correlates of these physiological phenomena, e.g., priming, and global precedence."

"It is fairly easy to show that both perceptual inference and learning rest on a minimisation of free energy or suppression of prediction error."

Mind Uploading

Whole brain emulation (WBE) or mind uploading (sometimes called "mind copying" or "mind transfer") is the hypothetical process of scanning mental state (including long-term memory and "self") of a particular brain substrate and copying it to a computational device, such as a digital, analog, quantum-based or software-based artificial neural network. The computational device could then run a simulation model of the brain's information processing, such that it responds in essentially the same way as the original brain (i.e., indistinguishable from the brain for all relevant purposes) and experiences having a conscious mind.

Mind uploading may potentially be accomplished by either of two methods: Copy-and-Transfer or gradual replacement of neurons. In the case of the former method, mind uploading would be achieved by scanning and mapping the salient features of a biological brain, and then by copying, transferring, and storing that information state into a computer system or another computational device. The simulated mind could be within a virtual reality or simulated world, supported by an anatomic 3D body simulation model. Alternatively, the simulated mind could reside in a computer that is inside (or connected to) a (not necessarily humanoid) robot or a biological body.

Among some futurists and within the transhumanist movement, mind uploading is treated as an important proposed life extension technology. Some believe mind uploading is our current best option for preserving who we are as opposed to cryonics.

Another aim of mind uploading is to provide a permanent backup to our "mind-file", and a means for functional copies of human minds to survive a global disaster or inter-stellar space travels. Whole brain emulation is discussed by some futurists as a "logical endpoint" of the topical computational neuroscience and neuroinformatics fields, both about brain simulation for medical research purposes. It is discussed in artificial intelligence research publications as an approach to strong AI. Computer-based intelligence such as an upload could think much faster than a biological human even if it were no more intelligent. A large-scale society of uploads might, according to futurists, give rise to a technological singularity, meaning a sudden time constant decrease in the exponential development of technology. Mind uploading is a central conceptual feature of numerous science fiction novels and films.

Substantial mainstream research in related areas is being conducted in animal brain mapping and simulation, development of faster super computers, virtual reality, brain–computer interfaces, connectomics and information extraction from dynamically functioning brains. According to supporters, many of the tools and ideas needed to achieve mind uploading already exist or are currently under active development; however, they will admit that others are, as yet, very speculative, but still in the realm of engineering possibility. Neuroscientist Randal Koene has formed a nonprofit organization called Carbon Copies to promote mind uploading research.

Overview

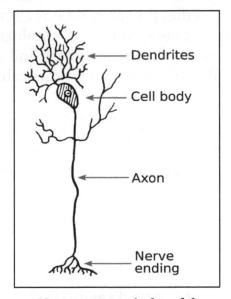

Neuron anatomical model.

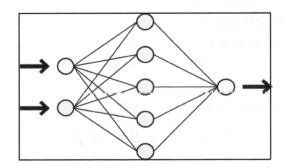

Simple artificial neural network.

The human brain contains about 86 billion nerve cells called neurons, each individually linked to other neurons by way of connectors called axons and dendrites. Signals at the junctures (synapses) of these connections are transmitted by the release and detection of chemicals known as neurotransmitters. The established neuroscientific consensus is that the human mind is largely an emergent property of the information processing of this neural network.

Importantly, neuroscientists have stated that important functions performed by the mind, such as learning, memory, and consciousness, are due to purely physical and electrochemical processes in the brain and are governed by applicable laws. For example, Christof Koch and Giulio Tononi wrote in IEEE Spectrum:

"Consciousness is part of the natural world. It depends, we believe, only on mathematics and logic and on the imperfectly known laws of physics, chemistry, and biology; it does not arise from some magical or otherworldly quality."

The concept of mind uploading is based on this mechanistic view of the mind, and denies the vitalist view of human life and consciousness.

Eminent computer scientists and neuroscientists have predicted that specially programmed computers will be capable of thought and even attain consciousness, including Koch and Tononi, Douglas Hofstadter, Jeff Hawkins, Marvin Minsky, Randal A. Koene, and Rodolfo Llinas.

Such an artificial intelligence capability might provide a computational substrate necessary for uploading.

However, even though uploading is dependent upon such a general capability, it is conceptually distinct from general forms of AI in that it results from dynamic reanimation of information derived from a specific human mind so that the mind retains a sense of historical identity (other forms are possible but would compromise or eliminate the life-extension feature generally associated with uploading). The transferred and reanimated information would become a form of artificial intelligence, sometimes called an infomorph or *"noömorph."*

Many theorists have presented models of the brain and have established a range of estimates of the amount of computing power needed for partial and complete simulations. Using these models, some have estimated that uploading may become possible within decades if trends such as Moore's Law continue.

Theoretical Benefits and Applications

"Immortality" or Backup

In theory, if the information and processes of the mind can be disassociated from the biological body, they are no longer tied to the individual limits and lifespan of that body. Furthermore, information within a brain could be partly or wholly copied or transferred to one or more other substrates (including digital storage or another brain), thereby - from a purely mechanistic perspective - reducing or eliminating "mortality risk" of such information. This general proposal appears to have been first made in the biomedical literature in 1971 by biogerontologist George M. Martin of the University of Washington.

Speedup

If Moore's law holds for several more decades, a supercomputer might be able to simulate a human brain at the neural level at a faster perceived speed than a biological brain. By that time, transistors will have reached sub-atomic size, as current experimental transistors are 10 nm across. However, even if simulation at such speeds should be possible, the exact date this would be achieved is difficult to estimate due to limited understanding of the required accuracy, and computational speed is not the only requirement for making full human brain simulation possible. Several contradictory predictions have been made about when a whole human brain can be emulated, for example 2029 has been suggested by Ray Kurzweil; some of the predicted dates have already passed.

Given that the electrochemical signals that brains use to achieve thought travel at about 150 meters per second, while the electronic signals in computers are sent at 2/3 the speed of light (three hundred million meters per second), this means that a massively parallel electronic counterpart of a human biological brain in theory might be able to think thousands to millions of times faster than our naturally evolved systems. Also, neurons can generate a maximum of about 200 to 1000 action potentials or "spikes" per second, whereas the clock speed of microprocessors has reached 5.5 GHz in 2013, which is about five million times faster.

However, the human brain contains roughly eighty-six billion neurons with eighty-six trillion synapses connecting them. Replicating each of these as separate electronic components using microchip-based semiconductor technology would require a computer enormously large in comparison with today's super-computers. In a less futuristic implementation, time-sharing would allow several neurons to be emulated sequentially by the same computational unit. Thus the size of the computer would be restricted, but the speedup would be lower. Assuming that cortical minicolumns organized into hypercolumns are the computational units, mammal brains can be emulated by today's supercomputers, but with slower speed than in a biological brain.

One obvious use of this technology is the possibility to speed up the development of even faster brains.

Uploaded Astronaut

An "uploaded astronaut" is the application of mind uploading to human spaceflight. An uploaded astronaut would consist of a human mental content transferred or copied to a space humanoid robot or a spacecraft's data storage device. This would eliminate the harms caused by a zero gravity environment, the vacuum of space and cosmic radiation to the human body since both a humanoid robot and a spacecraft can be more resistant than a biological entity in such conditions, permitting longer and farther voyages through outer space than manned spaceflight. Furthermore, an uploaded astronaut may not require a large spacecraft so spacecrafts at the scale of the StarChip might suffice. Alien uploaded astronauts are conceivable as well. In science fiction, Charlie Stross' *Accelerando* features a can-sized starship that visits a nearby star system with an "e-crew" of 63 uploaded astronauts.

Relevant Technologies and Techniques

The focus of mind uploading, in the case of copy-and-transfer, is on data acquisition, rather than data maintenance of the brain. A set of approaches known as loosely coupled off-loading (LCOL) may be used in the attempt to characterize and copy the mental contents of a brain. The LCOL approach may take advantage of self-reports, lifelogs and video recordings that can be analyzed by artificial intelligence. A bottom-up approach may focus on the specific resolution and morphology of neurons, the spike times of neurons, the times at which neurons produce action potential responses.

Computational Complexity

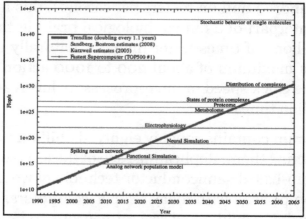

Estimates of how much processing power is needed to emulate a human brain at various levels (from Ray Kurzweil and the chart to the left), along with the fastest supercomputer from TOP500 mapped by year. Note the logarithmic scale and exponential trendline, which assumes the computational capacity doubles every 1.1 years. Kurzweil believes that mind uploading will be possible at neural simulation, while the Sandberg, Bostrom report is less certain about where consciousness arises.

Advocates of mind uploading point to Moore's law to support the notion that the necessary computing power is expected to become available within a few decades. However, the actual computational requirements for running an uploaded human mind are very difficult to quantify, potentially rendering such an argument specious.

Regardless of the techniques used to capture or recreate the function of a human mind, the processing demands are likely to be immense, due to the large number of neurons in the human brain along with the considerable complexity of each neuron.

In 2004, Henry Markram, lead researcher of the "Blue Brain Project", stated that "it is not [their] goal to build an intelligent neural network", based solely on the computational demands such a project would have.

It will be very difficult because, in the brain, every molecule is a powerful computer and we would need to simulate the structure and function of trillions upon trillions of molecules as well as all the rules that govern how they interact. You would literally need computers that are trillions of times bigger and faster than anything existing today.

Five years later, after successful simulation of part of a rat brain, the same scientist was much more bold and optimistic. In 2009, when he was director of the Blue Brain Project, he claimed that

A detailed, functional artificial human brain can be built within the next 10 years

Required computational capacity strongly depend on the chosen level of simulation model scale:

Level	CPU demand (FLOPS)	Memory demand (Tb)	$1 million super-computer (Earliest year of making)
Analog network population model	10^{15}	10^2	2008
Spiking neural network	10^{18}	10^4	2019
Electrophysiology	10^{22}	10^4	2033
Metabolome	10^{25}	10^6	2044
Proteome	10^{26}	10^7	2048
States of protein complexes	10^{27}	10^8	2052
Distribution of complexes	10^{30}	10^9	2063
Stochastic behavior of single molecules	10^{43}	10^{14}	2111
Estimates from *Sandberg, Bostrom, 2008*			

Simulation Model Scale

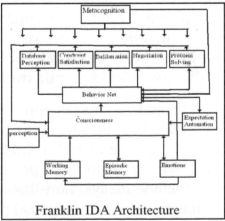

Franklin IDA Architecture

A high-level cognitive AI model of the brain architecture is not required for brain emulation.

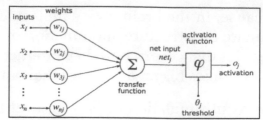

Simple neuron model: Black-box dynamic non-linear signal processing system.

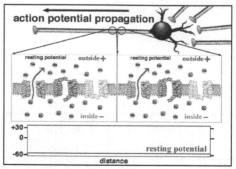

Metabolism model: The movement of positively charged ions through the ion channels controls the membrane electrical action potential in an axon.

Since the function of the human mind, and how it might arise from the working of the brain's neural network, are poorly understood issues, mind uploading relies on the idea of neural network emulation. Rather than having to understand the high-level psychological processes and large-scale structures of the brain, and model them using classical artificial intelligence methods and cognitive psychology models, the low-level structure of the underlying neural network is captured, mapped and emulated with a computer system. In computer science terminology, rather than analyzing and reverse engineering the behavior of the algorithms and data structures that resides in the brain, a blueprint of its source code is translated to another programming language. The human mind and the personal identity then, theoretically, is generated by the emulated neural network in an identical fashion to it being generated by the biological neural network.

On the other hand, a molecule-scale simulation of the brain is not expected to be required, provided that the functioning of the neurons is not affected by quantum mechanical processes. The neural network emulation approach only requires that the functioning and interaction of neurons and synapses are understood. It is expected that it is sufficient with a black-box signal processing model of how the neurons respond to nerve impulses (electrical as well as chemical synaptic transmission).

A sufficiently complex and accurate model of the neurons is required. A traditional artificial neural network model, for example multi-layer perceptron network model, is not considered as sufficient. A dynamic spiking neural network model is required, which reflects that the neuron fires only when a membrane potential reaches a certain level. It is likely that the model must include delays, non-linear functions and differential equations describing the relation between electrophysical parameters such as electrical currents, voltages, membrane states (ion channel states) and neuromodulators.

Since learning and long-term memory are believed to result from strengthening or weakening the synapses via a mechanism known as synaptic plasticity or synaptic adaptation, the model should include this mechanism. The response of sensory receptors to various stimuli must also be modelled.

Furthermore, the model may have to include metabolism, i.e. how the neurons are affected by hormones and other chemical substances that may cross the blood–brain barrier. It is considered likely that the model must include currently unknown neuromodulators, neurotransmitters and ion channels. It is considered unlikely that the simulation model has to include protein interaction, which would make it computationally complex.

A digital computer simulation model of an analog system such as the brain is an approximation that introduces random quantization errors and distortion. However, the biological neurons also suffer from randomness and limited precision, for example due to background noise. The errors of the discrete model can be made smaller than the randomness of the biological brain by choosing a sufficiently high variable resolution and sample rate, and sufficiently accurate models of non-linearities. The computational power and computer memory must however be sufficient to run such large simulations, preferably in real time.

Scanning and Mapping Scale of an Individual

When modelling and simulating the brain of a specific individual, a brain map or connectivity database showing the connections between the neurons must be extracted from an anatomic model of the brain. For whole brain simulation, this network map should show the connectivity of the whole nervous system, including the spinal cord, sensory receptors, and muscle cells. Destructive scanning of a small sample of tissue from a mouse brain including synaptic details is possible as of 2010.

However, if short-term memory and working memory include prolonged or repeated firing of neurons, as well as intra-neural dynamic processes, the electrical and chemical signal state of the synapses and neurons may be hard to extract. The uploaded mind may then perceive a memory loss of the events and mental processes immediately before the time of brain scanning.

A full brain map has been estimated to occupy less than 2×10^{16} bytes (20,000 TB) and would store the addresses of the connected neurons, the synapse type and the synapse "weight" for each of the brains' 10^{15} synapses. However, the biological complexities of true brain function (e.g. the epigenetic states of neurons, protein components with multiple functional states, etc.) may preclude an accurate prediction of the volume of binary data required to faithfully represent a functioning human mind.

Serial Sectioning

A possible method for mind uploading is serial sectioning, in which the brain tissue and perhaps other parts of the nervous system are frozen and then scanned and analyzed layer by layer, which for frozen samples at nano-scale requires a cryo-ultramicrotome, thus capturing the structure of the neurons and their interconnections. The exposed surface of frozen nerve tissue would be scanned and recorded, and then the surface layer of tissue removed. While this would be a very slow and labor-intensive process, research is currently underway to automate the collection and microscopy of serial sections. The scans would then be analyzed, and a model of the neural net recreated in the system that the mind was being uploaded into.

There are uncertainties with this approach using current microscopy techniques. If it is possible to replicate neuron function from its visible structure alone, then the resolution afforded by a scanning electron microscope would suffice for such a technique. However, as the function of brain tissue is partially determined by molecular events (particularly at synapses, but also at other places on the neuron's cell membrane), this may not suffice for capturing and simulating neuron functions. It may be possible to extend the techniques of serial sectioning and to capture the internal molecular makeup of neurons, through the use of sophisticated immunohistochemistry staining methods that could then be read via confocal laser scanning microscopy. However, as the physiological genesis of 'mind' is not currently known, this method may not be able to access all of the necessary biochemical information to recreate a human brain with sufficient fidelity.

Brain Imaging

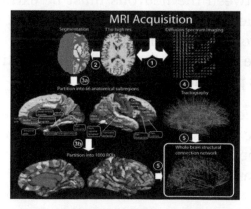

Process from MRI acquisition to whole brain structural network.

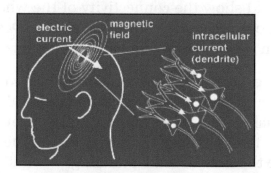

Magnetoencephalography.

It may also be possible to create functional 3D maps of the brain activity, using advanced neuroimaging technology, such as functional MRI (fMRI, for mapping change in blood flow), Magnetoencephalography (MEG, for mapping of electrical currents), or combinations of multiple methods, to build a detailed three-dimensional model of the brain using non-invasive and non-destructive methods. Today, fMRI is often combined with MEG for creating functional maps of human cortex during more complex cognitive tasks, as the methods complement each other. Even though current imaging technology lacks the spatial resolution needed to gather the information needed for such a scan, important recent and future developments are predicted to substantially improve both spatial and temporal resolutions of existing technologies.

Brain Simulation

There is ongoing work in the field of brain simulation, including partial and whole simulations of some animals. For example, the *C. elegans* roundworm, Drosophila fruit fly, mouse have all been simulated to various degrees.

The Blue Brain Project by the Brain and Mind Institute of the *École Polytechnique Fédérale de Lausanne,* Switzerland is an attempt to create a synthetic brain by reverse-engineering mammalian brain circuitry.

Issues

Philosophical Issues

Underlying the concept of "mind uploading" (more accurately "mind transferring") is the broad philosophy that consciousness lies within the brain's information processing and is in essence an emergent feature that arises from large neural network high-level patterns of organization, and that the same patterns of organization can be realized in other processing devices. Mind uploading also relies on the idea that the human mind (the "self" and the long-term memory), just like non-human minds, is represented by the current neural network paths and the weights of the brain synapses rather than by a dualistic and mystic soul and spirit. The mind or "soul" can be defined as the information state of the brain, and is immaterial only in the same sense as the information content of a data file or the state of a computer software currently residing in the work-space memory of the computer. Data specifying the information state of the neural network can be captured and copied as a "computer file" from the brain and re-implemented into a different physical form. This is not to deny that minds are richly adapted to their substrates. An analogy to the idea of mind uploading is to copy the temporary information state (the variable values) of a computer program from the computer memory to another computer and continue its execution. The other computer may perhaps have different hardware architecture but emulates the hardware of the first computer.

These issues have a long history. In 1775 Thomas Reid wrote:

I would be glad to know... whether when my brain has lost its original structure, and when some hundred years after the same materials are fabricated so curiously as to become an intelligent being, whether, I say that being will be me; or, if, two or three such beings should be formed out of my brain; whether they will all be me, and consequently one and the same intelligent being.

A considerable portion of transhumanists and singularitarians place great hope into the belief that they may become immortal, by creating one or many non-biological functional copies of their brains, thereby leaving their "biological shell". However, the philosopher and transhumanist Susan Schneider claims that at best, uploading would create a copy of the original persons mind. Susan Schneider agrees that consciousness has a computational basis, but this doesn't mean we can upload and survive. According to her views, "uploading" would probably result in the death of the original person's brain, while only outside observers can maintain the illusion of the original person still being alive. For it is implausible to think that one's consciousness would leave one's brain and travel to a remote location; ordinary physical objects do not behave this way. Ordinary objects (rocks, tables, etc.) are not simultaneously here, and somewhere else. At best, a copy of the original mind is created. Others have argued against such conclusions. For example, buddhist transhumanist James Hughes has pointed out that this consideration only goes so far: if one believes the self is an illusion, worries about survival are not reasons to avoid uploading, and Keith Wiley has presented an argument wherein all resulting minds of an uploading procedure are granted equal primacy in their claim to the original identity, such that survival of the self is determined retroactively from a strictly subjective position.

Another potential consequence of mind uploading is that the decision to "upload" may then create a mindless symbol manipulator instead of a conscious mind. Are we to assume that an Upload is conscious if it displays behaviors that are highly indicative of consciousness? Are we to assume that an Upload is conscious if it verbally insists that it is conscious? Could there be an absolute upper limit in processing speed above which consciousness cannot be sustained? The mystery of consciousness precludes a definitive answer to this question. Numerous scientists, including Kurzweil, strongly believe that determining whether a separate entity is conscious (with 100% confidence) is fundamentally unknowable, since consciousness is inherently subjective. Regardless, some scientists strongly believe consciousness is the consequence of computational processes which are substrateneutral. On the contrary, numerous scientists believe consciousness may be the result of some form of quantum computation dependent on substrate.

In light of uncertainty on whether to regard uploads as conscious, Sandberg proposes a cautious approach:

Principle of assuming the most (PAM): Assume that any emulated system could have the same mental properties as the original system and treat it correspondingly.

It is argued that if a computational copy of one's mind did exist, it would be impossible for one to recognize it as their own mind. The argument for this stance is the following: for a computational mind to recognize an emulation of itself, it must be capable of deciding whether two Turing Machines (namely, itself and the proposed emulation) are functionally equivalent. This task is uncomputable, and thus there cannot exist a computational procedure in the mind that is capable of recognizing an emulation of itself.

Copying vs. Moving

A philosophical issue with mind uploading is whether the newly generated digital mind is really the "same" sentience, or simply an exact copy with the same memories and personality. This issue is especially obvious when the original remains essentially unchanged by the procedure, thereby resulting in a copy which could potentially have rights separate from the unaltered, obvious original.

Most projected brain scanning technologies, such as serial sectioning of the brain, would necessarily be destructive, and the original brain would not survive the brain scanning procedure. But if it can be kept intact, the computer-based consciousness could be a copy of the still-living biological person. It is in that case implicit that copying a consciousness could be as feasible as literally moving it into one or several copies, since these technologies generally involve simulation of a human brain in a computer of some sort, and digital files such as computer programs can be copied precisely. It is assumed that once the versions are exposed to different sensory inputs, their experiences would begin to diverge, but all their memories up until the moment of the copying would remain the same.

The problem is made even more apparent through the possibility of creating a potentially infinite number of initially identical copies of the original person, which would of course all exist simultaneously as distinct beings with their own emotions and thoughts. The most parsimonious view of this phenomenon is that the two (or more) minds would share memories of their past but from the point of duplication would simply be distinct minds.

Toward the goal of resolving the copy-vs-move debate, some have argued for a third way of conceptualizing the process, which is described by such terms as *split* and *divergence*. The distinguishing feature of this third terminological option is that while *moving* implies that a single instance relocates in space and while *copying* invokes problematic connotations (a *copy* is often denigrated in status relative to its *original*), the notion of a *split* better illustrates that some kinds of entities might become two separate instances, but without the imbalanced associations assigned to originals and copies, and that such equality may apply to minds.

Depending on computational capacity, the simulation's subjective time may be faster or slower than elapsed physical time, resulting in that the simulated mind would perceive that the physical world is running in slow motion or fast motion respectively, while biological persons will see the simulated mind in fast or slow motion respectively.

A brain simulation can be started, paused, backed-up and rerun from a saved backup state at any time. The simulated mind would in the latter case forget everything that has happened after the instant of backup, and perhaps not even be aware that it is repeating itself. An older version of a simulated mind may meet a younger version and share experiences with it.

One proposed route for mind uploading is gradual transfer of functions from an "aging biological brain" into an exocortex.

Ethical and Legal Implications

The process of developing emulation technology raises ethical issues related to animal welfare and artificial consciousness. The neuroscience required to develop brain emulation would require animal experimentation, first on invertebrates and then on small mammals before moving on to humans. Sometimes the animals would just need to be euthanized in order to extract, slice, and scan their brains, but sometimes behavioral and *in vivo* measures would be required, which might cause pain to living animals.

In addition, the resulting animal emulations themselves might suffer, depending on one's views about consciousness. Bancroft argues for the plausibility of consciousness in brain simulations on the basis of the "fading qualia" thought experiment of David Chalmers. He then concludes:

If, as I argue above, a sufficiently detailed computational simulation of the brain is potentially operationally equivalent to an organic brain, it follows that we must consider extending protections against suffering to simulations.

It might help reduce emulation suffering to develop virtual equivalents of anaesthesia, as well as to omit processing related to pain and/or consciousness. However, some experiments might require a fully functioning and suffering animal emulation. Animals might also suffer by accident due to flaws and lack of insight into what parts of their brains are suffering. Questions also arise regarding the moral status of *partial* brain emulations, as well as creating neuromorphic emulations that draw inspiration from biological brains but are built somewhat differently.

Brain emulations could be erased by computer viruses or malware, without need to destroy the underlying hardware. This may make assassination easier than for physical humans. The attacker might take the computing power for its own use.

Many questions arise regarding the legal personhood of emulations. Would they be given the rights of biological humans? If a person makes an emulated copy of himself and then dies, does the emulation inherit his property and official positions? Could the emulation ask to "pull the plug" when its biological version was terminally ill or in a coma? Would it help to treat emulations as adolescents for a few years so that the biological creator would maintain temporary control? Would criminal emulations receive the death penalty, or would they be given forced data modification as a form of "rehabilitation"? Could an upload have marriage and child-care rights?

If simulated minds would come true and if they were assigned rights of their own, it may be difficult to ensure the protection of "digital human rights". For example, social science researchers might be tempted to secretly expose simulated minds, or whole isolated societies of simulated minds, to controlled experiments in which many copies of the same minds are exposed (serially or simultaneously) to different test conditions.

Political and Economic Implications

Emulations could create a number of conditions that might increase risk of war, including inequality, changes of power dynamics, a possible technological arms race to build emulations first, first-strike advantages, strong loyalty and willingness to "die" among emulations, and triggers for racist, xenophobic, and religious prejudice. If emulations run much faster than humans, there might not be enough time for human leaders to make wise decisions or negotiate. It's possible that humans would react violently against growing power of emulations, especially if they depress human wages. Or maybe emulations wouldn't trust each other, and even well intentioned defensive measures might be interpreted as offense.

Emulation Timelines and AI risk

There are very few feasible technologies that humans have refrained from developing. The neuroscience and computer-hardware technologies that may make brain emulation possible are widely desired for other reasons, so cutting off funding doesn't seem to be an option. If we assume that emulation technology will arrive, a question becomes whether we should accelerate or slow its advance.

Arguments for speeding up brain-emulation research:

- If neuroscience is the bottleneck on brain emulation rather than computing power, emulation advances may be more erratic and unpredictable based on when new scientific discoveries happen. Limited computing power would mean the first emulations would run slower and so would be easier to adapt to, and there would be more time for the technology to transition through society.

- Improvements in manufacturing, 3D printing, and nanotechnology may accelerate hardware production, which could increase the "computing overhang" from excess hardware relative to neuroscience.

- If one AI-development group had a lead in emulation technology, it would have more subjective time to win an arms race to build the first superhuman AI. Because it would be less rushed, it would have more freedom to consider AI risks.

Arguments for slowing down brain-emulation research:

- Greater investment in brain emulation and associated cognitive science might enhance the ability of artificial intelligence (AI) researchers to create "neuromorphic" (brain-inspired) algorithms, such as neural networks, reinforcement learning, and hierarchical perception. This could accelerate risks from uncontrolled AI. Participants at a 2011 AI workshop estimated an 85% probability that neuromorphic AI would arrive before brain emulation. This was based on the idea that brain emulation would require understanding some brain components, and it would be easier to tinker with these than to reconstruct the entire brain in its original form. By a very narrow margin, the participants on balance leaned toward the view that accelerating brain emulation would increase expected AI risk.

- Waiting might give society more time to think about the consequences of brain emulation and develop institutions to improve cooperation.

Emulation research would also speed up neuroscience as a whole, which might accelerate medical advances, cognitive enhancement, lie detectors, and capability for psychological manipulation.

Emulations might be easier to control than *de novo* AI because

- We understand better human abilities, behavioral tendencies, and vulnerabilities, so control measures might be more intuitive and easier to plan for.

- Emulations could more easily inherit human motivations.

- Emulations are harder to manipulate than *de novo* AI, because brains are messy and complicated; this could reduce risks of their rapid takeoff. Also, emulations may be bulkier and require more hardware than AI, which would also slow the speed of a transition. Unlike AI, an emulation wouldn't be able to rapidly expand beyond the size of a human brain. Emulations running at digital speeds would have less intelligence differential vis-à-vis AI and so might more easily control AI.

As counterpoint to these considerations, Bostrom notes some downsides:

- Even if we better understand human behavior, the *evolution* of emulation behavior under self-improvement might be much less predictable than the evolution of safe *de novo* AI under self-improvement.

- Emulations may not inherit all human motivations. Perhaps they would inherit our darker motivations or would behave abnormally in the unfamiliar environment of cyberspace.

- Even if there's a slow takeoff toward emulations, there would still be a second transition to *de novo* AI later on. Two intelligence explosions may mean more total risk.

Mind Uploading Advocates

Ray Kurzweil, director of engineering at Google, claims to know and foresee that people will be able to "upload" their entire brains to computers and become "digitally immortal" by 2045. Kurzweil made this claim for many years, e.g. during his speech in

2013 at the Global Futures 2045 International Congress in New York, which claims to subscribe to a similar set of beliefs. Mind uploading is also advocated by a number of researchers in neuroscience and artificial intelligence, such as Marvin Minsky while he was still alive. In 1993, Joe Strout created a small web site called the Mind Uploading Home Page, and began advocating the idea in cryonics circles and elsewhere on the net. That site has not been actively updated in recent years, but it has spawned other sites including MindUploading.org, run by Randal A. Koene, Ph.D., who also moderates a mailing list on the topic. These advocates see mind uploading as a medical procedure which could eventually save countless lives.

Many transhumanists look forward to the development and deployment of mind uploading technology, with transhumanists such as Nick Bostrom predicting that it will become possible within the 21st century due to technological trends such as Moore's Law.

Michio Kaku, in collaboration with Science hosted a documentary, Sci Fi Science: Physics of the Impossible based on his book Physics of the Impossible and in episode 4 on "How to teleport" mentions that mind uploading via techniques such as quantum entanglement and whole brain emulation using an advanced MRI machine may enable people to be transported to vast distances at near light-speed.

The book *Beyond Humanity: CyberEvolution and Future Minds* by Gregory S. Paul & Earl D. Cox, is about the eventual (and, to the authors, almost inevitable) evolution of computers into sentient beings, but also deals with human mind transfer. Richard Doyle's *Wetwares: Experiments in PostVital Living* deals extensively with uploading from the perspective of distributed embodiment, arguing for example that humans are currently part of the "artificial life phenotype." Doyle's vision reverses the polarity on uploading, with artificial life forms such as uploads actively seeking out biological embodiment as part of their reproductive strategy.

Mind Uploading Skeptics

Kenneth D. Miller, a professor of neuroscience at Columbia and a co-director of the Center for Theoretical Neuroscience, raised doubts about the practicality of mind uploading.

Neurocomputational Speech Processing

Neurocomputational speech processing is computer-simulation of speech production and speech perception by referring to the natural neuronal processes of speech production and speech perception, as they occur in the human nervous system (central nervous system and peripheral nervous system). This topic is based on neuroscience and computational neuroscience.

Overview

Neurocomputational models of speech processing are complex. They comprise at least a cognitive part, a motor part and a sensory part.

The cognitive or linguistic part of a neurocomputational model of speech processing comprises the neural activation or generation of a phonemic representation on the side of speech production (e.g. neurocomputational and extended version of the Levelt model developed by Ardi Roelofs: WEAVER++ as well as the neural activation or generation of an intention or meaning on the side of speech perception or speech comprehension.

The motor part of a neurocomputational model of speech processing starts with a phonemic representation of a speech item, activates a motor plan and ends with the articulation of that particular speech item.

The sensory part of a neurocomputational model of speech processing starts with an acoustic signal of a speech item (acoustic speech signal), generates an auditory representation for that signal and activates a phonemic representations for that speech item.

Neurocomputational Speech Processing Topics

Neurocomputational speech processing is speech processing by artificial neural networks. Neural maps, mappings and pathways as described below, are model structures, i.e. important structures within artificial neural networks.

Neural Maps

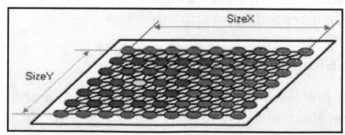

2D neuronal map with a local activation pattern. magenta: neuron with highest degree of activation; blue: neurons with no activation.

A neural network can be separated in three types of neural maps, also called "layers":

1. Input maps (in the case of speech processing: primary auditory map within the auditory cortex, primary somatosensory map within the somatosensory cortex).

2. Output maps (primary motor map within the primary motor cortex).

3. Higher level cortical maps (also called "hidden layers", see neural networks).

The term "neural map" is favoured here over the term "neural layer", because a cortial neural map should be modeled as a 2D-map of interconnected neurons (e.g. like a self-organizing map; see also Fig.). Thus, each "model neuron" or "artificial neuron" within this 2D-map is physiologically represented by a cortical column since the cerebral cortex anatomically exhibits a layered structure.

Neural Representations (Neural States)

A neural representation within an artificial neural network is a temporarily activated (neural) state within a specific neural map. Each neural state is represented by a specific neural activation pattern. This activation pattern changes during speech processing (e.g. from syllable to syllable).

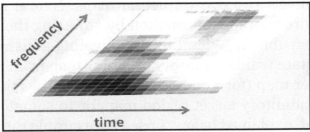

2D neuronal map with a distributed activation pattern. Example: "neural spectrogram" (This auditory neural representation is speculative; ACT model, below).

In the ACT model, it is assumed that an auditory state can be represented by a "neural spectrogram" within an auditory state map. This auditory state map is assumed to be located in the auditory association cortex.

A somatosensory state can be divided in a tactile and proprioceptive state and can be represented by a specific neural activation pattern within the somatosensory state map. This state map is assumed to be located in the somatosensory association cortex (see cerebral cortex, somatosensory system, somatosensory cortex).

A motor plan state can be assumed for representing a motor plan, i.e. the planning of speech articulation for a specific syllable or for a longer speech item (e.g. word, short phrase). This state map is assumed to be located in the premotor cortex, while the instantaneous (or lower level) activation of each speech articulator occurs within the primary motor cortex.

The neural representations occurring in the sensory and motor maps (as introduced above) are distributed representations (Hinton et al. 1968): Each neuron within the sensory or motor map is more or less activated, leading to a specific activation pattern.

The neural representation for speech units occurring in the speech sound map is a punctual or local representation. Each speech item or speech unit is represented here by a specific neuron.

Neural Mappings (Synaptic Projections)

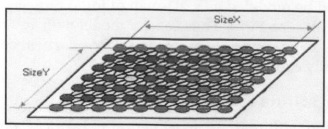

Fig. Neural mapping between phonetic map (local activation pattern for a specific phonetic state), motor plan state map (distributed activation pattern) and auditory state map (distributed activation pattern) as part of the ACT model. Only neural connections with the winner neuron within the phonetic map are shown.

A neural mapping connects two cortical neural maps. Neural mappings (in contrast to neural pathways) store training information by adjusting their neural link weights. Neural mappings are capable of generating or activating a distributed representation of a sensory or motor state within a sensory or motor map from a punctual or local activation within the other map (for example the synaptic projection from speech sound map to motor map, to auditory target region map, or to somatosensory target region map in the DIVA model, explained below; or see for example the neural mapping from phonetic map to auditory state map and motor plan state map in the ACT model, explained below and Fig.).

Neural mapping between two neural maps are compact or dense: Each neuron of one neural map is interconnected with (nearly) each neuron of the other neural map (many-to-many-connection). Because of this density criterion for neural mappings, neural maps which are interconnected by a neural mapping are not far apart from each other.

Neural Pathways

In contrast to neural mappings neural pathways can connect neural maps which are far apart (e.g. in different cortical lobes). From the functional or modeling viewpoint, neural pathways mainly forward information without processing this information. A neural pathway in comparison to a neural mapping need much less neural connections. A neural pathway can be modelled by using a one-to-one connection of the neurons of both neural maps.

Example: In the case of two neural maps, each comprising 1,000 model neurons, a neural mapping needs up to 1,000,000 neural connections (many-to-many-connection), while only 1,000 connections are needed in the case of a neural pathway connection.

Furthermore the link weights of the connections within a neural mapping are adjusted during training, while the neural connections in the case of a neural pathway need not to be trained (each connection is maximal exhibitory).

DIVA Model

The leading approach in neurocomputational modeling of speech production is the DIVA model developed by Frank H. Guenther and his group at Boston University. The model accounts for a wide range of phonetic and neuroimaging data but - like each neurocomputational model - remains speculative to some extent.

Structure of the Model

The organization or structure of the DIVA model is shown in Fig.

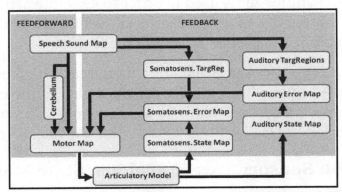

Fig. Organization of the DIVA model; This figure is an adaptation following Guenther et al. 2006.

Speech Sound Map: The Phonemic Representation as a Starting Point

The speech sound map - assumed to be located in the inferior and posterior portion of Broca's area (left frontal operculum) - represents (phonologically specified) language-specific speech units (sounds, syllables, words, short phrases). Each speech unit (mainly syllables; e.g. the syllable and word "palm" /pam/, the syllables /pa/, /ta/, /ka/, ...) is represented by a specific model cell within the speech sound map (i.e. punctual neural representations). Each model cell corresponds to a small population of neurons which are located at close range and which fire together.

Feedforward Control: Activating Motor Representations

Each neuron (model cell, artificial neuron) within the speech sound map can be activated and subsequently activates a forward motor command towards the motor map, called articulatory velocity and position map. The activated neural representation on the level of that motor map determines the articulation of a speech unit, i.e. controls all articulators (lips, tongue, velum, glottis) during the time interval for producing that speech unit. Forward control also involves subcortical structures like the cerebellum, not modelled in detail here.

A speech *unit* represents an amount of speech *items* which can be assigned to the same phonemic category. Thus, each speech unit is represented by one specific neuron with in the speech sound map, while the realization of a speech unit may exhibit some articulatory and acoustic variability. This phonetic variability is the motivation to define sensory target *regions* in the DIVA model.

Articulatory Model: Generating Somatosensory and Auditory Feedback Information

The activation pattern within the motor map determines the movement pattern of all model articulators (lips, tongue, velum, glottis) for a speech item. In order not to overload the model, no detailed modeling of the neuromuscular system is done. The Maeda articulatory speech synthesizer is used in order to generate articulator movements, which allows the generation of a time-varying vocal tract form and the generation of the acoustic speech signal for each particular speech item.

In terms of artificial intelligence the articulatory model can be called plant (i.e. the system, which is controlled by the brain); it represents a part of the embodiement of the neuronal speech processing system. The articulatory model generates sensory output which is the basis for generating feedback information for the DIVA model.

Feedback Control: Sensory Target Regions, State Maps, and Error Maps

On the one hand the articulatory model generates sensory information, i.e. an auditory state for each speech unit which is neurally represented within the auditory state map (distributed representation), and a somatosensory state for each speech unit which is neurally represented within the somatosensory state map (distributed representation as well). The auditory state map is assumed to be located in the superior temporal cortex while the somatosensory state map is assumed to be located in the inferior parietal cortex.

On the other hand the speech sound map, if activated for a specific speech unit (single neuron activation; punctual activation), activates sensory information by synaptic projections between speech sound map and auditory target region map and between speech sound map and somatosensory target region map. Auditory and somatosensory target regions are assumed to be located in higher-order auditory cortical regions and in higher-order somatosensory cortical regions respectively. These target region sensory activation patterns - which exist for each speech unit - are learned during speech acquisition.

Consequently two types of sensory information are available if a speech unit is activated at the level of the speech sound map: (i) learned sensory target regions (i.e. *intended* sensory state for a speech unit) and (ii) sensory state activation patterns resulting from a possibly imperfect execution (articulation) of a specific speech unit (i.e. *current* sensory state, reflecting the current production and articulation of that particular speech unit). Both types of sensory information is projected to sensory error maps, i.e. to an auditory error map which is assumed to be located in the superior temporal cortex (like the auditory state map) and to a somatosensosry error map which is assumed to be located in the inferior parietal cortex (like the somatosensory state map).

If the current sensory state deviates from the intended sensory state, both error maps are generating feedback commands which are projected towards the motor map and which are capable to correct the motor activation pattern and subsequently the articulation of a speech unit under production. Thus, in total, the activation pattern of the motor map is not only influenced by a specific feedforward command learned for a speech unit (and generated by the synaptic projection from the speech sound map) but also by a feedback command generated at the level of the sensory error maps.

Learning (Modeling Speech Acquisition)

While the *structure* of a neuroscientific model of speech processing (given in Fig. for the DIVA model) is mainly determined by evolutionary processes, the (language-specific) *knowledge* as well as the (language-specific) *speaking skills* are learned and trained during speech acquisition. In the case of the DIVA model it is assumed that the newborn has not available an already structured (language-specific) speech sound map; i.e. no neuron within the speech sound map is related to any speech unit. Rather the organization of the speech sound map as well as the tuning of the projections to the motor map and to the sensory target region maps is learned or trained during speech acquisition. Two important phases of early speech acquisition are modeled in the DIVA approach: Learning by babbling and by imitation.

Babbling

During babbling the synaptic projections between sensory error maps and motor map are tuned. This training is done by generating an amount of semi-random feedforward commands, i.e. the DIVA model "babbles". Each of these babbling commands leads to the production of an "articulatory item", also labeled as "pre-linguistic (i.e. non language-specific) speech item" (i.e. the articulatory model generates an articulatory movement pattern on the basis of the babbling motor command). Subsequently an acoustic signal is generated.

On the basis of the articulatory and acoustic signal, a specific auditory and somatosensory state pattern is activated at the level of the sensory state maps for each (pre-linguistic) speech item. At this point the DIVA model has available the sensory and associated motor activation pattern for different speech items, which enables the model to tune the synaptic projections between sensory error maps and motor map. Thus, during babbling the DIVA model learns feedback commands (i.e. how to produce a proper (feedback) motor command for a specific sensory input).

Imitation

During imitation the DIVA model organizes its speech sound map and tunes the synaptic projections between speech sound map and motor map - i.e. tuning of forward motor commands - as well as the synaptic projections between speech sound map and sensory target regions (see Fig.). Imitation training is done by exposing the model to an amount of acoustic speech signals representing realizations of language-specific speech units (e.g. isolated speech sounds, syllables, words, short phrases).

The tuning of the synaptic projections between speech sound map and auditory target region map is accomplished by assigning one neuron of the speech sound map to the phonemic representation of that speech item and by associating it with the auditory representation of that speech item, which is activated at the auditory target region map. Auditory *regions* (i.e. a specification of the auditory vairiability of a speech unit) occur, because one specific speech unit (i.e. one specific phonemic representation) can be realized by several (slightly) different acoustic (auditory) realizations (for the difference between speech *item* and speech *unit* see above: feedforward control) .

The tuning of the synaptic projections between speech sound map and motor map (i.e. tunig of forward motor commands) is accomplished with the aid of feedback commands, since the projections between sensory error maps and motor map were already tuned during babbling training (see above). Thus the DIVA model tries to "imitate" an auditory speech item by attempting to find a proper feedforward motor command. Subsequently the model compares the resulting sensory output (*current* sensory state following the articulation of that attempt) with the already learned auditory target region (*intended* sensory state) for that speech item. Then the model updates the current feedforward motor command by the current feedback motor command generated from the auditory error map of the auditory feedback system. This process may be repeated several times (several attempts). The DIVA model is capable of producing the speech item with a decreasing auditory difference between curren and intended auditory state from attempt to attempt.

During imitation the DIVA model is also capable of tuning the synaptic projections from speech sound map to somatosensory target region map, since each new imitation attempt produces a new articulation of the speech item and thus produces a somatosensory state pattern which is associated with the phonemic representation of that speech item.

Perturbation Experiments

Real-time Perturbation of F1: the Influence of Auditory Feedback

While auditory feedback is most important during speech acquisition, it may be activated less if the model has learned a proper feedforward motor command for each speech unit. But it has been shown that auditory feedback needs to be strongly coactivated in the case of auditory perturbation (e.g. shifting a formant frequency, Tourville et al. 2005). This is comparable to the strong influence of visual feedback on reaching movements during visual perturbation (e.g. shifting the location of objects by viewing through a prism).

Unexpected Blocking of the Jaw: The Influence of Somatosensory Feedback

In a comparable way to auditory feedback, also somatosensory feedback can be strongly coactivated during speech production, e.g. in the case of unexpected blocking of the jaw (Tourville et al. 2005).

ACT Model

A further approach in neurocomputational modeling of speech processing is the ACT model developed by Bernd J. Kröger and his group at RWTH Aachen University, Germany (Kröger et al. 2014, Kröger et al. 2009, Kröger et al. 2011). The ACT model is in accord with the DIVA model in large parts. The ACT model focuses on the "action repository" (i.e. repository for sensorimotor speaking skills, comparable to the mental syllablary, Levelt and Wheeldon 1994), which is not spelled out in detail in the DIVA model. Moreover the ACT model explicitly introduces a level of motor plans, i.e. a high-level motor description for the production of speech items. The ACT model - like any neurocomputational model - remains speculative to some extent.

Structure

The organization or structure of the ACT model is given in Fig.

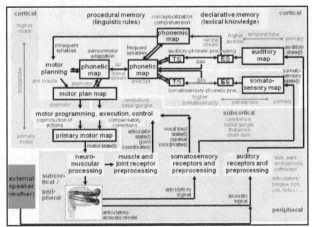

Organization of the ACT model.

For speech production, the ACT model starts with the activation of a phonemic representation of a speech item (phonemic map). In the case of a *frequent syllable*, a co-activation occurs at the level of the phonetic map, leading to a further co-activation of the intended sensory state at the level of the sensory state maps and to a co-activation of a motor plan state at the level of the motor plan map. In the case of an *infrequent syllable*, an attempt for a motor plan is generated by the motor planning module for that speech item by activating motor plans for phonetic similar speech items via the phonetic map. The motor plan or vocal tract action score comprises temporally overlapping vocal tract actions, which are programmed and subsequently executed by the motor programming, execution, and control module. This module gets real-time somatosensory feedback information for controlling the correct execution of the (intended) motor plan. Motor programing leads to activation pattern at the level lof the primary motor map and subsequently activates neuromuscular processing. Motoneuron activation patterns generate muscle forces and subsequently movement patterns of all model articulators (lips, tongue, velum, glottis). The Birkholz 3D articulatory synthesizer is used in order to generate the acoustic speech signal.

Articulatory and acoustic feedback signals are used for generating somatosensory and auditory feedback information via the sensory preprocessing modules, which is forwarded towards the auditory and somatosensory map. At the level of the sensory-phonetic processing modules, auditory and somatosensory information is stored in short-term memory and the external sensory signal (ES, Fig., which are activated via the sensory feedback loop) can be compared with the already trained sensory signals (TS, Fig., which are activated via the phonetic map). Auditory and somatosensory error signals can be generated if external and intended (trained) sensory signals are noticeably different (cf. DIVA model).

The light green area in Fig. indicates those neural maps and processing modules, which process a syllable as a whole unit (specific processing time window around 100 ms and more). This processing comprises the phonetic map and the directly connected sensory state maps within the sensory-phonetic processing modules and the directly connected motor plan state map, while the primary motor map as well as the (primary) auditory and (primary) somatosensory map process smaller time windows (around 10 ms in the ACT model).

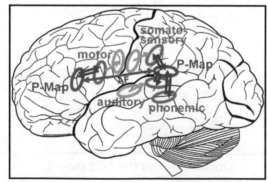

Fig. Hypothetical location of brain regions for neural maps of the ACT model.

The hypothetical cortical location of neural maps within the ACT model is shown in Fig. The hypothetical locations of primary motor and primary sensory maps are given in magenta, the hypothetical locations of motor plan state map and sensory state maps (within sensory-phonetic processing module, comparable to the error maps in DIVA) are given in orange, and the hypothetical locations for the mirrored phonetic map is given in red. Double arrows indicate neuronal mappings. Neural mappings connect neural maps, which are not far apart from each other. The two mirrored locations of the phonetic map are connected via a neural pathway, leading to a (simple) one-to-one mirroring of the current activation pattern for both realizations of the phonetic map. This neural pathway between the two locations of the phonetic map is assumed to be a part of the fasciculus arcuatus.

For speech perception, the model starts with an external acoustic signal (e.g. produced by an external speaker). This signal is preprocessed, passes the auditory map, and leads to an activation pattern for each syllable or word on the level of the auditory-phonetic processing module. The ventral path of speech perception would directly activate a lexical item, but is not implemented in ACT. Rather, in ACT the activation of a phonemic state occurs via the phonemic map and thus may lead to a coactivation of motor representations for that speech item (i.e. dorsal pathway of speech perception; ibid.).

Action Repository

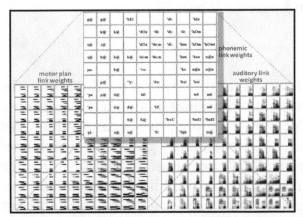

Visualization of synaptic link weights for a section of the phonetic map, trained for the 200 most frequent syllables of Standard German. Each box represents a neuron within the self-organizing phonetic map. Each of the three link weight representations refers to the same section within the phonetic map and thus refers to the same 10×10 neurons.

The phonetic map together with the motor plan state map, sensory state maps (occurring within the sensory-phonetic processing modules), and phonemic (state) map form the action repository. The phonetic map is implemented in ACT as a self-organizing neural map and different speech items are represented by different neurons within this map (punctual or local representation, see above: neural representations). The phonetic map exhibits three major characteristics:

- More than one phonetic realization may occur within the phonetic map for one phonemic state (phonemic link weights in Fig. e.g. the syllable /de:m/ is represented by three neurons within the phonetic map).

- Phonetotopy: The phonetic map exhibits an ordering of speech items with respect to different phonetic features (phonemic link weights in Fig. Three examples: (i) the syllables /p@/, /t@/, and /k@/ occur in an upward ordering at the left side within the phonetic map; (ii) syllable-initial plosives occur in the upper left part of the phonetic map while syllable initial fricatives occur in the lower right half; (iii) CV syllables and CVC syllables as well occur in different areas of the phonetic map.).

- The phonetic map is hypermodal or multimodal: The activation of a phonetic item at the level of the phonetic map coactivates (i) a phonemic state (phonemic link weights in Fig.), (ii) a motor plan state (motor plan link weights in Fig.), (iii) an auditory state (auditory link weights in Fig.), and (iv) a somatosensory state (not shown in Fig. 7). All these states are learned or trained during speech acquisition by tuning the synaptic link weights between each neuron within the phonetic map, representing a particular phonetic state and all neurons within the associated motor plan and sensory state maps.

The phonetic map implements the action-perception-link within the ACT model (The dual neural representation of the phonetic map in the frontal lobe and at the intersection of temporal lobe and parietal lobe).

Motor Plans

A motor plan is a high level motor description for the production and articulation of a speech items. In our neurocomputational model ACT a motor plan is quantified as a vocal tract action score. Vocal tract action scores quantitatively determine the number of vocal tract actions (also called articulatory gestures), which need to be activated in order to produce a speech item, their degree of realization and duration, and the temporal organization of all vocal tract actions building up a speech item. The detailed realization of each vocal tract action (articulatory gesture) depends on the temporal organization of all vocal tract actions building up a speech item and especially on their temporal overlap. Thus the detailed realization of each vocal tract action within an speech item is specified below the motor plan level in our neurocomputational model ACT.

Integrating Sensorimotor and Cognitive Aspects: The Coupling of Action Repository and Mental Lexicon

A severe problem of phonetic or sensorimotor models of speech processing (like DIVA or ACT) is that the development of the phonemic map during speech acquisition is not modeled. A possible solution of this problem could be a direct coupling of action repository and mental lexicon without explicitly introducing a phonemic map at the beginning of speech acquisition.

Experiments: Speech Acquisition

A very important issue for all neuroscientific or neurocomputational approaches is to separate structure and knowledge. While the structure of the model (i.e. of the human neuronal network, which is needed for processing speech) is mainly determined by evolutionary processes, the knowledge is gathered mainly during speech acquisition by processes of learning. Different learning experiments were carried out with the model ACT in order to learn (i) a five-vowel system /i, e, a, o, u/, (ii) a small consonant system (voiced plosives /b, d, g/ in combination with all five vowels acquired earlier as CV syllables (ibid.), (iii) a small model language comprising the five-vowel system, voiced and unvoiced plosives /b, d, g, p, t, k/, nasals /m, n/ and the lateral /l/ and three syllable types (V, CV, and CCV) and (iv) the 200 most frequent syllables of Standard German for a 6 year old child. In all cases, an ordering of phonetic items with respect to different phonetic features can be observed.

Experiments: Speech Perception

Despite the fact that the ACT model in its earlier versions was designed as a pure speech production model (including speech acquisition), the model is capable of exhibiting important basic phenomena of speech perception, i.e. categorical perception and the McGurk effect. In the case of categorical perception, the model is able to exhibit that categorical perception is stronger in the case of plosives than in the case of vowels. Furthermore the model ACT was able to exhibit the McGurk effect, if a specific mechanism of inhibition of neurons of the level of the phonetic map was implemented.

Brain–Reading

Brain-reading uses the responses of multiple voxels in the brain evoked by stimulus then detected by fMRI in order to decode the original stimulus. Brain reading studies differ in the type of decoding (i.e. classification, identification and reconstruction) employed, the target (i.e. decoding visual patterns, auditory patterns, cognitive states), and the decoding algorithms (linear classification, nonlinear classification, direct reconstruction, Bayesian reconstruction, etc.) employed.

Classification

In classification, a pattern of activity across multiple voxels is used to determine the particular class from which the stimulus was drawn. Many studies have classified visual stimuli, but this approach has also been used to classify cognitive states.

Reconstruction

In reconstruction brain reading the aim is to create a literal picture of the image that was presented. Early studies used voxels from early visual cortex areas (V1, V2, and V3) to reconstruct geometric stimuli made up of flickering checkerboard patterns.

Natural Images

More recent studies used voxels from early and anterior visual cortex areas forward of them (visual areas V3A, V3B, V4, and the lateral occipital) together with Bayesian inference techniques to reconstruct complex natural images. This brain reading approach uses three components: A structural encoding model that characterizes responses in early visual areas; a semantic encoding model that characterizes responses in anterior visual areas; and a Bayseian prior that describes the distribution of structural and semantic scene statistics.

Experimentally the procedure is for subjects to view 1750 black and white natural images that are correlated with voxel activation in their brains. Then subjects viewed another 120 novel target images, and information from the earlier scans is used reconstruct them. Natural images used include pictures of a seaside cafe and harbor, performers on a stage, and dense foliage.

Other Types

It is possible to track which of two forms of rivalrous binocular illusions a person was subjectively experiencing from fMRI signals. The category of event which a person freely recalls can be identified from fMRI before they say what they remembered. Statistical analysis of EEG brainwaves has been claimed to allow the recognition of phonemes, and at a 60% to 75% level color and visual shape words. It has also been shown that brain-reading can be achieved in a complex virtual environment.

Accuracy

Brain-reading accuracy is increasing steadily as the quality of the data and the complexity of the decoding algorithms improve. In one recent experiment it was possible to identify which single image was being seen from a set of 120. In another it was possible to correctly identify 90% of the time which of two categories the stimulus came and the specific semantic category (out of 23) of the target image 40% of the time.

Limitations

It has been noted that so far brain reading is limited. "In practice, exact reconstructions are impossible to achieve by any reconstruction algorithm on the basis of brain activity signals acquired by fMRI. This is because all reconstructions will inevitably be limited by inaccuracies in the encoding models and noise in the measured signals. Our results demonstrate that the natural image prior is a powerful (if unconventional) tool for mitigating the effects of these fundamental limitations. A natural image prior with only six million images is sufficient to produce reconstructions that are structurally and semantically similar to a target image."

Applications

Brain reading has been suggested as an alternative to polygraph machines as a form of lie detection. One neuroimaging method that has been proposed as a lie detector is EEG "brain-fingerprinting", in which event related potentials are supposedly used to determine whether a stimulus is familiar or unfamiliar. The inventor of brain fingerprinting, Lawrence Farwell, has attempted to demonstrate its use in a legal case, Harrington v. State of Iowa, although the state objected on the basis that the probes used by Farwell were too general for familiarity or unfamiliarity with them to prove innocence. Another alternative to polygraph machines is Blood Oxygenated Level Dependent functional MRI technology (BOLD fMRI). This technique involves the interpretation of the local change in the concentration of oxygenated hemoglobin in the brain, although the relationship between this blood flow and neural activity is not yet completely understood.

A number of concerns have been raised about the accuracy and ethical implications of brain reading for this purpose. Laboratory studies have found rates of accuracy of up to 85%; however, there are concerns about what this means for false positive results among non-criminal populations: "If the prevalence of "prevaricators" in the group being examined is low, the test will yield far more false-positive than true-positive results; about one person in five will be incorrectly identified by the test." Ethical problems involved in the use of brain reading as lie detection include misapplications due to adoption of the technology before its reliability and validity can be properly assessed and due to misunderstanding of the technology, and privacy concerns due to unprecedented access to individual's private thoughts. However, it has been noted that the use of polygraph lie detection carries similar concerns about the reliability of the results and violation of privacy.

Brain-reading has also been proposed as a method of improving human-machine interfaces, by the use of EEG to detect relevant brain states of a human. In recent years, there has been a rapid increase in patents for technology involved in reading brain-waves, rising from fewer than 400 from 2009-2012 to 1600 in 2014. These include proposed ways to control video games via brain waves and "neuro-marketing" to determine someone's thoughts about a new product or advertisement.

References

- Wiley, Keith (Sep 2014). A Taxonomy and Metaphysics of Mind-Uploading (1st ed.). Humanity+ Press and Alautun Press. ISBN 978-0692279847. Retrieved 24, March 2020

- Gürkök H., Nijholt A., Poel M. (2012). "Brain-Computer Interface Games: Towards a Framework". ICEC. Lecture Notes in Computer Science. 2012: 373–380. doi:10.1007/978-3-642-33542-6_33. ISBN 978-3-642-33541-9

- Naumann, J. Search for Paradise: A Patient's Account of the Artificial Vision Experiment (2012), Xlibris Corporation, ISBN 1-479-7092-04

- Wiley, Keith (March 20, 2014). "Response to Susan Schneider's "Philosophy of 'Her'"". H+Magazine. Retrieved 13, March 2020

- Prisco, Giulio (12 December 2012). "Uploaded e-crews for interstellar missions". kurzweilai.net. Retrieved 19, May 2020

- Anna Salamon; Luke Muehlhauser (2012). "Singularity Summit 2011 Workshop Report" (PDF). Machine Intelligence Research Institute. Retrieved 22, June 2020

- Shulman, Carl; Anders Sandberg (2010). Mainzer, Klaus, ed. "Implications of a Software-Limited Singularity" (PDF). ECAP10: VIII European Conference on Computing and Philosophy. Retrieved 20, May 2020

- Bostrom, Nick (2014). "Ch. 14: The strategic picture". Superintelligence: Paths, Dangers, Strategies. Oxford University Press. ISBN 978-0199678112

Understanding Artificial Neural Networks

The computing system designed in a way that it resembles the way of human brain to analyze and process information is known as artificial neural network. This chapter encompasses recurrent neural network, machine learning and perceptron. The topics elaborated in this chapter will help in gaining a better perspective about artificial neural networks.

Artificial Neural Network

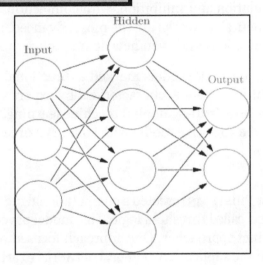

An artificial neural network is an interconnected group of nodes, akin to the vast network of neurons in a brain. Here, each circular node represents an artificial neuron and an arrow represents a connection from the output of one neuron to the input of another.

Artificial neural networks (ANNs) or connectionist systems are a computational model used in machine learning, computer science and other research disciplines, which is based on a large collection of connected simple units called artificial neurons, loosely analogous to axons in a biological brain. Connections between neurons carry an activation signal of varying strength. If the combined incoming signals are strong enough, the neuron becomes activated and the signal travels to other neurons connected to it. Such systems can be trained from examples, rather than explicitly programmed, and excel in areas where the solution or feature detection is difficult to express in a traditional computer program. Like other machine learning methods, neural networks have been used to solve a wide variety of tasks, like computer vision and speech recognition, that are difficult to solve using ordinary rule-based programming.

Typically, neurons are connected in layers, and signals travel from the first (input), to the last (output) layer. Modern neural network projects typically have a few thousand to a few million neural units and millions of connections; their computing power is similar to a worm brain, several orders of magnitude simpler than a human brain. The signals and state of artificial neurons are real numbers, typically between 0 and 1. There may be a threshold function or limiting function on each connection and on the unit itself, such that the signal must surpass the limit before propagating. Back propagation is the use of forward stimulation to modify connection weights, and is sometimes done to train the network using known correct outputs. However, the success is unpredictable: after training, some systems are good at solving problems while others are not. Training typically requires several thousand cycles of interaction.

The goal of the neural network is to solve problems in the same way that a human would, although several neural network categories are more abstract. New brain research often stimulates new patterns in neural networks. One new approach is use of connections which span further to connect processing layers rather than adjacent neurons. Other research being explored with the different types of signal over time that axons propagate, such as deep learning, interpolates greater complexity than a set of boolean variables being simply on or off. Newer types of network are more free flowing in terms of stimulation and inhibition, with connections interacting in more chaotic and complex ways. Dynamic neural networks are the most advanced, in that they dynamically can, based on rules, form new connections and even new neural units while disabling others.

Historically, the use of neural network models marked a directional shift in the late 1980s from high-level (symbolic) artificial intelligence, characterized by expert systems with knowledge embodied in *if-then* rules, to low-level (sub-symbolic) machine learning, characterized by knowledge embodied in the parameters of a cognitive model with some dynamical system.

History

Warren McCulloch and Walter Pitts (1943) created a computational model for neural networks based on mathematics and algorithms called threshold logic. This model paved the way for neural network research to split into two distinct approaches. One approach focused on biological processes in the brain and the other focused on the application of neural networks to artificial intelligence. This work led to the influential paper by Kleene on nerve networks and their link to finite automata.

1. "Representation of events in nerve nets and finite automata." In: Automata Studies, ed. by C.E. Shannon and J. McCarthy. Annals of Mathematics Studies, no. 34. Princeton University Press, Princeton, N. J.

Hebbian Learning

In the late 1940s psychologist Donald Hebb created a hypothesis of learning based on the mechanism of neural plasticity that is now known as Hebbian learning. Hebbian learning is considered to be a 'typical' unsupervised learning rule and its later variants were early models for long term potentiation. Researchers started applying these ideas to computational models in 1948 with Turing's B-type machines.

Farley and Wesley A. Clark (1954) first used computational machines, then called "calculators", to simulate a Hebbian network at MIT. Other neural network computational machines were created by Rochester, Holland, Habit, and Duda (1956).

Frank Rosenblatt (1958) created the perceptron, an algorithm for pattern recognition based on a two-layer computer learning network using simple addition and subtraction. With mathematical notation, Rosenblatt also described circuitry not in the basic perceptron, such as the exclusive-or circuit, a circuit which could not be processed by neural networks until after the backpropagation algorithm was created by Paul Werbos (1975).

Neural network research stagnated after the publication of machine learning research by Marvin Minsky and Seymour Papert (1969), who discovered two key issues with the computational machines that processed neural networks. The first was that basic perceptrons were incapable of processing the exclusive-or circuit. The second significant issue was that computers didn't have enough processing power to effectively handle the long run time required by large neural networks. Neural network research slowed until computers achieved greater processing power.

Backpropagation and Resurgence

A key advance that came later was the backpropagation algorithm which effectively solved the exclusive-or problem, and more generally the problem of quickly training multi-layer neural networks (Werbos 1975).

In the mid-1980s, parallel distributed processing became popular under the name connectionism. The textbook by David E. Rumelhart and James McClelland (1986) provided a full exposition of the use of connectionism in computers to simulate neural processes.

Neural networks, as used in artificial intelligence, have traditionally been viewed as simplified models of neural processing in the brain, even though the relation between this model and the biological architecture of the brain is debated; it's not clear to what degree artificial neural networks mirror brain function.

Support vector machines and other, much simpler methods such as linear classifiers gradually overtook neural networks in machine learning popularity. As earlier challenges in training deep neural networks were successfully addressed with methods such as Unsupervised Pre-training and computing power increased through the use of GPUs and distributed computing, neural networks were again deployed on a large scale, particularly in image and visual recognition problems. This became known as "deep learning", although deep learning is not strictly synonymous with deep neural networks.

Improvements Since 2006

Computational devices have been created in CMOS, for both biophysical simulation and neuromorphic computing. More recent efforts show promise for creating nanodevices for very large scale principal components analyses and convolution. If successful, it would create a new class of neural computing because it depends on learning rather than programming and because it is fundamentally analog rather than digital even though the first instantiations may in fact be with CMOS digital devices.

Between 2009 and 2012, the recurrent neural networks and deep feedforward neural networks developed in the research group of Jürgen Schmidhuber at the Swiss AI Lab IDSIA have won eight international competitions in pattern recognition and machine learning. For example, the bi-directional and multi-dimensional long short-term memory (LSTM) of Alex Graves et al. won three competitions in connected handwriting recognition at the 2009 International Conference on Document Analysis and Recognition (ICDAR), without any prior knowledge about the three different languages to be learned.

Fast GPU-based implementations of this approach by Dan Ciresan and colleagues at IDSIA have won several pattern recognition contests, including the IJCNN 2011 Traffic Sign Recognition Competition, the ISBI 2012 Segmentation of Neuronal Structures in Electron Microscopy Stacks challenge, and others. Their neural networks also were the first artificial pattern recognizers to achieve human-competitive or even superhuman performance on important benchmarks such as traffic sign recognition (IJCNN 2012), or the MNIST handwritten digits problem of Yann LeCun at NYU.

Deep, highly nonlinear neural architectures similar to the 1980 neocognitron by Kunihiko Fukushima and the "standard architecture of vision", inspired by the simple and complex cells identified by David H. Hubel and Torsten Wiesel in the primary visual cortex, can also be pre-trained by unsupervised methods of Geoff Hinton's lab at University of Toronto. A team from this lab won a 2012 contest sponsored by Merck to design software to help find molecules that might lead to new drugs.

Models

Neural network models in artificial intelligence are usually referred to as artificial neural networks (ANNs); these are essentially simple mathematical models defining a function $f : X \rightarrow Y$ or a distribution over X or both X and Y, but sometimes models are also intimately associated with a particular learning algorithm or learning rule. A common use of the phrase "ANN model" is really the definition of a *class* of such functions (where members of the class are obtained by varying parameters, connection weights, or specifics of the architecture such as the number of neurons or their connectivity).

Network Function

The word *network* in the term 'artificial neural network' refers to the interconnections between the neurons in the different layers of each system. An example system has three layers. The first layer has input neurons which send data via synapses to the second layer of neurons, and then via more synapses to the third layer of output neurons. More complex systems will have more layers of neurons, some having increased layers of input neurons and output neurons. The synapses store parameters called "weights" that manipulate the data in the calculations.

An ANN is typically defined by three types of parameters:

1. The interconnection pattern between the different layers of neurons.

2. The weights of the interconnections, which are updated in the learning process.

3. The activation function that converts a neuron's weighted input to its output activation.

Mathematically, a neuron's network function $f(x)$ is defined as a composition of other functions $g_i(x)$, which can further be defined as a composition of other functions. This can be conveniently represented as a network structure, with arrows depicting the dependencies between variables.

A widely used type of composition is the *nonlinear weighted sum*, where $f(x) = K\left(\sum_i w_i g_i(x)\right)$, where K (commonly referred to as the activation function) is some predefined function, such as the hyperbolic tangent or sigmoid function. The important characteristic of the activation function is that it provides a smooth transition as input values change, i.e. a small change in input produces a small change in output. It will be convenient for the following to refer to a collection of functions g_i as simply a vector $g = (g_1, g_2, \ldots, g_n)$.

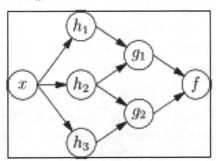

ANN dependency graph.

This figure depicts such a decomposition of f, with dependencies between variables indicated by arrows. These can be interpreted in two ways.

The first view is the functional view: the input x is transformed into a 3-dimensional vector h, which is then transformed into a 2-dimensional vector g, which is finally transformed into f. This view is most commonly encountered in the context of optimization.

The second view is the probabilistic view: the random variable $F = f(G)$ depends upon the random variable $G = g(H)$, which depends upon $H = h(X)$, which depends upon the random variable X. This view is most commonly encountered in the context of graphical models.

The two views are largely equivalent. In either case, for this particular network architecture, the components of individual layers are independent of each other (e.g., the components of g are independent of each other given their input h). This naturally enables a degree of parallelism in the implementation.

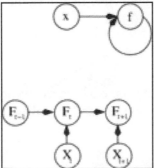

Two separate depictions of the recurrent ANN dependency graph.

Networks such as the previous one are commonly called feedforward, because their graph is a directed acyclic graph. Networks with cycles are commonly called recurrent. Such networks are commonly depicted in the manner shown at the top of the figure, where f is shown as being dependent upon itself. However, an implied temporal dependence is not shown.

Learning

What has attracted the most interest in neural networks is the possibility of *learning*. Given a specific *task* to solve, and a *class* of functions F, learning means using a set of *observations* to find $f^* \in F$ which solves the task in some *optimal* sense.

This entails defining a cost function $C : F \to \mathbb{R}$ such that, for the optimal solution f^*, $C(f^*) \le C(f)$ $\forall f \in F$ – i.e., no solution has a cost less than the cost of the optimal solution.

The cost function C is an important concept in learning, as it is a measure of how far away a particular solution is from an optimal solution to the problem to be solved. Learning algorithms search through the solution space to find a function that has the smallest possible cost.

For applications where the solution is dependent on some data, the cost must necessarily be a *function of the observations*, otherwise we would not be modelling anything related to the data. It is frequently defined as a statistic to which only approximations can be made. As a simple example, consider the problem of finding the model f, which minimizes $C = E\left[(f(x) - y)^2\right]$, for data pairs (x, y) drawn from some distribution $\mathcal{D}$. In practical situations we would only have N samples from $\mathcal{D}$ and thus, for the above example, we would only minimize $\hat{C} = \frac{1}{N}\sum_{i=1}^{N}(f(x_i) - y_i)^2$. Thus, the cost is minimized over a sample of the data rather than the entire distribution generating the data.

When $N \to \infty$ some form of online machine learning must be used, where the cost is partially minimized as each new example is seen. While online machine learning is often used when $\mathcal{D}$ is fixed, it is most useful in the case where the distribution changes slowly over time. In neural network methods, some form of online machine learning is frequently used for finite datasets.

Choosing a Cost Function

While it is possible to define some arbitrary ad hoc cost function, frequently a particular cost will be used, either because it has desirable properties (such as convexity) or because it arises naturally from a particular formulation of the problem (e.g., in a probabilistic formulation the posterior probability of the model can be used as an inverse cost). Ultimately, the cost function will depend on the desired task. An overview of the three main categories of learning tasks is provided below:

Learning Paradigms

There are three major learning paradigms, each corresponding to a particular abstract learning task. These are supervised learning, unsupervised learning and reinforcement learning.

Supervised Learning

In supervised learning, we are given a set of example pairs $(x, y), x \in X, y \in Y$ and the aim is to find a function $f : X \to Y$ in the allowed class of functions that matches the examples. In other words, we wish to *infer* the mapping implied by the data; the cost function is related to the mismatch between our mapping and the data and it implicitly contains prior knowledge about the problem domain.

A commonly used cost is the mean-squared error, which tries to minimize the average squared error between the network's output, $f(x)$, and the target value y over all the example pairs. When one tries to minimize this cost using gradient descent for the class of neural networks called multilayer perceptrons (MLP), one obtains the common and well-known backpropagation algorithm for training neural networks.

Tasks that fall within the paradigm of supervised learning are pattern recognition (also known as classification) and regression (also known as function approximation). The supervised learning paradigm is also applicable to sequential data (e.g., for speech and gesture recognition). This can be thought of as learning with a "teacher", in the form of a function that provides continuous feedback on the quality of solutions obtained thus far.

Unsupervised Learning

In unsupervised learning, some data x is given and the cost function to be minimized, that can be any function of the data x and the network's output, f.

The cost function is dependent on the task (what we are trying to model) and our *a priori* assumptions (the implicit properties of our model, its parameters and the observed variables).

As a trivial example, consider the model $f(x) = a$ where a is a constant and the cost $C = E[(x - f(x))^2]$. Minimizing this cost will give us a value of a that is equal to the mean of the data. The cost function can be much more complicated. Its form depends on the application: for example, in compression it could be related to the mutual information between x and $f(x)$, whereas in statistical modeling, it could be related to the posterior probability of the model given the data (note that in both of those examples those quantities would be maximized rather than minimized).

Tasks that fall within the paradigm of unsupervised learning are in general estimation problems; the applications include clustering, the estimation of statistical distributions, compression and filtering.

Reinforcement Learning

In reinforcement learning, data x are usually not given, but generated by an agent's interactions with the environment. At each point in time t, the agent performs an action y_t and the environment generates an observation x_t and an instantaneous cost c_t, according to some (usually unknown) dynamics. The aim is to discover a *policy* for selecting actions that minimizes some measure of a long-term cost, e.g., the expected cumulative cost. The environment's dynamics and the long-term cost for each policy are usually unknown, but can be estimated.

More formally the environment is modeled as a Markov decision process (MDP) with states $s_1, ..., s_n \in S$ and actions $a_1, ..., a_m \in A$ with the following probability distributions: the instantaneous cost distribution $P(c_t \mid s_t)$, the observation distribution $P(x_t \mid s_t)$ and the transition $P(s_{t+1} \mid s_t, a_t)$, while a policy is defined as the conditional distribution over actions given the observations. Taken together, the two then define a Markov chain (MC). The aim is to discover the policy (i.e., the MC) that minimizes the cost.

ANNs are frequently used in reinforcement learning as part of the overall algorithm. Dynamic programming has been coupled with ANNs (giving neurodynamic programming) by Bertsekas and Tsitsiklis and applied to multi-dimensional nonlinear problems such as those involved in vehicle routing, natural resources management or medicine because of the ability of ANNs to mitigate losses of accuracy even when reducing the discretization grid density for numerically approximating the solution of the original control problems.

Tasks that fall within the paradigm of reinforcement learning are control problems, games and other sequential decision making tasks.

Learning Algorithms

Training a neural network model essentially means selecting one model from the set of allowed models (or, in a Bayesian framework, determining a distribution over the set of allowed models) that minimizes the cost criterion. There are numerous algorithms available for training neural network models; most of them can be viewed as a straightforward application of optimization theory and statistical estimation.

Most of the algorithms used in training artificial neural networks employ some form of gradient descent, using backpropagation to compute the actual gradients. This is done by simply taking the derivative of the cost function with respect to the network parameters and then changing those parameters in a gradient-related direction. The backpropagation training algorithms are usually classified into three categories:

- Steepest descent (with variable learning rate and momentum, resilient backpropagation).

- Quasi-Newton (Broyden-Fletcher-Goldfarb-Shanno, one step secant).

- Levenberg-Marquardt and conjugate gradient (Fletcher-Reeves update, Polak-Ribiére update, Powell-Beale restart, scaled conjugate gradient).

Evolutionary methods, gene expression programming, simulated annealing, expectation-maximization, non-parametric methods and particle swarm optimization are some other methods for training neural networks.

Use

Perhaps the greatest advantage of ANNs is their ability to be used as an arbitrary function approximation mechanism that 'learns' from observed data. However, using them is not so straightforward, and a relatively good understanding of the underlying theory is essential:

- Choice of model: This will depend on the data representation and the application. Overly complex models tend to lead to challenges in learning.

- Learning algorithm: There are numerous trade-offs between learning algorithms. Almost any algorithm will work well with the *correct hyperparameters* for training on a particular fixed data set. However, selecting and tuning an algorithm for training on unseen data require a significant amount of experimentation.

- Robustness: If the model, cost function and learning algorithm are selected appropriately, the resulting ANN can be extremely robust.

With the correct implementation, ANNs can be used naturally in online learning and large data set applications. Their simple implementation and the existence of mostly local dependencies exhibited in the structure allows for fast, parallel implementations in hardware.

Applications

The utility of artificial neural network models lies in the fact that they can be used to infer a function from observations. This is particularly useful in applications where the complexity of the data or task makes the design of such a function by hand impracticable.

Real-life Applications

The tasks artificial neural networks are applied to tend to fall within the following broad categories:

- Function approximation, or regression analysis, including time series prediction, fitness approximation and modeling.

- Classification, including pattern and sequence recognition, novelty detection and sequential decision making.

- Data processing, including filtering, clustering, blind source separation and compression.

- Robotics, including directing manipulators, prosthesis.

- Control, including computer numerical control.

Application areas include the system identification and control (vehicle control, trajectory prediction, process control, natural resources management), quantum chemistry, game-playing and decision making (backgammon, chess, poker), pattern recognition (radar systems, face identification, object recognition and more), sequence recognition (gesture, speech, handwritten text recognition), medical diagnosis, financial applications (e.g. automated trading systems), data mining (or knowledge discovery in databases, "KDD"), visualization and e-mail spam filtering.

Artificial neural networks have also been used to diagnose several cancers. An ANN based hybrid lung cancer detection system named HLND improves the accuracy of diagnosis and the speed of lung cancer radiology. These networks have also been used to diagnose prostate cancer. The diagnoses can be used to make specific models taken from a large group of patients compared to information of one given patient. The models do not depend on assumptions about correlations of different variables. Colorectal cancer has also been predicted using the neural networks. Neural networks could predict the outcome for a patient with colorectal cancer with more accuracy than the current clinical methods. After training, the networks could predict multiple patient outcomes from unrelated institutions. ANN have been used to distinguish between high invasive cancer cell lines from low invasive lines using only cell shape information with almost perfect accuracy.

Neural Networks and Neuroscience

Theoretical and computational neuroscience is the field concerned with the theoretical analysis and the computational modeling of biological neural systems. Since neural systems are intimately related to cognitive processes and behavior, the field is closely related to cognitive and behavioral modeling.

The aim of the field is to create models of biological neural systems in order to understand how biological systems work. To gain this understanding, neuroscientists strive to make a link between observed biological processes (data), biologically plausible mechanisms for neural processing and learning (biological neural network models) and theory (statistical learning theory and information theory).

Types of Models

Many models are used in the field, defined at different levels of abstraction and modeling different aspects of neural systems. They range from models of the short-term behavior of individual neurons (e.g.), models of how the dynamics of neural circuitry arise from interactions between individual neurons and finally to models of how behavior can arise from abstract neural modules that represent complete subsystems. These include models of the long-term, and short-term plasticity, of neural systems and their relations to learning and memory from the individual neuron to the system level.

Networks with Memory

Integrating external memory components with artificial neural networks has a long history dating back to early research in distributed representations and self-organizing maps. E.g. in sparse distributed memory the patterns encoded by neural networks are used as memory addresses for content-addressable memory, with "neurons" essentially serving as address encoders and decoders.

More recently deep learning was shown to be useful in semantic hashing where a deep graphical model of the word-count vectors is obtained from a large set of documents. Documents are mapped to memory addresses in such a way that semantically similar documents are located at nearby addresses. Documents similar to a query document can then be found by simply accessing all the addresses that differ by only a few bits from the address of the query document.

Memory Networks is another extension to neural networks incorporating long-term memory which was developed by Facebook research. The long-term memory can be read and written to, with the goal of using it for prediction. These models have been applied in the context of question answering (QA) where the long-term memory effectively acts as a (dynamic) knowledge base, and the output is a textual response.

Neural Turing Machines developed by Google DeepMind extend the capabilities of deep neural networks by coupling them to external memory resources, which they can interact with by attentional processes. The combined system is analogous to a Turing Machine but is differentiable end-to-end, allowing it to be efficiently trained with gradient descent. Preliminary results demonstrate that Neural Turing Machines can infer simple algorithms such as copying, sorting, and associative recall from input and output examples.

Differentiable neural computers (DNC) are an extension of Neural Turing Machines, also from DeepMind. They have out-performed Neural turing machines, Long short-term memory systems and memory networks on sequence-processing tasks.

Software

Neural network software is used to simulate, research, develop and apply artificial neural networks, biological neural networks and, in some cases, a wider array of adaptive systems.

Types

Artificial neural network types vary from those with only one or two layers of single direction logic, to complicated multi–input many directional feedback loops and layers. On the whole, these systems use algorithms in their programming to determine control and organization of their functions. Most systems use "weights" to change the parameters of the throughput and the varying connections to the neurons. Artificial neural networks can be autonomous and learn by input from outside "teachers" or even self-teaching from written-in rules. Neural Cube style neural networks first pioneered by Gianna Giavelli provide a dynamic space in which networks dynamically recombine information and links across billions of self adapting nodes utilizing Neural Darwinism, a technique developed by Gerald Edelman which allows for more biologically modeled systems.

Theoretical Properties

Computational Power

The multilayer perceptron is a universal function approximator, as proven by the universal approximation theorem. However, the proof is not constructive regarding the number of neurons required, the network topology, the settings of the weights and the learning parameters.

Work by Hava Siegelmann and Eduardo D. Sontag has provided a proof that a specific recurrent architecture with rational valued weights (as opposed to full precision real number-valued weights) has the full power of a Universal Turing Machine using a finite number of neurons and standard linear connections. Further, it has been shown that the use of irrational values for weights results in a machine with super-Turing power.

Capacity

Artificial neural network models have a property called 'capacity', which roughly corresponds to their ability to model any given function. It is related to the amount of information that can be stored in the network and to the notion of complexity.

Convergence

Nothing can be said in general about convergence since it depends on a number of factors. Firstly, there may exist many local minima. This depends on the cost function and the model. Secondly, the optimization method used might not be guaranteed to converge when far away from a local minimum. Thirdly, for a very large amount of data or parameters, some methods become impractical.

In general, it has been found that theoretical guarantees regarding convergence are an unreliable guide to practical application.

Generalization and Statistics

In applications where the goal is to create a system that generalizes well in unseen examples, the problem of over-training has emerged. This arises in convoluted or over-specified systems when the capacity of the network significantly exceeds the needed free parameters. There are two schools of thought for avoiding this problem: The first is to use cross-validation and similar techniques to check for the presence of overtraining and optimally select hyperparameters such as to minimize the generalization error. The second is to use some form of *regularization*. This is a concept that emerges naturally in a probabilistic (Bayesian) framework, where the regularization can be performed by selecting a larger prior probability over simpler models; but also in statistical learning theory, where the goal is to minimize over two quantities: the 'empirical risk' and the 'structural risk', which roughly corresponds to the error over the training set and the predicted error in unseen data due to overfitting.

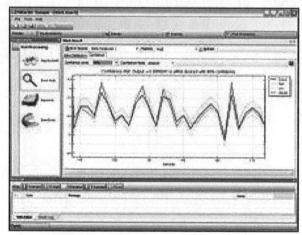

Confidence analysis of a neural network.

Supervised neural networks that use a mean squared error (MSE) cost function can use formal statistical methods to determine the confidence of the trained model. The MSE on a validation set can be used as an estimate for variance. This value can then be used to calculate the confidence interval of the output of the network, assuming a normal distribution. A confidence analysis made this way is statistically valid as long as the output probability distribution stays the same and the network is not modified.

By assigning a softmax activation function, a generalization of the logistic function, on the output layer of the neural network (or a softmax component in a component-based neural network) for categorical target variables, the outputs can be interpreted as posterior probabilities. This is very useful in classification as it gives a certainty measure on classifications.

The softmax activation function is:

$$y_i = \frac{e^{x_i}}{\sum_{j=1}^{c} e^{x_j}}$$

Criticism

Training Issues

A common criticism of neural networks, particularly in robotics, is that they require a large diversity of training for real-world operation. This is not surprising, since any learning machine needs sufficient representative examples in order to capture the underlying structure that allows it to generalize to new cases. Dean A. Pomerleau, in his research presented in the paper "Knowledge-based Training of Artificial Neural Networks for Autonomous Robot Driving", uses a neural network to train a robotic vehicle to drive on multiple types of roads (single lane, multi-lane, dirt, etc.). A large amount of his research is devoted to (1) extrapolating multiple training scenarios from a single training experience, and (2) preserving past training diversity so that the system does not become overtrained (if, for example, it is presented with a series of right turns – it should not learn to always turn right). These issues are common in neural networks that must decide from amongst a wide variety of responses, but can be dealt with in several ways, for example by randomly shuffling the training examples, by using a numerical optimization algorithm that does not take too large steps when changing the network connections following an example, or by grouping examples in so-called mini-batches.

Theoretical Issues

A. K. Dewdney, a mathematician and computer scientist at University of Western Ontario and former *Scientific American* columnist, wrote in 1997, "Although neural nets do solve a few toy problems, their powers of computation are so limited that I am surprised anyone takes them seriously as a general problem-solving tool". No neural network has ever been shown that solves computationally difficult problems such as the n-Queens problem, the travelling salesman problem, or the problem of factoring large integers.

Aside from their utility, a fundamental objection to artificial neural networks is that they fail to reflect how real neurons function. Back propagation is at the heart of most artificial neural networks and not only is there no evidence of any such mechanism in natural neural networks, it seems to contradict the fundamental principle of real neurons that information can only flow forward along the axon. How information is coded by real neurons is not yet known. What is known is that sensor neurons fire action potentials more frequently with sensor activation and muscle cells pull more strongly when their associated motor neurons receive action potentials more frequently. Other than the simplest case of just relaying information from a sensor neuron to a motor neuron almost nothing of the underlying general principles of how information is handled by real neural networks is known.

The motivation behind artificial neural networks is not necessarily to replicate real neural function but to use natural neural networks as an inspiration for an approach to computing that is inherently parallel and which provides solutions to problems that have up until now been considered intractable. A central claim of artificial neural networks is therefore that it embodies some new and powerful general principle for processing information. Unfortunately, these general principles are ill-defined and it is often claimed that they are *emergent* from the neural network itself. This allows simple statistical association (the basic function of artificial neural networks) to be described as *learning* or *recognition*. As a result, artificial neural networks have a "something-for-nothing quality, one that imparts a peculiar aura of laziness and a distinct lack of curiosity about just how good these computing systems are. No human hand (or mind) intervenes; solutions are found as if by magic; and no one, it seems, has learned anything".

Hardware Issues

To implement large and effective software neural networks, considerable processing and storage resources need to be committed. While the brain has hardware tailored to the task of processing signals through a graph of neurons, simulating even a most simplified form on von Neumann architecture may compel a neural network designer to fill many millions of database rows for its connections – which can consume vast amounts of computer memory and hard disk space. Furthermore, the designer of neural network systems will often need to simulate the transmission of signals through many of these connections and their associated neurons – which must often be matched with incredible amounts of CPU processing power and time.

Jürgen Schmidhuber notes that the resurgence of neural networks in the twenty-first century, and their renewed success at image recognition tasks is largely attributable to advances in hardware: from 1991 to 2015, computing power, especially as delivered by GPGPUs (on GPUs), has increased around a million-fold, making the standard backpropagation algorithm feasible for training networks that are several layers deeper than before (but adds that this doesn't overcome algorithmic problems such as vanishing gradients "in a fundamental way"). The use of GPUs instead of ordinary CPUs can bring training times for some networks down from months to mere days.

Computing power continues to grow roughly according to Moore's Law, which may provide sufficient resources to accomplish new tasks. Neuromorphic engineering addresses the hardware difficulty directly, by constructing non-von-Neumann chips with circuits designed to implement neural nets from the ground up. Google has also designed a chip optimized for neural network processing called a Tensor Processing Unit, or TPU.

Practical Counter Examples to Criticisms

Arguments against Dewdney's position are that neural networks have been successfully used to solve many complex and diverse tasks, ranging from autonomously flying aircraft to detecting credit card fraud.

Technology writer Roger Bridgman commented on Dewdney's statements about neural nets:

Neural networks, for instance, are in the dock not only because they have been hyped to high heaven, (what hasn't?) but also because you could create a successful net without understanding how it worked: the bunch of numbers that captures its behaviour would in all probability be "an opaque, unreadable table...valueless as a scientific resource".

In spite of his emphatic declaration that science is not technology, Dewdney seems here to pillory neural nets as bad science when most of those devising them are just trying to be good engineers. An unreadable table that a useful machine could read would still be well worth having.

Although it is true that analyzing what has been learned by an artificial neural network is difficult, it is much easier to do so than to analyze what has been learned by a biological neural network.

Furthermore, researchers involved in exploring learning algorithms for neural networks are gradually uncovering generic principles which allow a learning machine to be successful. For example, Bengio and LeCun (2007) wrote an article regarding local vs non-local learning, as well as shallow vs deep architecture.

Hybrid Approaches

Some other criticisms come from advocates of hybrid models (combining neural networks and symbolic approaches), who believe that the intermix of these two approaches can better capture the mechanisms of the human mind.

Types

- Dynamic Neural Network:
  - Feedforward neural network (FNN).
  - Recurrent neural network (RNN):
    - Hopfield network.
    - Boltzmann machine.
    - Simple recurrent networks.
    - Echo state network.
    - Long short-term memory.
    - Bi-directional RNN.
    - Hierarchical RNN.
    - Stochastic neural networks.
  - Kohonen Self-Organizing Maps.
  - Autoencoder.
  - Probabilistic neural network (PNN).
  - Time delay neural network (TDNN).
  - Regulatory feedback network (RFNN).
- Static Neural Network:
  - Neocognitron.
  - McCulloch-Pitts cell.
  - Radial basis function network (RBF).

- o Learning vector quantization.

- o Perceptron:

  - Adaline model.

  - Convolutional neural network (CNN).

- o Modular neural networks:

  - Committee of machines (COM).

  - Associative neural network (ASNN).

- Memory Network:

  - o Google / Deep Mind.

  - o Facebook / MemNN.

  - o Holographic associative memory.

  - o One-shot associative memory.

  - o Neural Turing Machine.

  - o Adaptive resonance theory.

  - o Hierarchical temporal memory.

- Other types of networks:

  - o Instantaneously trained neural networks (ITNN).

  - o Spiking neural network (SNN):

    - Pulse Coded Neural Networks (PCNN).

  - o Cascading neural networks.

  - o Neuro-fuzzy networks.

  - o Growing Neural Gas (GNG).

  - o Compositional pattern-producing networks.

  - o Counterpropagation network.

  - o Oscillating neural network.

  - o Hybridization neural network.

  - o Physical neural network:

    - Optical neural network.

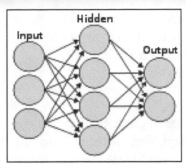

An artificial neural network.

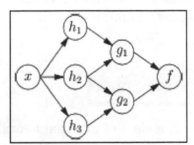

An ANN dependency graph.

Generative Adversarial Networks

Generative adversarial networks are a type of artificial intelligence algorithms used in unsupervised machine learning, implemented by a system of two neural networks competing against each other in a zero-sum game framework. They were first introduced by Ian Goodfellow *et al.* in 2014.

This technique can generate photographs that look authentic to human observers.

Method

One network is generative and one is discriminative. Typically, the generative network is taught to map from a latent space to a particular data distribution of interest, and the discriminative network is simultaneously taught to discriminate between instances from the true data distribution and synthesized instances produced by the generator. The generative network's training objective is to increase the error rate of the discriminative network (i.e., "fool" the discriminator network by producing novel synthesized instances that appear to have come from the true data distribution). These models are used for computer vision tasks.

In practice, a particular dataset serves as the training data for the discriminator. Training the discriminator involves presenting the discriminator with samples from the dataset and samples synthesized by the generator, and backpropagating from a binary classification loss. In order to produce a sample, typically the generator is seeded with a randomized input that is sampled from a predefined latent space (e.g., a multivariate normal distribution). Training the generator involves back-propagating the negation of the binary classification loss of the discriminator. The generator adjusts its parameters so that the training data and generated data cannot be distinguished by the discriminator model. The goal is to find a setting of parameters that makes generated data look like the training data to the discriminator network. In practice, the generator is typically a deconvolutional neural network, and the discriminator is a convolutional neural network.

The idea to infer models in a competitive setting (model versus discriminator) was first proposed by Li, Gauci and Gross in 2013. Their method is used for behavioral inference. It is termed Turing Learning, as the setting is akin to that of a Turing test.

Application

GANs can be used to produce samples of photorealistic images for the purposes of visualizing new interior/industrial design, shoes, bags and clothing items or items for computer games' scenes. These networks were reported to be used by Facebook. Recently, GANs have been able to model rudimentary patterns of motion in video. They have also been used to reconstruct 3D models of objects from images and to improve astronomical images.

Recurrent Neural Network

A recurrent neural network (RNN) is a class of artificial neural network where connections between units form a directed cycle. This creates an internal state of the network which allows it to exhibit dynamic temporal behavior. Unlike feedforward neural networks, RNNs can use their internal memory to process arbitrary sequences of inputs. This makes them applicable to tasks such as unsegmented connected handwriting recognition or speech recognition.

Architectures

Fully Recurrent Network

This is the basic architecture developed in the 1980s: a network of neuron-like units, each with a directed connection to every other unit. Each unit has a time-varying real-valued activation. Each connection has a modifiable real-valued weight. Some of the nodes are called input nodes, some output nodes, the rest hidden nodes. Most architectures below are special cases.

For supervised learning in discrete time settings, training sequences of real-valued input vectors become sequences of activations of the input nodes, one input vector at a time. At any given time step, each non-input unit computes its current activation as a nonlinear function of the weighted sum of the activations of all units from which it receives connections. There may be teacher-given target activations for some of the output units at certain time steps. For example, if the input sequence is a speech signal corresponding to a spoken digit, the final target output at the end of the sequence may be a label classifying the digit. For each sequence, its error is the sum of the deviations of all target signals from the corresponding activations computed by the network. For a training set of numerous sequences, the total error is the sum of the errors of all individual sequences. Algorithms for minimizing this error are mentioned in the section on training algorithms below.

In reinforcement learning settings, there is no teacher providing target signals for the RNN, instead a fitness function or reward function is occasionally used to evaluate the RNN's performance, which is influencing its input stream through output units connected to actuators affecting the environment. Again, compare the section on training algorithms below.

Recursive Neural Networks

A recursive neural network is created by applying the same set of weights recursively over a differentiable graph-like structure, by traversing the structure in topological order. Such networks are typically also trained by the reverse mode of automatic differentiation. They were introduced to learn distributed representations of structure, such as logical terms. A special case of recursive neural networks is the RNN itself whose structure corresponds to a linear chain. Recursive neural networks have been applied to natural language processing. The Recursive Neural Tensor Network uses a tensor-based composition function for all nodes in the tree.

Hopfield Network

The Hopfield network is of historic interest although it is not a general RNN, as it is not designed to process sequences of patterns. Instead it requires stationary inputs. It is a RNN in which all connections are symmetric. Invented by John Hopfield in 1982, it guarantees that its dynamics will converge. If the connections are trained using Hebbian learning then the Hopfield network can perform as robust content-addressable memory, resistant to connection alteration.

A variation on the Hopfield network is the bidirectional associative memory (BAM). The BAM has two layers, either of which can be driven as an input, to recall an association and produce an output on the other layer.

Elman Networks and Jordan Networks

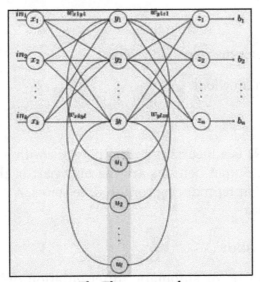

The Elman network.

The following special case of the basic architecture above was employed by Jeff Elman. A three-layer network is used (arranged horizontally as x, y, and z in the illustration), with the addition of a set of "context units" (u in the illustration). There are connections from the middle (hidden) layer to these context units fixed with a weight of one. At each time step, the input is propagated in a standard feed-forward fashion, and then a learning rule is applied. The fixed back connections result in the context units always maintaining a copy of the previous values of the hidden units (since they propagate over the connections before the learning rule is applied). Thus the network can maintain a sort of state, allowing it to perform such tasks as sequence-prediction that are beyond the power of a standard multilayer perceptron.

Jordan networks, due to Michael I. Jordan, are similar to Elman networks. The context units are however fed from the output layer instead of the hidden layer. The context units in a Jordan network are also referred to as the state layer, and have a recurrent connection to themselves with no other nodes on this connection.

Elman and Jordan networks are also known as "simple recurrent networks" (SRN).

Elman network

$$h_t = \sigma_h(W_h x_t + U_h h_{t-1} + b_h)$$
$$y_t = \sigma_y(W_y h_t + b_y)$$

Jordan network

$$h_t = \sigma_h(W_h x_t + U_h y_{t-1} + b_h)$$
$$y_t = \sigma_y(W_y h_t + b_y)$$

Variables and functions:

- x_t : input vector.

- h_t : hidden layer vector.

- y_t : output vector.

- W, U and b : parameter matrices and vector.

- σ_h and σ_y : Activation functions.

Echo State Network

The echo state network (ESN) is a recurrent neural network with a sparsely connected random hidden layer. The weights of output neurons are the only part of the network that can change and be trained. ESN are good at reproducing certain time series. A variant for spiking neurons is known as liquid state machines.

Neural History Compressor

The vanishing gradient problem of automatic differentiation or backpropagation in neural networks was partially overcome in 1992 by an early generative model called the neural history compressor, implemented as an unsupervised stack of recurrent neural networks (RNNs). The RNN at the input level learns to predict its next input from the previous input history. Only unpredictable inputs of some RNN in the hierarchy become inputs to the next higher level RNN which therefore recomputes its internal state only rarely. Each higher level RNN thus learns a compressed representation of the information in the RNN below. This is done such that the input sequence can be precisely reconstructed from the sequence representation at the highest level. The system effectively minimises the description length or the negative logarithm of the probability of the data. If there is a lot of learnable predictability in the incoming data sequence, then the highest level RNN can use supervised learning to easily classify even deep sequences with very long time intervals between important events. In 1993, such a system already solved a "Very Deep Learning" task that requires more than 1000 subsequent layers in an RNN unfolded in time.

It is also possible to distill the entire RNN hierarchy into only two RNNs called the "conscious" chunker (higher level) and the "subconscious" automatizer (lower level). Once the chunker has learned to predict and compress inputs that are still unpredictable by the automatizer, then the automatizer can be forced in the next learning phase to predict or imitate through special additional units the hidden units of the more slowly changing chunker. This makes it easy for the automatizer to learn appropriate, rarely changing memories across very long time intervals. This in turn helps the automatizer to make many of its once unpredictable inputs predictable, such that the chunker can focus on the remaining still unpredictable events, to compress the data even further.

Long Short-term Memory

Numerous researchers now use a deep learning RNN called the long short-term memory (LSTM) network, published by Hochreiter & Schmidhuber in 1997. It is a deep learning system that unlike traditional RNNs doesn't have the vanishing gradient problem (compare the section on training algorithms below). LSTM is normally augmented by recurrent gates called forget gates. LSTM RNNs prevent backpropagated errors from vanishing or exploding. Instead errors can flow backwards through unlimited numbers of virtual layers in LSTM RNNs unfolded in space. That is, LSTM can learn "Very Deep Learning" tasks that require memories of events that happened thousands or even millions of discrete time steps ago. Problem-specific LSTM-like topologies can be evolved. LSTM works even when there are long delays, and it can handle signals that have a mix of low and high frequency components.

Today, many applications use stacks of LSTM RNNs and train them by Connectionist Temporal Classification (CTC) to find an RNN weight matrix that maximizes the probability of the label sequences in a training set, given the corresponding input sequences. CTC achieves both alignment and recognition. Around 2007, LSTM started to revolutionise speech recognition, outperforming traditional models in certain speech applications. In 2009, CTC-trained LSTM was the first RNN to win pattern recognition contests, when it won several competitions in connected handwriting recognition. In 2014, the Chinese search giant Baidu used CTC-trained RNNs to break the Switchboard Hub5'00 speech recognition benchmark, without using any traditional speech processing methods. LSTM also improved large-vocabulary speech recognition, text-to-speech synthesis, also for Google Android, and photo-real talking heads. In 2015, Google's speech recognition reportedly experienced a dramatic performance jump of 49% through CTC-trained LSTM, which is now available through Google voice search to all smartphone users.

LSTM has also become very popular in the field of natural language processing. Unlike previous models based on HMMs and similar concepts, LSTM can learn to recognise context-sensitive languages. LSTM improved machine translation, Language Modeling and Multilingual Language Processing. LSTM combined with convolutional neural networks (CNNs) also improved automatic image captioning and a plethora of other applications.

Gated Recurrent Unit

Gated recurrent unit is one of the recurrent neural network introduced in 2014.

Bi-directional RNN

Invented by Schuster & Paliwal in 1997, bi-directional RNN or BRNN use a finite sequence to predict or label each element of the sequence based on both the past and the future context of the element. This is done by concatenating the outputs of two RNN, one processing the sequence from left to right, the other one from right to left. The combined outputs are the predictions of the teacher-given target signals. This technique proved to be especially useful when combined with LSTM RNN.

Continuous-time RNN

A continuous time recurrent neural network (CTRNN) is a dynamical systems model of biological neural networks. A CTRNN uses a system of ordinary differential equations to model the effects on a neuron of the incoming spike train.

For a neuron i in the network with action potential y_i the rate of change of activation is given by:

$$\tau_i \dot{y}_i = -y_i + \sum_{j=1}^{n} w_{ji}\sigma(y_j - \Theta_j) + I_i(t)$$

Where:

- τ_i : Time constant of postsynaptic node.

- y_i : Activation of postsynaptic node.

- $\dot{y}_i$: Rate of change of activation of postsynaptic node.

- w_{ji} : Weight of connection from pre to postsynaptic node.

- $\sigma(x)$: Sigmoid of x e.g. $\sigma(x) = 1/(1+e^{-x})$.

- y_j : Activation of presynaptic node.

- Θ_j : Bias of presynaptic node.

- $I_i(t)$: Input (if any) to node.

CTRNNs have frequently been applied in the field of evolutionary robotics, where they have been used to address, for example, vision, co-operation and minimally cognitive behaviour.

Note that by the Shannon sampling theorem, discrete time recurrent neural networks can be viewed as continuous time recurrent neural networks where the differential equation have transformed in an equivalent difference equation after that the postsynaptic node activation functions $y_i(t)$ have been low-pass filtered prior to sampling.

Hierarchical RNN

There are many instances of hierarchical RNN whose elements are connected in various ways to decompose hierarchical behavior into useful subprograms.

Recurrent Multilayer Perceptron

Generally, a Recurrent Multi-Layer Perceptron (RMLP) consists of a series of cascaded subnetworks, each of which consists of multiple layers of nodes. Each of these subnetworks is entirely feed-forward except for the last layer, which can have feedback connections among itself. Each of these subnets is connected only by feed forward connections.

Second Order RNN

Second order RNNs use higher order weights w_{ijk} instead of the standard w_{ij} weights, and inputs and states can be a product. This allows a direct mapping to a finite state machine both in training, stability, and representation. Long short-term memory is an example of this but has no such formal mappings or proof of stability.

Multiple Timescales Recurrent Neural Network (MTRNN) Model

MTRNN is a possible neural-based computational model that imitates to some extent the activity of the brain. It has the ability to simulate the functional hierarchy of the brain through self-organization that not only depends on spatial connection between neurons, but also on distinct types of neuron activities, each with distinct time properties. With such varied neuronal activities, continuous sequences of any set of behaviors are segmented into reusable primitives, which in turn are flexibly integrated into diverse sequential behaviors. The biological approval of such a type of hierarchy has been discussed on the memory-prediction theory of brain function by Jeff Hawkins in his book *On Intelligence*.

Pollack's Sequential Cascaded Networks

Neural Turing Machines

Neural Turing machine (NTMs) are a method of extending the capabilities of recurrent neural networks by coupling them to external memory resources, which they can interact with by attentional processes. The combined system is analogous to a Turing machine or Von Neumann architecture but is differentiable end-to-end, allowing it to be efficiently trained with gradient descent.

Neural Network Pushdown Automata

NNPDAs are similar to NTMs but tapes are replaced by analogue stacks that are differentiable and which are trained to control. In this way they are similar in complexity to recognizers of context free grammars (CFGs).

Bidirectional Associative Memory

First introduced by Kosko, BAM neural networks store associative data as a vector. The bi-directionality comes from passing information through a matrix and its transpose. Typically, bipolar encoding is preferred to binary encoding of the associative pairs. Recently, stochastic BAM models using Markov stepping were optimized for increased network stability and relevance to real-world applications.

Training

Gradient Descent

To minimize total error, gradient descent can be used to change each weight in proportion to the derivative of the error with respect to that weight, provided the non-linear activation functions are differentiable. Various methods for doing so were developed in the 1980s and early 1990s by Paul Werbos, Ronald J. Williams, Tony Robinson, Jürgen Schmidhuber, Sepp Hochreiter, Barak Pearlmutter, and others.

The standard method is called "backpropagation through time" or BPTT, and is a generalization of back-propagation for feed-forward networks, and like that method, is an instance of automatic differentiation in the reverse accumulation mode or Pontryagin's minimum principle. A more computationally expensive online variant is called "Real-Time Recurrent Learning" or RTRL, which is an instance of Automatic differentiation in the forward accumulation mode with stacked tangent vectors. Unlike BPTT this algorithm is *local in time but not local in space*.

In this context, *local in space* means that a unit's weight vector can be updated only using information stored in the connected units and the unit itself such that update complexity of a single unit is linear in the dimensionality of the weight vector. *Local in time* means that that the updates take place continually (on-line) and only depend on the most recent time step rather than on multiple time steps within a given time horizon as in BPTT. Biological neural networks appear to be local both with respect to time and space.

The downside of RTRL is that for recursively computing the partial derivatives, it has a time-complexity of O(number of hidden x number of weights) per time step for computing the Jacobian matrices, whereas BPTT only takes O(number of weights) per time step, at the cost, however, of storing all forward activations within the given time horizon.

There also is an online hybrid between BPTT and RTRL with intermediate complexity, and there are variants for continuous time. A major problem with gradient descent for standard RNN architectures is that error gradients vanish exponentially quickly with the size of the time lag between important events. The long short-term memory architecture together with a BPTT/RTRL hybrid learning method was introduced in an attempt to overcome these problems.

Moreover, the on-line algorithm called causal recursive BP (CRBP), implements and combines together BPTT and RTRL paradigms for locally recurrent network. It works with the most general locally recurrent networks. The CRBP algorithm can minimize the global error; this fact results in an improved stability of the algorithm, providing a unifying view on gradient calculation techniques for recurrent networks with local feedback.

An interesting approach to the computation of gradient information in RNNs with arbitrary architectures was proposed by Wan and Beaufays, is based on signal-flow graphs diagrammatic derivation to obtain the BPTT batch algorithm while, based on Lee theorem for networks sensitivity calculations, its fast online version was proposed by Campolucci, Uncini and Piazza.

Global Optimization Methods

Training the weights in a neural network can be modeled as a non-linear global optimization problem. A target function can be formed to evaluate the fitness or error of a particular weight vector as follows: First, the weights in the network are set according to the weight vector. Next, the network is evaluated against the training sequence. Typically, the sum-squared-difference between the predictions and the target values specified in the training sequence is used to represent the error of the current weight vector. Arbitrary global optimization techniques may then be used to minimize this target function.

The most common global optimization method for training RNNs is genetic algorithms, especially in unstructured networks.

Initially, the genetic algorithm is encoded with the neural network weights in a predefined manner where one gene in the chromosome represents one weight link, henceforth; the whole network is represented as a single chromosome. The fitness function is evaluated as follows: 1) each weight encoded in the chromosome is assigned to the respective weight link of the network; 2) the training set of examples is then presented to the network which propagates the input signals forward; 3) the mean-squared-error is returned to the fitness function; 4) this function will then drive the genetic selection process.

There are many chromosomes that make up the population; therefore, many different neural networks are evolved until a stopping criterion is satisfied. A common stopping scheme is: 1) when the neural network has learnt a certain percentage of the training data or 2) when the minimum value of the mean-squared-error is satisfied or 3) when the maximum number of training generations has been reached. The stopping criterion is evaluated by the fitness function as it gets the reciprocal of the mean-squared-error from each neural network during training. Therefore, the goal of the genetic algorithm is to maximize the fitness function, hence, reduce the mean-squared-error.

Other global (and/or evolutionary) optimization techniques may be used to seek a good set of weights such as simulated annealing or particle swarm optimization.

Related Fields and Models

RNNs may behave chaotically. In such cases, dynamical systems theory may be used for analysis.

Recurrent neural networks are in fact recursive neural networks with a particular structure: that of a linear chain. Whereas recursive neural networks operate on any hierarchical structure, combining child representations into parent representations, recurrent neural networks operate on the linear progression of time, combining the previous time step and a hidden representation into the representation for the current time step.

In particular, recurrent neural networks can appear as nonlinear versions of finite impulse response and infinite impulse response filters and also as a nonlinear autoregressive exogenous model (NARX).

Common RNN Libraries

- Apache Singa.

- Caffe: Created by the Berkeley Vision and Learning Center (BVLC). It supports both CPU and GPU. Developed in C++, and has Python and MATLAB wrappers.

- Deeplearning4j: Deep learning in Java and Scala on multi-GPU-enabled Spark. A general-purpose deep learning library for the JVM production stack running on a C++ scientific computing engine. Allows the creation of custom layers. Integrates with Hadoop and Kafka.

- Keras.

- Microsoft Cognitive Toolkit.

- TensorFlow: Apache 2.0-licensed Theano-like library with support for CPU, GPU and Google's proprietary TPU, mobile.

- Theano: The reference deep-learning library for Python with an API largely compatible with the popular NumPy library. Allows user to write symbolic mathematical expressions, then automatically generates their derivatives, saving the user from having to code gradients or backpropagation. These symbolic expressions are automatically compiled to CUDA code for a fast, on-the-GPU implementation.

- Torch: A scientific computing framework with wide support for machine learning algorithms, written in C and lua. The main author is Ronan Collobert.

Neural Network Software

Neural network software is used to simulate, research, develop, and apply artificial neural networks, software concepts adapted from biological neural networks, and, in some cases, a wider array of adaptive systems such as artificial intelligence and machine learning.

Simulators

Neural network simulators are software applications that are used to simulate the behavior of artificial or biological neural networks. They focus on one or a limited number of specific types of neural networks. They are typically stand-alone and not intended to produce general neural networks that can be integrated in other software. Simulators usually have some form of built-in visualization to monitor the training process. Some simulators also visualize the physical structure of the neural network.

Research Simulators

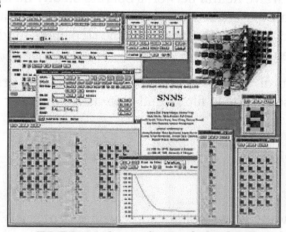

SNNS research neural network simulator.

Historically, the most common type of neural network software was intended for researching neural network structures and algorithms. The primary purpose of this type of software is, through simulation, to gain a better understanding of the behavior and properties of neural networks. Today in the study of artificial neural networks, simulators have largely been replaced by more general component based development environments as research platforms.

Commonly used artificial neural network simulators include the Stuttgart Neural Network Simulator (SNNS), Emergent and Neural Lab.

In the study of biological neural networks however, simulation software is still the only available approach. In such simulators the physical biological and chemical properties of neural tissue, as well as the electromagnetic impulses between the neurons are studied.

Commonly used biological network simulators include Neuron, GENESIS, NEST and Brian.

Data Analysis Simulators

Unlike the research simulators, data analysis simulators are intended for practical applications of artificial neural networks. Their primary focus is on data mining and forecasting. Data analysis simulators usually have some form of preprocessing capabilities. Unlike the more general development environments data analysis simulators use a relatively simple static neural network that can be configured. A majority of the data analysis simulators on the market use backpropagating networks or self-organizing maps as their core. The advantage of this type of software is that it is relatively easy to use. Neural Designer is one example of a data analysis simulator.

Simulators for Teaching Neural Network Theory

When the Parallel Distributed Processing volumes were released in 1986-87, they provided some relatively simple software. The original PDP software did not require any programming skills, which led to its adoption by a wide variety of researchers in diverse fields. The original PDP software was developed into a more powerful package called PDP++, which in turn has become an even more powerful platform called Emergent. With each development, the software has become more powerful, but also more daunting for use by beginners.

In 1997, the tLearn software was released to accompany a book. This was a return to the idea of providing a small, user-friendly, simulator that was designed with the novice in mind. tLearn allowed basic feed forward networks, along with simple recurrent networks, both of which can be trained by the simple back propagation algorithm. tLearn has not been updated since 1999.

In 2011, the Basic Prop simulator was released. Basic Prop is a self-contained application, distributed as a platform neutral JAR file, that provides much of the same simple functionality as tLearn.

In 2012, Wintempla included a namespace called NN with a set of C++ classes to implement: feed forward networks, probabilistic neural networks and Kohonen networks. Neural Lab is based on Wintempla classes. Neural Lab tutorial and Wintempla tutorial explains some of these clases for neural networks. The main disadvantage of Wintempla is that it compiles only with Microsoft Visual Studio.

Development Environments

Development environments for neural networks differ from the software described above primarily on two accounts – they can be used to develop custom types of neural networks and they support deployment of the neural network outside the environment. In some cases they have advanced preprocessing, analysis and visualization capabilities.

Component Based

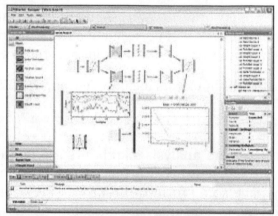

Peltarion Synapse component based development environment.

A more modern type of development environments that are currently favored in both industrial and scientific use are based on a component based paradigm. The neural network is constructed by connecting adaptive filter components in a pipe filter flow. This allows for greater flexibility as custom networks can be built as well as custom components used by the network. In many cases this allows a combination of adaptive and non-adaptive components to work together. The data flow is controlled by a control system which is exchangeable as well as the adaptation algorithms. The other important feature is deployment capabilities.

With the advent of component-based frameworks such as .NET and Java, component based development environments are capable of deploying the developed neural network to these frameworks as inheritable components. In addition some software can also deploy these components to several platforms, such as embedded systems.

Component based development environments include: Peltarion Synapse, NeuroDimension NeuroSolutions, Scientific Software Neuro Laboratory, and the LIONsolver integrated software. Free open source component based environments include Encog and Neuroph.

Criticism

A disadvantage of component-based development environments is that they are more complex than simulators. They require more learning to fully operate and are more complicated to develop.

Custom Neural Networks

The majority implementations of neural networks available are however custom implementations in various programming languages and on various platforms. Basic types of neural networks are simple to implement directly. There are also many programming libraries that contain neural network functionality and that can be used in custom implementations (such as tensorflow, theano, etc., typically providing bindings to languages such as python, C++, Java).

Standards

In order for neural network models to be shared by different applications, a common language is necessary. The Predictive Model Markup Language (PMML) has been proposed to address this need. PMML is an XML-based language which provides a way for applications to define and share neural network models (and other data mining models) between PMML compliant applications.

PMML provides applications a vendor-independent method of defining models so that proprietary issues and incompatibilities are no longer a barrier to the exchange of models between applications. It allows users to develop models within one vendor's application, and use other vendors' applications to visualize, analyze, evaluate or otherwise use the models. Previously, this was very difficult, but with PMML, the exchange of models between compliant applications is now straightforward.

PMMl Consumers and Producers

A range of products are being offered to produce and consume PMML. This ever-growing list includes the following neural network products:

- R: produces PMML for neural nets and other machine learning models via the package pmml.

- SAS Enterprise Miner: produces PMML for several mining models, including neural networks, linear and logistic regression, decision trees, and other data mining models.

- SPSS: produces PMML for neural networks as well as many other mining models.

- STATISTICA: produces PMML for neural networks, data mining models and traditional statistical models.

Machine Learning

Machine learning is the subfield of computer science that, according to Arthur Samuel in 1959, gives "computers the ability to learn without being explicitly programmed." Evolved from the study of pattern recognition and computational learning theory in artificial intelligence, machine learning explores the study and construction of algorithms that can learn from and make predictions on data – such algorithms overcome following strictly static program instructions by making data-driven predictions or decisions, through building a model from sample inputs. Machine learning is employed in a range of computing tasks where designing and programming explicit algorithms with good performance is difficult or unfeasible; example applications include email filtering, detection of network intruders or malicious insiders working towards a data breach, optical character recognition (OCR), learning to rank and computer vision.

Machine learning is closely related to (and often overlaps with) computational statistics, which also focuses on prediction-making through the use of computers. It has strong ties to mathematical optimization, which delivers methods, theory and application domains to the field. Machine learning is sometimes conflated with data mining, where the latter subfield focuses more on exploratory data analysis and is known as unsupervised learning. Machine learning can also be unsupervised and be used to learn and establish baseline behavioral profiles for various entities and then used to find meaningful anomalies.

Within the field of data analytics, machine learning is a method used to devise complex models and algorithms that lend themselves to prediction; in commercial use, this is known as predictive analytics. These analytical models allow researchers, data scientists, engineers, and analysts to "produce reliable, repeatable decisions and results" and uncover "hidden insights" through learning from historical relationships and trends in the data.

As of 2016, machine learning is a buzzword, and according to the Gartner hype cycle of 2016, at its peak of inflated expectations. Because finding patterns is hard, often not enough training data is available, and also because of the high expectations it often fails to deliver.

Overview

Tom M. Mitchell provided a widely quoted, more formal definition: "A computer program is said to learn from experience E with respect to some class of tasks T and performance measure P if its performance at tasks in T, as measured by P, improves with experience E." This definition is notable for its defining machine learning in fundamentally operational rather than cognitive terms, thus following Alan Turing's proposal in his paper "Computing Machinery and Intelligence", that the question "Can machines think?" be replaced with the question "Can machines do what we (as thinking entities) can do?". In the proposal he explores the various characteristics that could be possessed by a *thinking machine* and the various implications in constructing one.

Types of Problems and Tasks

Machine learning tasks are typically classified into three broad categories, depending on the nature of the learning "signal" or "feedback" available to a learning system. These are:

- Supervised learning: The computer is presented with example inputs and their desired outputs, given by a "teacher", and the goal is to learn a general rule that maps inputs to outputs.

- Unsupervised learning: No labels are given to the learning algorithm, leaving it on its own to find structure in its input. Unsupervised learning can be a goal in itself (discovering hidden patterns in data) or a means towards an end (feature learning).

- Reinforcement learning: A computer program interacts with a dynamic environment in which it must perform a certain goal (such as driving a vehicle or playing a game against an opponent). The program is provided feedback in terms of rewards and punishments as it navigates its problem space.

Between supervised and unsupervised learning is semi-supervised learning, where the teacher gives an incomplete training signal: a training set with some (often many) of the target outputs missing. Transduction is a special case of this principle where the entire set of problem instances is known at learning time, except that part of the targets are missing.

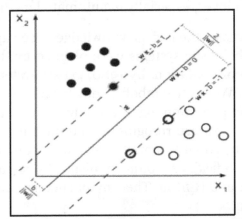

A support vector machine is a classifier that divides its input space into two regions, separated by a linear boundary. Here, it has learned to distinguish black and white circles.

Among other categories of machine learning problems, learning to learn learns its own inductive bias based on previous experience. Developmental learning, elaborated for robot learning, generates its own sequences (also called curriculum) of learning situations to cumulatively acquire repertoires of novel skills through autonomous self-exploration and social interaction with human teachers and using guidance mechanisms such as active learning, maturation, motor synergies, and imitation.

Another categorization of machine learning tasks arises when one considers the desired *output* of a machine-learned system:

- In classification, inputs are divided into two or more classes, and the learner must produce a model that assigns unseen inputs to one or more (multi-label classification) of these classes. This is typically tackled in a supervised way. Spam filtering is an example of classification, where the inputs are email (or other) messages and the classes are "spam" and "not spam".

- In regression, also a supervised problem, the outputs are continuous rather than discrete.

- In clustering, a set of inputs is to be divided into groups. Unlike in classification, the groups are not known beforehand, making this typically an unsupervised task.

- Density estimation finds the distribution of inputs in some space.

- Dimensionality reduction simplifies inputs by mapping them into a lower-dimensional space. Topic modeling is a related problem, where a program is given a list of human language documents and is tasked to find out which documents cover similar topics.

History and Relationships to Other Fields

As a scientific endeavour, machine learning grew out of the quest for artificial intelligence. Already in the early days of AI as an academic discipline, some researchers were interested in having machines learn from data. They attempted to approach the problem with various symbolic methods, as well as what were then termed "neural networks"; these were mostly perceptrons and other models that were later found to be reinventions of the generalized linear models of statistics. Probabilistic reasoning was also employed, especially in automated medical diagnosis.

However, an increasing emphasis on the logical, knowledge-based approach caused a rift between AI and machine learning. Probabilistic systems were plagued by theoretical and practical problems of data acquisition and representation. By 1980, expert systems had come to dominate AI, and statistics was out of favor. Work on symbolic/knowledge-based learning did continue within AI, leading to inductive logic programming, but the more statistical line of research was now outside the field of AI proper, in pattern recognition and information retrieval. Neural networks research had been abandoned by AI and computer science around the same time. This line, too, was continued outside the AI/CS field, as "connectionism", by researchers from other disciplines including Hopfield, Rumelhart and Hinton. Their main success came in the mid-1980s with the reinvention of backpropagation.

Machine learning, reorganized as a separate field, started to flourish in the 1990s. The field changed its goal from achieving artificial intelligence to tackling solvable problems of a practical nature. It shifted focus away from the symbolic approaches it had inherited from AI, and toward methods and models borrowed from statistics and probability theory. It also benefited from the increasing availability of digitized information, and the possibility to distribute that via the Internet.

Machine learning and data mining often employ the same methods and overlap significantly, but while machine learning focuses on prediction, based on *known* properties learned from the training data, data mining focuses on the discovery of (previously) *unknown* properties in the data (this is the analysis step of Knowledge Discovery in Databases). Data mining uses many machine learning methods, but with different goals; on the other hand, machine learning also employs data mining methods as "unsupervised learning" or as a preprocessing step to improve learner accuracy. Much of the confusion between these two research communities (which do often have separate conferences and separate journals, ECML PKDD being a major exception) comes from the basic assumptions they work with: in machine learning, performance is usually evaluated with respect to the ability to *reproduce known* knowledge, while in Knowledge Discovery and Data Mining (KDD) the key task is the discovery of previously *unknown* knowledge. Evaluated with respect to known knowledge, an uninformed (unsupervised) method will easily be outperformed by other supervised methods, while in a typical KDD task, supervised methods cannot be used due to the unavailability of training data.

Machine learning also has intimate ties to optimization: many learning problems are formulated as minimization of some loss function on a training set of examples. Loss functions express the discrepancy between the predictions of the model being trained and the actual problem instances (for example, in classification, one wants to assign a label to instances, and models are trained to correctly predict the pre-assigned labels of a set examples). The difference between the two fields arises from the goal of generalization: while optimization algorithms can minimize the loss on a training set, machine learning is concerned with minimizing the loss on unseen samples.

Relation to Statistics

Machine learning and statistics are closely related fields. According to Michael I. Jordan, the ideas of machine learning, from methodological principles to theoretical tools, have had a long pre-history in statistics. He also suggested the term data science as a placeholder to call the overall field.

Leo Breiman distinguished two statistical modelling paradigms: data model and algorithmic model, wherein 'algorithmic model' means more or less the machine learning algorithms like Random forest.

Some statisticians have adopted methods from machine learning, leading to a combined field that they call *statistical learning*.

Theory

A core objective of a learner is to generalize from its experience. Generalization in this context is the ability of a learning machine to perform accurately on new, unseen examples/tasks after having experienced a learning data set. The training examples come from some generally unknown probability distribution (considered representative of the space of occurrences) and the learner has to build a general model about this space that enables it to produce sufficiently accurate predictions in new cases.

The computational analysis of machine learning algorithms and their performance is a branch of theoretical computer science known as computational learning theory. Because training sets are finite and the future is uncertain, learning theory usually does not yield guarantees of the performance of algorithms. Instead, probabilistic bounds on the performance are quite common. The bias–variance decomposition is one way to quantify generalization error.

For the best performance in the context of generalization, the complexity of the hypothesis should match the complexity of the function underlying the data. If the hypothesis is less complex than the function, then the model has underfit the data. If the complexity of the model is increased in response, then the training error decreases. But if the hypothesis is too complex, then the model is subject to overfitting and generalization will be poorer.

In addition to performance bounds, computational learning theorists study the time complexity and feasibility of learning. In computational learning theory, a computation is considered feasible if it can be done in polynomial time. There are two kinds of time complexity results. Positive results show that a certain class of functions can be learned in polynomial time. Negative results show that certain classes cannot be learned in polynomial time.

Approaches

Decision Tree Learning

Decision tree learning uses a decision tree as a predictive model, which maps observations about an item to conclusions about the item's target value.

Association Rule Learning

Association rule learning is a method for discovering interesting relations between variables in large databases.

Artificial Neural Networks

An artificial neural network (ANN) learning algorithm, usually called "neural network" (NN), is a learning algorithm that is inspired by the structure and functional aspects of biological neural networks. Computations are structured in terms of an interconnected group of artificial neurons, processing information using a connectionist approach to computation. Modern neural networks are non-linear statistical data modeling tools. They are usually used to model complex relationships between inputs and outputs, to find patterns in data, or to capture the statistical structure in an unknown joint probability distribution between observed variables.

Deep Learning

Falling hardware prices and the development of GPUs for personal use in the last few years have contributed to the development of the concept of Deep learning which consists of multiple hidden layers in an artificial neural network. This approach tries to model the way the human brain processes light and sound into vision and hearing. Some successful applications of deep learning are computer vision and speech recognition.

Inductive Logic Programming

Inductive logic programming (ILP) is an approach to rule learning using logic programming as a uniform representation for input examples, background knowledge, and hypotheses. Given an encoding of the known background knowledge and a set of examples represented as a logical database of facts, an ILP system will derive a hypothesized logic program that entails all positive and no negative examples. Inductive programming is a related field that considers any kind of programming languages for representing hypotheses (and not only logic programming), such as functional programs.

Support Vector Machines

Support vector machines (SVMs) are a set of related supervised learning methods used for classification and regression. Given a set of training examples, each marked as belonging to one of two categories, an SVM training algorithm builds a model that predicts whether a new example falls into one category or the other.

Clustering

Cluster analysis is the assignment of a set of observations into subsets (called *clusters*) so that observations within the same cluster are similar according to some predesignated criterion or criteria, while observations drawn from different clusters are dissimilar. Different clustering techniques make different assumptions on the structure of the data, often defined by some *similarity metric* and evaluated for example by *internal compactness* (similarity between members of the same cluster) and *separation* between different clusters. Other methods are based on *estimated density* and *graph connectivity*. Clustering is a method of unsupervised learning, and a common technique for statistical data analysis.

Bayesian Networks

A Bayesian network, belief network or directed acyclic graphical model is a probabilistic graphical model that represents a set of random variables and their conditional independencies via a directed acyclic graph (DAG). For example, a Bayesian network could represent the probabilistic relationships between diseases and symptoms. Given symptoms, the network can be used to compute the probabilities of the presence of various diseases. Efficient algorithms exist that perform inference and learning.

Reinforcement Learning

Reinforcement learning is concerned with how an *agent* ought to take *actions* in an *environment* so as to maximize some notion of long-term *reward*. Reinforcement learning algorithms attempt to find a *policy* that maps *states* of the world to the actions the agent ought to take in those states. Reinforcement learning differs from the supervised learning problem in that correct input/output pairs are never presented, nor sub-optimal actions explicitly corrected.

Representation Learning

Several learning algorithms, mostly unsupervised learning algorithms, aim at discovering better representations of the inputs provided during training. Classical examples include principal components analysis and cluster analysis. Representation learning algorithms often attempt to preserve the information in their input but transform it in a way that makes it useful, often as a pre-processing step before performing classification or predictions, allowing reconstruction of the inputs coming from the unknown data generating distribution, while not being necessarily faithful for configurations that are implausible under that distribution.

Manifold learning algorithms attempt to do so under the constraint that the learned representation is low-dimensional. Sparse coding algorithms attempt to do so under the constraint that the learned representation is sparse (has many zeros). Multilinear subspace learning algorithms aim to learn low-dimensional representations directly from tensor representations for multidimensional data, without reshaping them into (high-dimensional) vectors. Deep learning algorithms discover multiple levels of representation, or a hierarchy of features, with higher-level, more abstract features defined in terms of (or generating) lower-level features. It has been argued that an intelligent machine is one that learns a representation that disentangles the underlying factors of variation that explain the observed data.

Similarity and Metric Learning

In this problem, the learning machine is given pairs of examples that are considered similar and pairs of less similar objects. It then needs to learn a similarity function (or a distance metric function) that can predict if new objects are similar. It is sometimes used in Recommendation systems.

Sparse Dictionary Learning

In this method, a datum is represented as a linear combination of basis functions, and the coefficients are assumed to be sparse. Let x be a d-dimensional datum, D be a d by n matrix, where each column of D represents a basis function. r is the coefficient to represent x using D. Mathematically, sparse dictionary learning means solving $x \approx Dr$ where r is sparse. Generally speaking, n is assumed to be larger than d to allow the freedom for a sparse representation.

Learning a dictionary along with sparse representations is strongly NP-hard and also difficult to solve approximately. A popular heuristic method for sparse dictionary learning is K-SVD.

Sparse dictionary learning has been applied in several contexts. In classification, the problem is to determine which classes a previously unseen datum belongs to. Suppose a dictionary for each class has already been built. Then a new datum is associated with the class such that it's best sparsely represented by the corresponding dictionary. Sparse dictionary learning has also been applied in image de-noising. The key idea is that a clean image patch can be sparsely represented by an image dictionary, but the noise cannot.

Genetic Algorithms

A genetic algorithm (GA) is a search heuristic that mimics the process of natural selection, and uses methods such as mutation and crossover to generate new genotype in the hope of finding good solutions to a given problem. In machine learning, genetic algorithms found some uses in the 1980s and 1990s. Vice versa, machine learning techniques have been used to improve the performance of genetic and evolutionary algorithms.

Rule-based Machine Learning

Rule-based machine learning is a general term for any machine learning method that identifies, learns, or evolves `rules' to store, manipulate or apply, knowledge. The defining characteristic of a rule-based machine learner is the identification and utilization of a set of relational rules that collectively represent the knowledge captured by the system. This is in contrast to other machine learners that commonly identify a singular model that can be universally applied to any instance in order to make a prediction. Rule-based machine learning approaches include learning classifier systems, association rule learning, and artificial immune systems.

Learning Classifier Systems

Learning classifier systems (LCS) are a family of rule-based machine learning algorithms that combine a discovery component (e.g. typically a genetic algorithm) with a learning component (performing either supervised learning, reinforcement learning, or unsupervised learning). They seek to identify a set of context-dependent rules that collectively store and apply knowledge in a piecewise manner in order to make predictions.

Applications

Applications for machine learning include:

- Adaptive websites
- Affective computing
- Bioinformatics
- Brain-machine interfaces
- Cheminformatics

- Classifying DNA sequences
- Computational anatomy
- Computer vision, including object recognition
- Detecting credit card fraud
- Game playing
- Information retrieval
- Internet fraud detection
- Marketing
- Machine learning control
- Machine perception
- Medical diagnosis
- Economics
- Natural language processing
- Natural language understanding
- Optimization and metaheuristic
- Online advertising
- Recommender systems
- Robot locomotion
- Search engines
- Sentiment analysis (or opinion mining)
- Sequence mining
- Software engineering
- Speech and handwriting recognition
- Financial market analysis
- Structural health monitoring
- Syntactic pattern recognition
- User behavior analytics
- Translation

In 2006, the online movie company Netflix held the first "Netflix Prize" competition to find a program to better predict user preferences and improve the accuracy on its existing Cinematch movie recommendation algorithm by at least 10%. A joint team made up of researchers from AT&T

Labs-Research in collaboration with the teams Big Chaos and Pragmatic Theory built an ensemble model to win the Grand Prize in 2009 for $1 million. Shortly after the prize was awarded, Netflix realized that viewers' ratings were not the best indicators of their viewing patterns ("everything is a recommendation") and they changed their recommendation engine accordingly.

In 2010 The Wall Street Journal wrote about money management firm Rebellion Research's use of machine learning to predict economic movements. The article describes Rebellion Research's prediction of the financial crisis and economic recovery.

In 2012 co-founder of Sun Microsystems Vinod Khosla predicted that 80% of medical doctors jobs would be lost in the next two decades to automated machine learning medical diagnostic software.

In 2014 it has been reported that a machine learning algorithm has been applied in Art History to study fine art paintings, and that it may have revealed previously unrecognized influences between artists.

Model Assessments

Classification machine learning models can be validated by accuracy estimation techniques like the Holdout method, which splits the data in a training and test set (conventionally 2/3 training set and 1/3 test set designation) and evaluates the performance of the training model on the test set. In comparison, the N-fold-cross-validation method randomly splits the data in k subsets where the k-1 instances of the data are used to train the model while the kth instance is used to test the predictive ability of the training model. In addition to the holdout and cross-validation methods, bootstrap, which samples n instances with replacement from the dataset, can be used to assess model accuracy. In addition to accuracy, sensitivity and specificity (True Positive Rate: TPR and True Negative Rate: TNR, respectively) can provide modes of model assessment. Similarly False Positive Rate (FPR) as well as the False Negative Rate (FNR) can be computed. Receiver operating characteristic (ROC) along with the accompanying Area Under the ROC Curve (AUC) offer additional tools for classification model assessment. Higher AUC is associated with a better performing model.

Ethics

Machine Learning poses a host of ethical questions. Systems which are trained on datasets collected with biases may exhibit these biases upon use, thus digitizing cultural prejudices. Responsible collection of data thus is a critical part of machine learning.

Because language contains biases, machines trained on language corpora will necessarily also learn bias.

Perceptron

In machine learning, the perceptron is an algorithm for supervised learning of binary classifiers (functions that can decide whether an input, represented by a vector of numbers, belongs to some specific class or not). It is a type of linear classifier, i.e. a classification algorithm that makes its predictions based on a linear predictor function combining a set of weights with the feature vector. The algorithm allows for online learning, in that it processes elements in the training set one at a time.

The perceptron algorithm dates back to the late 1950s; its first implementation, in custom hardware, was one of the first artificial neural networks to be produced.

History

The Mark I Perceptron machine was the first implementation of the perceptron algorithm. The machine was connected to a camera that used 20×20 cadmium sulfide photocells to produce a 400-pixel image. The main visible feature is a patchboard that allowed experimentation with different combinations of input features. To the right of that are arrays of potentiometers that implemented the adaptive weights.

The perceptron algorithm was invented in 1957 at the Cornell Aeronautical Laboratory by Frank Rosenblatt, funded by the United States Office of Naval Research. The perceptron was intended to be a machine, rather than a program, and while its first implementation was in software for the IBM 704, it was subsequently implemented in custom-built hardware as the "Mark 1 perceptron". This machine was designed for image recognition: it had an array of 400 photocells, randomly connected to the "neurons". Weights were encoded in potentiometers, and weight updates during learning were performed by electric motors.

In a 1958 press conference organized by the US Navy, Rosenblatt made statements about the perceptron that caused a heated controversy among the fledgling AI community; based on Rosenblatt's statements, *The New York Times* reported the perceptron to be "the embryo of an electronic computer that [the Navy] expects will be able to walk, talk, see, write, reproduce itself and be conscious of its existence."

Although the perceptron initially seemed promising, it was quickly proved that perceptrons could not be trained to recognise many classes of patterns. This caused the field of neural network research to stagnate for many years, before it was recognised that a feedforward neural network with two or more layers (also called a multilayer perceptron) had far greater processing power than perceptrons with one layer (also called a single layer perceptron). Single layer perceptrons are only capable of learning linearly separable patterns; in 1969 a famous book entitled *Perceptrons* by Marvin Minsky and Seymour Papert showed that it was impossible for these classes of network to learn an XOR function. It is often believed that they also conjectured (incorrectly) that a similar result would hold for a multi-layer perceptron network. However, this is not true, as both Minsky and Papert already knew that multi-layer perceptrons were capable of producing an XOR function. Three years later Stephen Grossberg published a series of papers introducing networks capable of modelling differential, contrast-enhancing and XOR functions. (The papers were published in 1972 and 1973, see e.g.:*Grossberg (1973). "Contour enhancement, short-term memory, and constancies in reverberating neural networks" (PDF). Studies in Applied Mathematics. 52: 213–257.*). Nevertheless, the often-miscited Minsky/Papert text caused a significant decline in interest and funding of neural network research. It took ten more years until neural network research experienced a resurgence in the 1980s. This text was reprinted in 1987 as "Perceptrons - Expanded Edition" where some errors in the original text are shown and corrected.

The kernel perceptron algorithm was already introduced in 1964 by Aizerman et al. Margin bounds guarantees were given for the Perceptron algorithm in the general non-separable case first by Freund and Schapire (1998), and more recently by Mohri and Rostamizadeh (2013) who extend previous results and give new L1 bounds.

Definition

In the modern sense, the perceptron is an algorithm for learning a binary classifier: a function that maps its input x (a real-valued vector) to an output value $f(x)$ (a single binary value):

$$f(x) = \begin{cases} 1 & \text{if } w \cdot x + b > 0 \\ 0 & \text{otherwise} \end{cases}$$

where w is a vector of real-valued weights, $w \cdot x$ is the dot product $\sum_{i=1}^{m} w_i x_i$, where m is the number of inputs to the perceptron and b is the *bias*. The bias shifts the decision boundary away from the origin and does not depend on any input value.

The value of $f(x)$ (0 or 1) is used to classify x as either a positive or a negative instance, in the case of a binary classification problem. If b is negative, then the weighted combination of inputs must produce a positive value greater than $|b|$ in order to push the classifier neuron over the 0 threshold. Spatially, the bias alters the position (though not the orientation) of the decision boundary. The perceptron learning algorithm does not terminate if the learning set is not linearly separable. If the vectors are not linearly separable learning will never reach a point where all vectors are classified properly. The most famous example of the perceptron's inability to solve problems with linearly nonseparable vectors is the Boolean exclusive-or problem. The solution spaces of decision boundaries for all binary functions and learning behaviors are studied in the reference.

In the context of neural networks, a perceptron is an artificial neuron using the Heaviside step function as the activation function. The perceptron algorithm is also termed the single-layer perceptron, to distinguish it from a multilayer perceptron, which is a misnomer for a more complicated neural network. As a linear classifier, the single-layer perceptron is the simplest feedforward neural network.

Learning Algorithm

Below is an example of a learning algorithm for a (single-layer) perceptron. For multilayer perceptrons, where a hidden layer exists, more sophisticated algorithms such as backpropagation must be used. Alternatively, methods such as the delta rule can be used if the function is non-linear and differentiable, although the one below will work as well.

When multiple perceptrons are combined in an artificial neural network, each output neuron operates independently of all the others; thus, learning each output can be considered in isolation.

Definitions

We first define some variables:

- $y = f(\mathbf{z})$ denotes the *output* from the perceptron for an input vector $\mathbf{z}$.

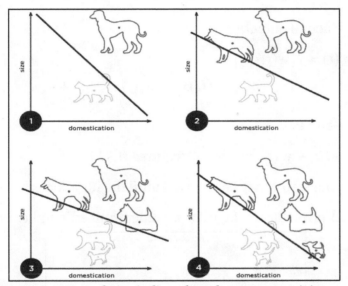

A diagram showing a perceptron updating its linear boundary as more training examples are added.

- $D = \{(\mathbf{x}_1, d_1), \ldots, (\mathbf{x}_s, d_s)\}$ is the *training set* of s samples, where:

  o $\mathbf{x}_j$ is the n-dimensional input vector.

  o d_j is the desired output value of the perceptron for that input.

We show the values of the features as follows:

- $x_{j,i}$ is the value of the ith feature of the jth training *input vector*.

- $x_{j,0} = 1$.

To represent the weights:

- w_i is the ith value in the *weight vector*, to be multiplied by the value of the ith input feature.

- Because $x_{j,0} = 1$, the w_0 is effectively a bias that we use instead of the bias constant b.

To show the time-dependence of w, we use:

- $w_i(t)$ is the weight i at time t.

Unlike other linear classification algorithms such as logistic regression, there is no need for a *learning rate* in the perceptron algorithm. This is because multiplying the update by any constant simply rescales the weights but never changes the sign of the prediction.

Steps

1. Initialize the weights and the threshold. Weights may be initialized to 0 or to a small random value. In the example below, we use 0.

2. For each example j in our training set D, perform the following steps over the input $\mathbf{x}_j$ and desired output d_j :

   a. Calculate the actual output:

   $$y_j(t) = f[\mathbf{w}(t) \cdot \mathbf{x}_j]$$
   $$= f[w_0(t)x_{j,0} + w_1(t)x_{j,1} + w_2(t)x_{j,2} + \cdots + w_n(t)x_{j,n}]$$

   b. Update the weights:

   $$w_i(t+1) = w_i(t) + (d_j - y_j(t))x_{j,i} \text{ , for all features } 0 \leq i \leq n.$$

3. For offline learning, the step 2 may be repeated until the iteration error $\dfrac{1}{s}\sum_{j=1}^{s}|d_j - y_j(t)|$ is less than a user-specified error threshold γ, or a predetermined number of iterations have been completed.

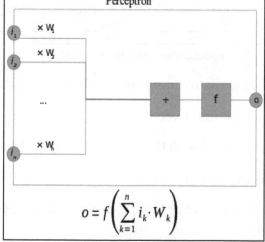

The appropriate weights are applied to the inputs, and the resulting weighted sum passed to a function that produces the output o.

The algorithm updates the weights after steps 2a and 2b. These weights are immediately applied to a pair in the training set, and subsequently updated, rather than waiting until all pairs in the training set have undergone these steps.

Convergence

The perceptron is a linear classifier, therefore it will never get to the state with all the input vectors classified correctly if the training set D is not linearly separable, i.e. if the positive examples can not be separated from the negative examples by a hyperplane. In this case, no "approximate" solution will be gradually approached under the standard learning algorithm, but instead learning will fail completely. Hence, if linear separability of the training set is not known a priori, one of the training variants below should be used.

But if the training set *is* linearly separable, then the perceptron is guaranteed to converge, and there is an upper bound on the number of times the perceptron will adjust its weights during the training.

Suppose that the input vectors from the two classes can be separated by a hyperplane with a margin γ, i.e. there exists a weight vector $\mathbf{w}, \|\mathbf{w}\|=1$, and a bias term b such that $\mathbf{w} \cdot \mathbf{x}_j > \gamma$ for all $j : d_j = 1$ and $\mathbf{w} \cdot \mathbf{x}_j < -\gamma$ for all $j : d_j = 0$. And also let R denote the maximum norm of an input vector. Novikoff (1962) proved that in this case the perceptron algorithm converges after making $O(R^2 / \gamma^2)$ updates. The idea of the proof is that the weight vector is always adjusted by a bounded amount in a direction with which it has a negative dot product, and thus can be bounded above by

$O\left(\sqrt{t}\right)$ where t is the number of changes to the weight vector. But it can also be bounded below

by $O(t)$ because if there exists an (unknown) satisfactory weight vector, then every change makes progress in this (unknown) direction by a positive amount that depends only on the input vector.

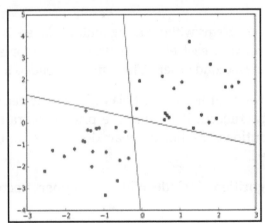

Two classes of points, and two of the infinitely many linear boundaries that separate them. Even though the boundaries are at nearly right angles to one another, the perceptron algorithm has no way of choosing between them.

While the perceptron algorithm is guaranteed to converge on *some* solution in the case of a linearly separable training set, it may still pick *any* solution and problems may admit many solutions of varying quality. The *perceptron of optimal stability*, nowadays better known as the linear support vector machine, was designed to solve this problem.

Variants

The pocket algorithm with ratchet (Gallant, 1990) solves the stability problem of perceptron learning by keeping the best solution seen so far "in its pocket". The pocket algorithm then returns the solution in the pocket, rather than the last solution. It can be used also for non-separable data sets, where the aim is to find a perceptron with a small number of misclassifications. However, these solutions appear purely stochastically and hence the pocket algorithm neither approaches them gradually in the course of learning, nor are they guaranteed to show up within a given number of learning steps.

The Maxover algorithm (Wendemuth, 1995) is "robust" in the sense that it will converge regardless of (prior) knowledge of linear separability of the data set. In the linear separable case, it will solve the training problem – if desired, even with optimal stability (maximum margin between the classes). For non-separable data sets, it will return a solution with a small number of misclassifications. In all cases, the algorithm gradually approaches the solution in the course of learning, without memorizing previous states and without stochastic jumps. Convergence is to global optimality for separable data sets and to local optimality for non-separable data sets.

In separable problems, perceptron training can also aim at finding the largest separating margin between the classes. The so-called perceptron of optimal stability can be determined by means of iterative training and optimization schemes, such as the Min-Over algorithm (Krauth and Mezard, 1987) or the AdaTron (Anlauf and Biehl, 1989)) . AdaTron uses the fact that the corresponding quadratic optimization problem is convex. The perceptron of optimal stability, together with the kernel trick, are the conceptual foundations of the support vector machine.

The α -perceptron further used a pre-processing layer of fixed random weights, with thresholded output units. This enabled the perceptron to classify analogue patterns, by projecting them into a binary space. In fact, for a projection space of sufficiently high dimension, patterns can become linearly separable.

Another way to solve nonlinear problems without using multiple layers is to use higher order networks (sigma-pi unit). In this type of network, each element in the input vector is extended with each pairwise combination of multiplied inputs (second order). This can be extended to an n-order network.

It should be kept in mind, however, that the best classifier is not necessarily that which classifies all the training data perfectly. Indeed, if we had the prior constraint that the data come from equi-variant Gaussian distributions, the linear separation in the input space is optimal, and the nonlinear solution is overfitted.

Other linear classification algorithms include Winnow, support vector machine and logistic regression.

Multiclass Perceptron

Like most other techniques for training linear classifiers, the perceptron generalizes naturally to multiclass classification. Here, the input x and the output y are drawn from arbitrary sets. A feature representation function $f(x, y)$ maps each possible input/output pair to a finite-dimensional real-valued feature vector. As before, the feature vector is multiplied by a weight vector w, but now the resulting score is used to choose among many possible outputs:

$$\hat{y} = \text{argmax}_y \, f(x, y) \cdot w.$$

$\approx$ Learning again iterates over the examples, predicting an output for each, leaving the weights unchanged when the predicted output matches the target, and changing them when it does not. The update becomes:

$$w_{t+1} = w_t + f(x, y) - f(x, \hat{y}).$$

This multiclass feedback formulation reduces to the original perceptron when x is a real-valued vector, y is chosen from $\{0,1\}$, and $f(x,y)=yx$.

For certain problems, input/output representations and features can be chosen so that $\text{argmax}_y f(x,y)\cdot w$ can be found efficiently even though y is chosen from a very large or even infinite set.

In recent years, perceptron training has become popular in the field of natural language processing for such tasks as part-of-speech tagging and syntactic parsing (Collins, 2002).

In a progressive simplification of single neuron models, we arrived at the McCulloch-Pitts neuron model which takes inputs from many neurons and produces a single output. If the net effect of the external inputs is greater than a threshold, the neuron goes into excited state (1), else it remains in its resting state (0).

Using this model, in 1943, its inventors Warren S. McCulloch, a neuroscientist, and Walter Pitts, a logician, set out to construct a model of brain function. Note that it was the time of World War- II. It was also a time when use of computing power was being tested for the first time on a large scale for war purposes – for calculating missile trajectories and breaking enemy codes. T he power of computing technology was just being realized by the world. Therefore it was natural to think of brain as a computer. Since the digital computer works on the basis of Boolean algebra, McCulloch and Pitts thought if it is possible for the brain also to use some form of Boolean algebra.

Since the MP neurons are binary units it seemed worthwhile to check if the basic logical operations can be performed by these neurons. McCulloch and Pitts quickly showed that the MP neuron can implement the basic logic gates AND, OR and NOT simply by proper choice of the weights:

OR Gate

The truth table of an OR gate is:

X1	X2	Y
0	0	0
0	1	1
1	0	1
1	1	1

Note that the function below, which represents a MP neuron with two inputs, x_1 and x_2, implements an OR gate.

$$y = g(x_1 + x_2 - b)$$

where b = 0.5; g(.) is the step function; $x_1, x_2 \in \{\ ,1\}$. Actually any value of the bias term b, 0 < b < 1, should work.

AND Gate

The truth table of an AND gate.

X1	X2	Y
0	0	0
0	1	0
1	0	0
1	1	1

Note that the function below implements an AND gate.

$$y = g(x_1 + x_2 - b)$$

Where $b = 1.5$; $g(.)$ is the step function; $x_1, x_2 \in \{0,1\}$. Actually any value of the bias term b, $1 < b < 2$, should work.

NOT Gate

$$y = g(-x + 0.5)$$

The truth table of a NOT gate is:

X	Y
0	1
1	0

Note that the function below implements a NOT gate.

$$y = g(-x + 0.5)$$

More generally, in $y = g(-x + b)$ any value of b in, $0 < b < 1$, would give a NOT gate.

Thus it became clear that by connecting properly designed MP neurons in specific architectures, any complex Boolean circuit can be constructed. Thus we have a theory of how brain can perform logical operations. McCulloch and Pitts explained their ideas in a paper titled, "A logical calculus of the ideas immanent in nervous activity" which appeared in the Bulletin of Mathematical Biophysics.

Although the idea of considering neurons as logic gates and the brain itself as a large Boolean circuit is quite tempting, it does not satisfy other important requirements of a good theory of the brain. There are some crucial differences between the brain and a digital computer (Table).

Table: Difference between the brain and a digital Computer.

Property	Computer	Brain
Shape	2d Sheets of inorganic matter	3d volume of organic matter
Power	Powered by DC mains	Powered by ATP
Signal	Digital	pulsed
Clock	Centralized clock	No centralized clock
Clock speed	Gigahertz	100s of Hz

Fault tolerance	Highly fault-sensitive	Very fault-tolerant
Performance	By programming	By learning

Thus there are some fundamental differences between the computer and the brain. The signals used in the two systems are very different. There is no centralized clock in the brain. Each neuron fires at its own frequency which further changes with time. A brain is very fault tolerant which can be seen by the manner in which a stroke patient recovers. Most importantly a computer has to be programmed whereas the brain can learn by a progressive trial-and-error process.

These considerations led to the feeling that something is wrong with the McCulloch-Pitts approach to the brain.

As an answer to the above need, Frank Rosenblatt developed the Perceptron in 1957. A Perceptron is essentially a network of MP neurons.

Thus a Perceptron maps an m-dimensional input vector, onto a n-dimensional output vector. A distinct feature of a Perceptron is that the weights are not pre-calculated as in a MP neuron but are adjusted by a iterative process called training. The general approach to training, not only of a Perceptron, but of a larger class of neural networks (feedforward networks which will be defined later) is depicted in the figure below.

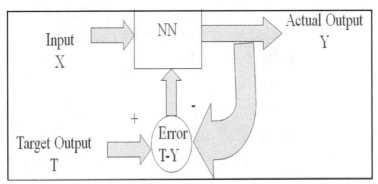

Training a neural network.

The network is initialized with random weights.

When an input X is presented to a neural network (NN), it responds with an output vector Y. Since the weights are random, the network output is likely to be wrong and therefore different from a Desired or a Target output T. Error defined as E = T-Y, is used to adjust the weights in the Perceptron (or NN in general) in such a way that the next time when X is presented to the network, the response Y is likely to be closer to T than before. This iterative procedure is continued with a large number of patterns until the error is minimum on all patterns.

The mechanism by which the weights are adjusted as a function of the error is called the learning rule.

The learning rule can vary depending on the precise architectural details of the Neural Network (NN) used in the above scheme.

Instead of directly taking up the task of deriving the learning rule for a Perceptron, let us begin with a very simple neuron model and derive the learning rule. In the process, we would introduce a few terms. The same procedure, with all its jargon, will be used to derive the learning rule for more complex architectures.

Case 1: Linear Neuron model: $\mathbf{y} = w^T x$

Procedure to find the weights:

1) Noniterative , 2) Iterative.

Output Error:

$$E = \frac{1}{2}\sum_{n}\left(y(p) - w^T x(p)\right)^2$$

$$\nabla_w E = \sum_{p}\left(-x(p)\right)\left(y(p) - w^T x(p)\right) = 0$$

1) Noniterative:

Pseudoinverse:

Let

$$X = \begin{bmatrix} x(1) \\ \cdot \\ \cdot \\ x(N) \end{bmatrix} = \begin{bmatrix} x_1(1) & x_m(1) \\ & \\ x_1(N) & x_m(N) \end{bmatrix}_{NXm}$$

$$Y = XW$$

$$w = \begin{bmatrix} w_1 & ... & w_m \end{bmatrix}^T$$

$$y = \begin{bmatrix} y(1) & ... & y(N) \end{bmatrix}^T$$

$$d = \begin{bmatrix} d(1) & ... & d(N) \end{bmatrix}^T$$

$$E = (1/2)(d - XW)^T(d - XW) = (1/2)d^T d - (x^T d)^T w + (1/2)w^T(X^T X)w$$

$$W = (X^T X)^{-1} X^T d$$

$$R_x = (X^T X) \qquad correlation\,matrix$$

$$r_{xd} = X^T d \qquad cross - correlation\,matrix$$

$$(X^T X)^{-1} \qquad pseudo - inverse$$

1) Iterative:

a) Steepest Descent:

$$w(t+1) = w(t) + \eta \sum_{p}(x(p))(d(p) - w^T x(p))$$

$$w(t+1) = w(t) + \eta\left(r_{xd} - R_x\,w(t)\right)$$

In the method of steepest descent, all the training data is used at the same time (packed into R_x and r_{xd}) to update every single weight. This can involve a large memory requirement and can be computationally expensive.

a) Least Mean Square Rule:

$$w(t+1) = w(t) + (x(p))(d(p) - w^T x(p))$$

Also called the Delta Rule, Widrow-Hoff Rule.

Note that the key difference between the steepest descent rule above and the delta rule is the absence of summation over all training patterns in the latter.

In this case the weight vector does not smoothly converge on the final solution. Instead, it performs a random walk around the final solution and converges only in a least square sense.

Issues:

1. Convergence.

1a. Shape of Error function, E (Single minimum for quadratic Error function).

Note that the dominant term in the error function of eqn. is a quadratic form associated with the correlation matrix, R_x.

Since R_x is a positive definite matrix the error function always has a unique minimum. It also has real, positive eigenvalues (λ_i).

1b. Effect of eigenvalues of correlation matrix.

Condition number: $\lambda_{max} / \lambda_{min}$

where λ_{max} is the largest eigenvalue and λ_{min} is the smallest eigenvalue of the correlation matrix R_x.

Slows down the descent over the error function if the condition number is too large.

1. The need to choose η.

    Large $\eta \rightarrow$ oscillations, instability

    Small $\eta \rightarrow$ slow convergence

    Bounds over the learning rate, η:

$$0 < \eta < 2/(\eta_{max})$$

Proof:

$R_x = (X^T X)$ correlation matrix

$r_{xd} = X^T d$ cross-correlation matrix

$(X^T X)^{-1}$ pseudo-inverse

$E = (1/2)(d - XW)^T (d - XW) = (1/2)d^T d - (X^T d)^T w + (1/2)w^T (X^T X)w$

$= (1/2)d^T d - r^T_{xd} w + (1/2)w^T (R_x)w$

Final value of w, $w* = R_x^{-1} r_{xd}$,

$$E = Emin + (1/2)(w-w*)^T R_x (w-w*)$$
$$\text{Grad}(E) = R_x(w-w*)$$
$$\text{Delta } w = -\eta \ \text{grad}(E)$$
$$= -\eta \ w(t+1) = w(t) - \eta \ R_x(w(t)-w*)$$
$$w(t+1) - w* = (I - \eta R_x)(w(t) - w*)$$

$$\text{Let,} v(t) = (w(t) - w*)$$
$$v(t+1) = (I - \eta R_x) v(t)$$

Let $v' = Qv$, where Q is an orthogonal matrix that diagonalizes R_x,

$$v'(t+1) = (I - \eta D)v'(t)$$

$$D = \begin{bmatrix} \lambda_1 & 0 & 0 & 0 \\ 0 & \lambda_2 & 0 & 0 \\ 0 & 0 & \ddots & 0 \\ 0 & 0 & 0 & \lambda_n \end{bmatrix}$$

If we consider the individual components, v_i, of eqn. above,

$$v_i(t+1) = (1 - \eta \lambda_i)v_i(t)$$

The condition for stability of the last equation, is
$|1 - \eta \lambda_i| < 1$. Let us consider the two possible cases of this inequality,

a) $1 - \eta \lambda_i < 1 \rightarrow \eta > 0$ which is trivial.

b) $-(1 - \eta \lambda_i) < 1 \rightarrow \eta < 2/\lambda_i$ for all i.

Therefore,

$$\eta < 2/\lambda_{max}$$

3. The need to reduce η with time:

There are obvious tradeoffs between use of a large vs. small η. Large η speeds up learning but can be unstable. Small η is stable but results in slower learning.

Therefore, it is desirable to begin with a large η and reduce it with time.

Learning rate variation schedules:

$$a) \eta = c/n; \quad b) \eta = \eta_o / (1 + (n/\tau))$$

Case 2: Perceptron: MP Neuron which has Sigmoid Nonlinearity

With the hard-limiting or threshold nonlinearity the neuron acts as a classifier.

Final solution is not unique.

Convergence only if linearly separable.

$$y = g(\sum_{i=1}^{n} w_i x_i - b)$$

Hardlimiter characteristics:

$$g(v) = 1, v \geq 0$$
$$= 0, v < 0$$

For a Perceptron with a single output neuron, the regions corresponding to the 2 classes are separated by a hyperplane given by:

$$\sum w_i x_i - b = 0$$

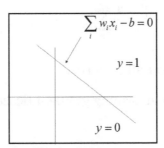

Classification by a perceptron.

In other words, a Perceptron classifies input patterns by dividing the input space into two semi-infinite regions using a hyperplane.

Perceptron Learning Rule

It is also called the LMS Rule or Delta Rule or Widrow-Hoff Rule.

The steps involved in Perceptron learning are as follows:

1. Initialization of weights: Set the initial values of the weights to 0. w(0) = 0.

2. Present the p'th training pattern, x, and calculate the network output, y.

3. Using the desired output, d, for the input pattern x, adjust the weights by a small amount using the following learning rule:

$$w(t+1) = w(t) + \eta[d(t) - y(t)]x(t)$$
where,
$$d(n) = +1, x(t) \in C1$$
$$d(n) = -1, x(t) \in C2$$

4. Go back to step 2 and continue until the network output error, e = d-y, is 0 for all patterns.

The above training process will converge after N_{max} iterations where,

$$\alpha = \min_{x(n) \in C1} w_0^T x(n)$$

$$\beta = \max_{x(k) \in C1} \| x(k) \|^2$$

$$N^{max} = \beta \| w_0 \|^2 / \alpha$$

Range of η:

$0 < \eta < 1$

1   Averaging of past inputs leads to stable weight dynamics, which requires small η.

2   Fast adaptation requires large η.

Learning rule can also be derived from an error function:

$$E = \frac{1}{2} \sum_p [(d_p - y_p)^2$$

where E denotes the squared error over all patterns.

The learning rule may be derived by performing gradient descent over the error function.

Gradient of Error:

$$\Delta w = -\eta \nabla_w E$$

$$\Delta w_i = -\eta \frac{\partial E}{\partial w_i}$$

$$\frac{\partial E}{\partial w_i} = -[d - y] \frac{\partial y}{\partial w_i} = -[d - y] g' x_i$$

The last term in the above equation has g', which is zero everywhere except at the origin if g is a hardlimiting nonlinearity. But if we take a smoother version of g(), which saturate at +1 and -1, like the tanh() function, the learning rule becomes,

$$\Delta w_i = \eta [d - y] g' x_i$$

Since g' > 0 always for tanh() function, we can absorb it into h, considering it as a quantity that varies with x. We then have,

$$\Delta w_i = \eta' [d - y] x_i$$

Which is identical to the Perceptron learning rule given in eqn. above.

Features of Perceptron

- The Perceptrons can only classify linearly separable classes.

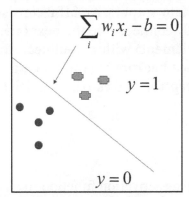

Classification of linear separable classes by a perceptron.

- When the training data is linearly separable, there can be an infinite number of solutions.

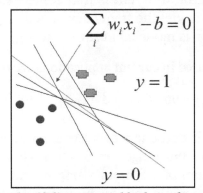

Solutions to classify linear separable classes by a perceptron.

Critique of Perceptrons

- Perceptrons cannot even solve simple problems like Xor problem.

- Linear model: Can only discriminate linearly separable classes.

- Even the multi-layered versions may be afflicted by these weaknesses (Minsky & Papert, 1969).

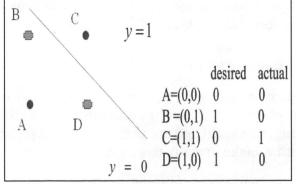

Inability to solve Xor by a perceptron.

Multilayer Perceptron

A multilayer perceptron (MLP) is a feedforward artificial neural network model that maps sets of input data onto a set of appropriate outputs. An MLP consists of multiple layers of nodes in a directed graph, with each layer fully connected to the next one. Except for the input nodes, each node is a neuron (or processing element) with a nonlinear activation function. MLP utilizes a supervised learning technique called backpropagation for training the network. MLP is a modification of the standard linear perceptron and can distinguish data that is not linearly separable.

Theory

Activation Function

If a multilayer perceptron has a linear activation function in all neurons, that is, a linear function that maps the weighted inputs to the output of each neuron, then it is easily proven with linear algebra that any number of layers can be reduced to the standard two-layer input-output model. What makes a multilayer perceptron different is that some neurons use a *nonlinear* activation function which was developed to model the frequency of action potentials, or firing, of biological neurons in the brain. This function is modeled in several ways.

The two main activation functions used in current applications are both sigmoids, and are described by,

$$y(v_i) = \tanh(v_i) \text{ and } y(v_i) = (1 + e^{-v_i})^{-1},$$

in which the former function is a hyperbolic tangent which ranges from -1 to 1, and the latter, the logistic function, is similar in shape but ranges from 0 to 1. Here y_i is the output of the ith node (neuron) and v_i is the weighted sum of the input synapses. Alternative activation functions have been proposed, including the rectifier and softplus functions. More specialized activation functions include radial basis functions which are used in another class of supervised neural network models.

Layers

The multilayer perceptron consists of three or more layers (an input and an output layer with one or more *hidden layers*) of nonlinearly-activating nodes and is thus considered a deep neural network. Since an MLP is a Fully Connected Network, each node in one layer connects with a certain weight w_{ij} to every node in the following layer. Some people do not include the input layer when counting the number of layers and there is disagreement about whether w_{ij} should be interpreted as the weight from i to j or the other way around.

Learning Through Backpropagation

Learning occurs in the perceptron by changing connection weights after each piece of data is processed, based on the amount of error in the output compared to the expected result. This is an example of supervised learning, and is carried out through backpropagation, a generalization of the least mean squares algorithm in the linear perceptron.

We represent the error in output node j in the nth data point (training example) by

$e_j(n) = d_j(n) - y_j(n)$, where d is the target value and y is the value produced by the perceptron. We then make corrections to the weights of the nodes based on those corrections which minimize the error in the entire output, given by:

$$\mathcal{E}(n) = \frac{1}{2} \sum_j e_j^2(n).$$

Using gradient descent, we find our change in each weight to be:

$$\Delta w_{ji}(n) = -\eta \frac{\partial \mathcal{E}(n)}{\partial v_j(n)} y_i(n)$$

where y_i is the output of the previous neuron and η is the *learning rate*, which is carefully selected to ensure that the weights converge to a response fast enough, without producing oscillations.

The derivative to be calculated depends on the induced local field v_j, which itself varies. It is easy to prove that for an output node this derivative can be simplified to:

$$-\frac{\partial \mathcal{E}(n)}{\partial v_j(n)} = e_j(n)\phi'(v_j(n))$$

where ϕ' is the derivative of the activation function described above, which itself does not vary. The analysis is more difficult for the change in weights to a hidden node, but it can be shown that the relevant derivative is:

$$-\frac{\partial \mathcal{E}(n)}{\partial v_j(n)} = \phi'(v_j(n)) \sum_k -\frac{\partial \mathcal{E}(n)}{\partial v_k(n)} w_{kj}(n)$$

This depends on the change in weights of the k th nodes, which represent the output layer. So to change the hidden layer weights, we must first change the output layer weights according to the derivative of the activation function, and so this algorithm represents a *backpropagation of the activation function.*

Terminology

The term "multilayer perceptron" often causes confusion. It is argued the model is not a single perceptron that has multiple layers. Rather, it contains many perceptrons that are organised into layers, leading some to believe that a more fitting term might therefore be "multilayer perceptron network". Moreover, these "perceptrons" are not really perceptrons in the strictest possible sense, as true perceptrons are a special case of artificial neurons that use a threshold activation function such as the Heaviside step function, whereas the artificial neurons in a multilayer perceptron are free to take on any arbitrary activation function. Consequently, whereas a true perceptron performs binary classification, a neuron in a multilayer perceptron is free to either perform classification or regression, depending upon its activation function.

The two arguments raised above can be reconciled with the name "multilayer perceptron" if "perceptron" is simply interpreted to mean a binary classifier, independent of the specific mechanistic implementation of a classical perceptron. In this case, the entire network can indeed be considered to be a binary classifier with multiple layers. Furthermore, the term "multilayer perceptron" now does not specify the nature of the layers; the layers are free to be composed of general artificial neurons, and not perceptrons specifically. This interpretation of the term "multilayer perceptron" avoids the loosening of the definition of "perceptron" to mean an artificial neuron in general.

Applications

Multilayer perceptrons using a backpropagation algorithm are the standard algorithm for any supervised learning pattern recognition process and the subject of ongoing research in computational neuroscience and parallel distributed processing. They are useful in research in terms of their ability to solve problems stochastically, which often allows one to get approximate solutions for extremely complex problems like fitness approximation.

MLPs are universal function approximators as showed by Cybenko's theorem, so they can be used to create mathematical models by regression analysis. As classification is a particular case of regression when the response variable is categorical, MLPs are also good classifier algorithms.

MLPs were a popular machine learning solution in the 1980s, finding applications in diverse fields such as speech recognition, image recognition, and machine translation software, but have since the 1990s faced strong competition from the much simpler (and related) support vector machines. More recently, there has been some renewed interest in backpropagation networks due to the successes of deep learning.

Improvements over Perceptron:

1) Smooth nonlinearity - sigmoid

2) 1 or more hidden layers

Adding a Hidden Layer

The perceptron, which has no hidden layers, can classify only linearly separable patterns. The MLP, with at least 1 hidden layer can classify *any* linearly non-separable classes also. An MLP can approximate any continuous multivariate function to any degree of accuracy, provided there are sufficiently many hidden neurons (Cybenko, 1988; Hornik et al, 1989). A more precise formulation is given below.

A serious limitation disappears suddenly by adding a single hidden layer.

It can easily be shown that the XOR problem which was not solvable by a Perceptron can be solved by a MLP with a single hidden layer containing two neurons.

XOR Example:

Neuron 1:

$$V_1 = \sigma(x_1 + x_2 - 1.5)$$

$$V_2 = \sigma(x_1 + x_2 - 0.5)$$

$$y = \sigma(V_1 - V_2 - 0.5)$$

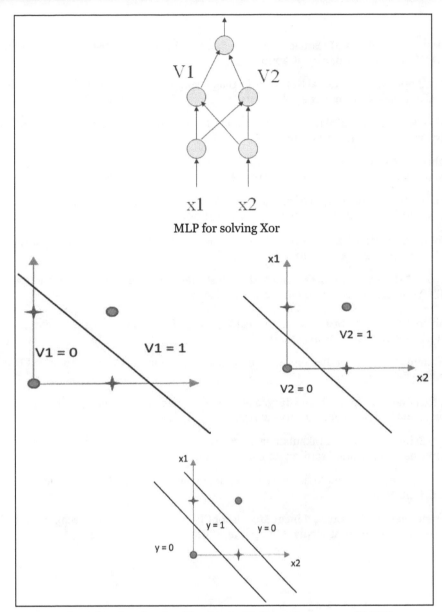

Plots showing the classification by V1,V2 and y(output of MLP).

Training the Hidden Layer

Not obvious how to train the hidden layer parameters.

The error term is meaningful only to the weights connected to the output layer. How to adjust hidden layer connections so as to reduce output error? – *credit assignment* problem.

Any connection can be adapted by taking a full partial derivative over the error function, but then to update a single weight in the first stage we need information about distant neurons/connections close to the output layer (locality rule is violated). In a large network with many layers, this implies that information is exchanged over distant elements of the network though they are not directly connected. Such an algorithm may be mathematically valid, but is biologically unrealistic.

References

- Burgess, Matt. "DeepMind's AI learned to ride the London Underground using human-like reason and memory". WIRED UK. Retrieved 06, August 2020

- Ganesan, N. "Application of Neural Networks in Diagnosing Cancer Disease Using Demographic Data" (PDF). International Journal of Computer Applications

- "CiteSeerX — Recurrent Multilayer Perceptrons for Identification and Control: The Road to Applications". Citeseerx.ist.psu.edu. Retrieved 15, July 2020

- Mohri, Mehryar; Rostamizadeh, Afshin; Talwalkar, Ameet (2012). Foundations of Machine Learning. USA, Massachusetts: MIT Press. ISBN 9780262018258

- Salakhutdinov, Ruslan; Hinton, Geoffrey (2009). "Semantic hashing". International Journal of Approximate Reasoning. 50 (7): 969–978. doi:10.1016/j.ijar.2008.11.006

- Mannes, John. "DeepMind's differentiable neural computer helps you navigate the subway with its memory". TechCrunch. Retrieved 20, May 2020

- Simonite, Tom. "Microsoft says its racist chatbot illustrates how AI isn't adaptable enough to help most businesses". MIT Technology Review. Retrieved 13, April 2020

- Cornell University Library. "Breiman : Statistical Modeling: The Two Cultures (with comments and a rejoinder by the author)". Retrieved 27, March 2020

- Alpaydin, Ethem (2010). Introduction to Machine Learning. London: The MIT Press. ISBN 978-0-262-01243-0. Retrieved 01, February 2020

- Felix Gers, Nicholas Schraudolph, and Jürgen Schmidhuber (2002). Learning precise timing with LSTM recurrent networks. Journal of Machine Learning Research 3:115–143

- F. Gomez, J. Schmidhuber, R. Miikkulainen. Accelerated Neural Evolution through Cooperatively Coevolved Synapses. Journal of Machine Learning Research (JMLR), 9:937-965, 2008

- "With QuickType, Apple wants to do more than guess your next text. It wants to give you an AI.". WIRED. Retrieved 11, June 2020

- Bishop, Christopher M. "Chapter 4. Linear Models for Classification". Pattern Recognition and Machine Learning. Springer Science+Business Media, LLC. p. 194. ISBN 978-0387-31073-2

Diverse Aspects of Computational Neuroscience

The assembly of instruments and methods that establish a connection between nervous system and technical devices is known as neurotechnology. In order to completely understand computational neuroscience, it is necessary to understand the processes related to it. The following chapter elucidates the varied aspects associated with this area of study such as artificial intelligence, neurophysiology and computational neuroanatomy.

Neurotechnology

Neurotechnology could be seen as any artificial means to interact with the workings of the brain. This version includes pharmacological adjustment of the activity of the brain, for example drugs treating Parkinson's disease or senile dementia, or alcohol and nicotine, if one wants to stretch it. In a more technically inclined definition, we would see Neurotechnology as:

- Technical and computational tools that measure and analyze chemical and electrical signals in the nervous system, be it the brain or nerves in the limbs. These may be used to identify the properties of nervous activity, understand how the brain works, diagnose pathological conditions, or control external devices (neuroprostheses, 'brain machine interfaces').

- Technical tools to interact with the nervous system to change its activity, for example to restore sensory input such as with cochlea implants to restore hearing or deep brain stimulation to stop tremor and treat other pathological conditions.

Neurotechnology research in this context includes all research that contributes to these systems, including, e.g. solving problems of encapsulation of electronic circuits, simulations of neuronal networks and culture biological networks to understand their properties, and the development of surgical implantation techniques. Not least, interacting with the brain requires a high level of ethical responsibility towards the patient, but also to society due to its influence on our concept of the human being as such. Consequently, Neurotechnology includes the discourse on the ethics of Neurotechnology.

Yet, these technical descriptions do not always provide a clear understanding of how neurotechnologies are used in practice. Without a strong public understanding of what neurotechnologies are and what they can do, it becomes difficult to have an inclusive discussion about their risks, benefits, and potential impacts on society. To follow is a look at the neurotechnologies that exist today, which we have categorized by three different functions: those that alter, extend, and monitor brain function.

Altering Brain Function

Neurotechnologies can be used to regulate certain aspects of brain function. A popular neurotechnological method that alters brain activity is deep brain stimulation (DBS). DBS is most commonly applied as a treatment for Parkinson's disease, a progressive neurodegenerative disease that affects movement. A device is implanted beneath the skull and is connected to an external device used to modulate the treatment. The device delivers electrical currents to stimulate the connection between the neurons that control motor function, or body movements. This can help reduce tremors and stiffness usually associated with Parkinsons. Other methods to alter brain function have been marketed for nonmedical purposes. Externally wearable neurotechnologies, such as the Oasis Pro device, use low level electrical currents to modulate mood, improve sleep, or enhance focus.

Current neurology research suggests that more direct manipulation of brain activity will be possible in the future. In Rafael Yuste's Lab at Columbia University, scientists successfully compelled mice to perform a licking behavior by using a neurotechnology mechanism that controls the activation of specific brain cells. With this technology, researchers "wrote" a specific neural code and fed it into a mouse's brain, thus altering its behavior in predicted ways. While there is no neurotechnology equivalent for human brains as of yet, this experiment indicates that brain function can be altered with extremely high precision. This enables elements of a subject's brain activity and resulting behaviors to be controlled externally by another entity.

Extending Brain Function

This next type of neurotechnology works in reverse of the previous category. Rather than using a neurotechnology device to control the brain function of a subject, this category of neurotechnology enables brain function to control an external device. For example, at Brown Institute for Brain Science, a parapalegic woman was able to control the movement of a robotic arm by thinking about the action she wished to accomplish. Her neural activity directed the robotic arm to pick up a cup of coffee and lift it to her mouth for a sip. There are a wide variety of external devices that could potentially be controlled through a neurotechnology including a prosthetic limb, the mouse of a computer, or the actions of a video game character. Many neurotechnologies are used by individuals without speech to answer questions by mentally directing a computer mouse at "yes" or "no".

Brain activity within one subject can even be extended to connect with other individuals. Scientists at Rice University embarked on a project in 2019 to facilitate human-to-human brain connections. This group of scientists are developing wearable neurotechnology with the capability to transfer visual images from one subject to another at the speed of thought. This means the device will have to decode neural activity from one subject's mind and transfer it into the visual cortex of another subject's mind within one twentieth of a second.

Monitoring Brain Function

In addition to altering and extending brain function, neurotechnologies can monitor brain activity. These technologies do not require active thinking to guide an external device and they do not alter the functioning of the brain. Rather, they passively monitor brain function and record data, which can be analyzed to provide insights into brain activity. An example of this type of neurotechnology are EEG headbands, which can extract various cognitive insights by tracking the electrical impulses that brain cells use to communicate with one another. This variety of neurotechnology was controversially used within some schools to monitor student's attentiveness. Depending on the subject's level of focus, a different color lights up on the head band. While a blue light indicates that the wearer is distracted, a red light means they are focused. In addition to monitoring students' focus level, these headbands also collect brain data for analysis. A Massachusetts based company produces these devices has a secondary mission: to build a massive database of brain data collected through their devices, then to synthesize that data into valuable information about the human brain.

A variety of wearable brains monitoring neurotechnologies are sold on consumer markets. Companies like Emotiv and Neurable sell headbands that can record brain activity with EEG. Both of these companies also produce software programs that enable individuals to analyze their own brain data. Technologies like this, which are used to monitor brain activity and collect brain data are the most common and accessible neurotechnologies today.

Neurotechnology, AI and Beyond

The above examples are only the beginning of neurotechnology's potential. In the years to come, neurotechnological capabilities across all three categories will be further enhanced by the application of Artificial Intelligence (AI). As AI becomes increasingly popular within the realms of science and technology, some neurotechnologies are beginning to utilize machine intelligence to expedite certain processes. In cases where neurotechnology is used to alter brain function, implanted devices can be imbued with semi-autonomous attributes that could, for example, perceive a downturn in mood and consequently trigger a stimulation treatment independently. When neurotechnology is used to extend the brain's control to an external device, AI can help reduce the lag between the subject thinking of an action and the action being performed. In such instances, predictive algorithms could allow the device to intuit the intentions of the subject.

These kinds of technologies are still in their early stages, but are on the path to becoming realities within the next few decades. More imminently, AI can be used to comb through the vast amounts of data generated from the brain activity recorded by neurotechnologies. The use of AI within these contexts has the potential to glean endless insights about the inner workings of the mind; from low level inferences about personality, to high level inferences about intentions and consciousness, to population-wide insights about human behavior.

Each of these neurotechnology categories, particularly when paired with AI, bring new potentials for medical advancement and increased self-understanding for humanity. Further developments within neurotechnology and AI will bring big scientific and societal changes; changes that certainly merit public consideration and input. Broadening civic understanding of these critical topics is the first step towards responsible and inclusive innovation.

Artificial Intelligence

Computational Intelligence and Artificial Intelligence are both aiming at building machines and software capable of intelligent behavior. They are consequently prone to interactions, even if the latter is not necessarily interested in understanding how cognition emerges from the brain substrate. One of the greatest challenges to effective brain-based therapies is our inability to monitor and modulate neural activity in real time. Moving beyond the relatively simple open-loop neurostimulation devices that are currently the standard in clinical practice (e.g., epilepsy) requires a closed-loop approach in which the therapeutic application of neurostimulation is determined by characterizing the moment-to-moment state of the brain. However, there remain major obstacles to progress for such a closed-loop approach. For one, we do not know how to objectively characterize mental states or even detect pathological activity associated with most psychiatric disorders. Second, we do not know the most effective way to improve maladaptive behaviors by means of neurostimulation.

The solutions to these problems require innovative experimental frameworks leveraging intelligent computational approaches able to sense, interpret, and modulate large amount of data from behaviorally relevant neural circuits at the speed of thoughts. New approaches such as computational psychiatry or ML are emerging. However, current ML approaches that are applied to neural data typically do not provide an understanding of the underlying neural processes or how they contributed to the outcome (i.e., prediction or classifier). For example, significant progress has been made using ML to effectively classify EEG patterns, but the understanding of brain function and mechanisms derived from such approaches still remain relatively limited. Such an understanding, be it correlational or causal, is key to improving ML methods and to suggesting new therapeutic targets or protocols using different techniques. Explainable Artificial Intelligence (XAI) is a relatively new set of techniques that combines sophisticated AI and ML algorithms with effective explanatory techniques to develop explainable solutions that have proven useful in many domain areas. Recent work has suggested that XAI may be a promising avenue to guide basic neural circuit manipulations and clinical interventions.

Explainable Artificial Intelligence for neurostimulation in mental health can be seen as an extension in the design of BMI. BMI are generally understood as combinations of hardware and software systems designed to rapidly transfer information between one or more brain area and an external device. While there is a long history of research in the decoding, analyses and production of neural signal in non-human primates and rodents, a lot of progress has recently been made to develop these techniques for the human brain both invasively and non-invasively, unidirectionally or bi-directionally. Motor decision making for example, has been shown to involve a network of brain areas, before and during movement execution, so that BMI intervention can inhibit movement up to 200 ms after its initiation. The advantage of this type of motor-decision BMI is that it is not bound to elementary motor commands (e.g., turn the wheel of a car), but rather to the high-level decision to initiate and complete a movement. That decision can potentially be affected by environmental factors (e.g., AI vision system detecting cars on the neighboring lane) and internal state (e.g., AI system assessing the state of fatigue of the driver).

The current consensus is that response inhibition is an emergent property of a network of discrete brain areas that include the right inferior frontal gyrus and that leverage basic wide-spread elementary neural circuits such a local-lateral-inhibition. This gyrus, as with many other cortical structures, is dynamically recruited so that individual neurons may code for drastically different aspects of the behavior, depending of the task at hand. Consequently, designing a BMI targeting such an area requires the ability for the system to rapidly switch its decoding and stimulation paradigms as a function of environmental or internal state information. Such online adaptability needs of course to be learned and personalized to each individual patient, a task that is ideally suited for AI/ML approaches. In the sensory domain, some have shown that BMI can be used to generate actionable entirely artificial tactile sensations to trigger complex motor decisions. Most of the BMI research work has, however, focused on the sensory motor system because of the relatively focused and well-defined nature of the neural circuits.

Consequently, most of the clinical applications are focused on neurological disorders. Interestingly, new generations of BMIs are emerging that are focused on more cognitive functions such as detecting and manipulating reward expectations using reinforcement learning paradigms, memory enhancement or collective problem solving using multi-brain interfacing in rats or humans. All these applications can potentially benefit from the adaptive properties of AI/ML algorithms and, as mentioned, explainable AI approaches have the promise of yielding basic mechanistic insights about the neural systems being targeted. However, the use of these approaches in the context of psychiatric or neurodevelopmental disorders have not been realized though their potential is clear.

In computational neuroscience and computational psychiatry there is a contrast between theory-driven (e.g., reinforcement learning, biophysically inspired network models) and data-driven models (e.g., deep-learning or ensemble methods). While the former models are highly explainable in terms of biological mechanisms, the latter are high performing in terms of predictive accuracy. In general, high performing methods tend to be the least explainable, while explainable methods tend to be the least accurate. Mathematically, the relationship between the two is still not fully formalized or understood. These are the type of issues that occupy the ML community beyond neuroscience and neurostimulation. XAI models in neuroscience might be created by combining theory- and data-driven models. This combination could be achieved by associating explanatory semantic information with features of the model; by using simpler models that are easier to explain; by using richer models that contain more explanatory content; or by building approximate models, solely for the purpose of explanation. Current efforts in this area include:

- Identify how explainable learning solutions can be applied to neuroscience and neuropsychiatric datasets for neurostimulation.

- Foster the development of a community of scholars working in the field of explainable learning applied to basic neuroscience and clinical neuropsychiatry.

- Stimulate an open exchange of data and theories between investigators in this nascent field.

Intelligent Decoding and Modulation of Behaviorally Activated Brain Circuits

A variety of perspectives for how ML and, more generally AI could contribute to closed-loop brain circuit interventions are worth investigating. From a purely signal processing stand point, an XAI system can be an active stimulation artifact rejection component. In parallel, the XAI system should have the ability to discover – in a data-driven manner – neuro-behavioral markers of the computational process or condition under consideration. Remarkable efforts are currently underway to derive biomarkers for mental health, as is the case for example for depression. Once these biomarkers are detected, and the artifacts rejected, the XAI system can generate complex feedback stimulation patterns designed and monitored (human in-the loop) to improve behavioral or cognitive performance.

XAI approaches have also the potential to address outstanding biological and theoretical questions in neuroscience, as well as to address clinical applications. They seem well-suited for extracting actionable information from highly complex neural systems, moving away from traditional correlational analyses and toward a causal understanding of network activity. However, even with XAI approaches, one should not assume that understanding the statistical causality of neural interactions is equivalent to understanding behavior; a highly sophisticated knowledge of neural activity and neural connectivity is not generally synonymous with understanding their role in causing behavior.

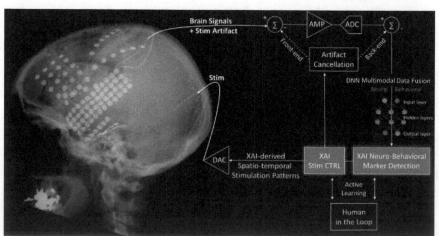

An XAI-enabled closed-loop neurostimulation process can be described in four phases:

- System-level recording of brain signals (e.g., spikes, LFPs, ECoG, EEG, neuromodulators, optical voltage/calcium indicators).

- Multimodal fusion of neural data and dense behavioral/cognitive assessment measures.

- XAI algorithm using unbiasedly discovered biomarkers to provide mechanistic explanations on how to improve behavioral/cognitive performance and reject stimulation artifacts.

- Complex XAI-derived spatio-temporal brain stimulation patterns (e.g., TMS, ECT, DBS, ECoG, VNS, TDCS, ultrasound, optogenetics) that will validate the model and affect subsequent recordings. ADC, Analog to Digital Converter; AMP, Amplifier; CTRL, Control; DAC, Digital to Analog Converter; DNN, Deep Neural Network.

Neurophysiology

Neurophysiology is the branch of physiology dealing with the functions of the nervous system i.e. the study of the functional properties of neurones, glia, and networks.

- Historically it has been dominated by electrophysiology—the electrical recording of neuronal events ranging from the molar (the electroencephalogram, EEG) to the cellular (intracellular recording of the properties of single neurons).

- As the neuron is an electrochemical machine, it is impossible to separate electrical events from the biochemical and molecular processes that bring them about.

- Neurophysiologists today use techniques from chemistry (calcium imaging), physics (functional magnetic resonance imaging, fMRI), and molecular biology (site directed mutations) to study brain function.

Ion Channels

An ion channel is a protein macromolecule that crosses the breadth of a membrane and allows molecules to pass through. The ions move in a direction determined by the electrochemical gradient across the membrane.

- Ions tend to flow from an area of high concentration to an area of low concentration.

- In the presence of a voltage gradient, there may be no flow of ions despite unequal concentrations.

- Ion channels can be open or closed.

- Opening is brought about by changing the voltage across the membrane, or binding a chemical substance to a receptor.

- Most important role is that they provide the neuron with electrical excitability.

- Found in all parts of the neuron and to a lesser extent in the neuroglial cells.

Types of Channel

- Voltage Gated,
- Chemically Activated,
- Mechanical Stretch/Pressure.

Fundamental Properties of an Ion Channel

- It is made up of a number of protein sub units, sitting across the membrane, allowing ions to cross from one side to the other (Transmembrane pore).

- The channel must be able to move from open to closed state, and back.

- Must be able to open in response to the appropriate stimuli.

- Some channels respond to chemical stimulus (particularly at the synapse). These channels have specific receptors for that chemical that leads to channel opening.

Resting Membrane and Action Potential

- In the resting state, the neuronal cell membrane is fairly impermeable to ions. This is crucial for the generation of the resting membrane potential.

- The major intracellular ion is Potassium (It is sodium in the extracellular fluid).

- The natural flow of ions by way of their concentration gradients is for K^+ to leave the cell and Na^+ to enter.

- This movement of ions out of the cell leads to a negative membrane potential - Hyperpolarisation.

- The opposite is true for a relative influx of ions - Hypopolarisation.

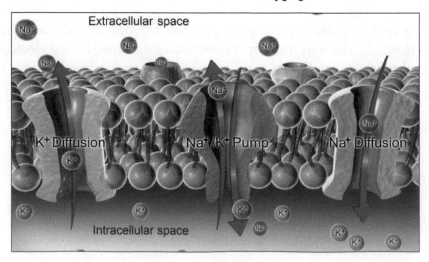

The resting membrane is relatively impermeable to Na+ ions, while remaining permeable to K^+ ions. So when the membrane is at rest, there will tend to be an efflux of K^+ ions out of the cell, down its concentration gradient, leaving excess negative charge behind. This continues until the chemical concentration gradient that is driving out the K^+ from the cell is exactly at the point where it is offset by the electrical potential difference generated by this efflux. (the membrane potential) K^+ is then drawn back into the cell. This steady state of the membrane is called the Equilibrium Potential. The equation for deriving the equilibrium potential is called the Nernst equation.

There is actually a slightly unexpected increased positive charge in axons due to a small permeability to Na^+ ions of the membrane in the resting state. This is offset by ATP dependent Na^+/K^+ exchange pump. I pumps out 3 Na^+ ions for every $3K^+$ ions brought in to the cell. However, it makes only a tiny contribution to the resting membrane potential of the cell.

Action Potential

Defined as a "single electrical impulse passing down an axon". It is all or nothing in its action. This means that once the threshold stimulus intensity is reached, an action potential will be generated. Information in the nervous system is coded and interpreted by the frequency of firing, not by the size of action potential.

Threshold Stimulus Intensity: The value at which the net inward current(determined by Na^+ ions) is just greater than the net outward current (carried by K^+ ions). It is normally -55mV (critical firing threshold). The AP most readily occurs at the axon hillock because this is where there is a greater density of Na^+ ion channels. It is for this reason that this is the site of AP initiation in the neuron. If the threshold is not reached, the action potential will not be generated, and transmission of the signal is terminated at that point.

Sequence of Events for an Action Potential to be Generated

- Depolorising voltage activates the voltage sensitive Na^+ ion channels in the neuronal membrane: Na^+ ions flow down the electrochemical gradient. Membrane is depolarised further. Further Na^+ channels open in a Positive feedback loop. When there is a greater inward current of sodium ions compared to the efflux of K^+ ions, there is fast opening of all Na^+ channels. This depolarises the membrane towards the equilibrium potential for Na^+(+55mV). Spike of AP is generated, but fails to reach equilibrium. Potential for Na^+ due to the increasing K^+ efflux.

- As the Na^+ channels become less active the AP falls. This inactivation is voltage dependent. During the falling phase the K^+ current is important as it leads to a short period of membrane hyperpolarisation before it deactivates.

- Membrane potential returns to the resting state.

Neuromuscular Junction/Synapse

Synapse

A synapse is the junction of two neurons. The chemical synapse is the predominate one found in the nervous system, however electrical synapses are found in cardiac muscle and glial cells.

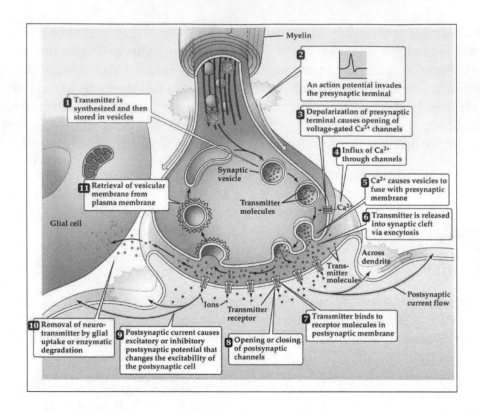

Synaptic Transmission

- Action potential arrives, leads to depolarisation of the presynaptic terminal. Voltage dependent Ca^{2+} channels open in the active zones of the terminal. This leads to influx of Ca^{2+}.

- Influx of Ca^{2+} leads to phosphorylation and alteration of amount of presynaptic calcium binding proteins. This liberates the vesicle from its presynaptic actin network, It then binds to the presynaptic membrane.

- The fusion of the vesicle to the membrane leads to the formation of a small channel, which quickly expands and releases its contents into the synaptic cleft. The vesicle membrane is recycled by endocytosis.

- Released neurotransmitter diffuses across synaptic cleft with the goal of binding to the postsynaptic receptor.

- Activation of the postsynaptic receptor leads to a change in the postsynaptic membrane potential.

- There are alternative theories that suggest that the neurotransmitter is delivered via molecules or membrane channels rather than vesicles.

Nerve Conduction

Action potential propagation is achieved by local current spread. The nerve is insulated with myelin if its size is above a certain diameter, with the Nodes of Ranvier at various intervals along its length.

Unmyelinated Axons

Action potential leads to depolarisation of the membrane immediately in front (and behind). The membrane is in a refractory state, so the action potential is only conducted in 1 direction. This is feasible in small axons, but the spread of current is slow.

Myelinated Axons

Same sequence of events as in the unmyelinated axons. There is however a significant difference. The progressing action potential encounters high resistance, low-capacitance structure - myelin wrapped around the axon. The depolarising current passes along the axoplasm, until it reaches the low resistance Node of Ranvier with its large amount of Na^+ channels. The action potential is then generated at this site. Action potential is conducted from node to node. This is called Saltatory Conduction.

Advantages of Myelination

- Allows for rapid conduction of action potential.

- Minimises metabolic demands on the cell.

- Increases packing capacity of the NS, allowing more fibres to be crammed into 1 nerve.

Most nerves greater than 1 micron are myelinated. Disturbances in conduction are normally due to demyelination pathologies. They include Guillan Barre syndrome and Multiple sclerosis.

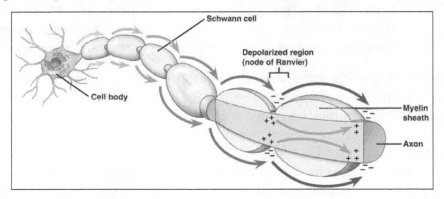

Postsynaptic Integration

Each central neuron receives many hundreds of synapses. Each of these inputs is than integrated into a response by that particular neuron. This involves processing all the inputs that arrive at any one time. This is called spatial summation. Processing inputs over a set period of time is called temporal summation. There will be a mix of excitatory and inhibitory synapses acting at this point.

Excitatory Post Synaptic Potentials

- Binding of neurotransmitter leads to opening of ion channels.

- There is cation influx in post-synaptic process.

- Depolarisation of the membrane occurs.

- EPSPs depolarisations recorded in the post-synaptic cell to a particular excitatory stimulus.

- Depolarisations assoc. with EPSPs can go on to trigger APs if summation occurs at the synapse.

Inhibitory Postsynaptic Potentials

- Ion channels allow postsynaptic anion influx when open.

- Hyperpolarisations of the membrane occur due to influx of CL- and efflux of K^+.

- Important for modulating the neurons response to excitatory input at the synapse.

- Found in strategically important sites of the neuron such as the proximal dendrite and soma.

- They have a large influence on the dendritic tree.

- Some neurons provide their own inhibitory influence by having axon collaterals and their own inhibitory interneurons. This is termed feedback inhibition. E.g. motorneurons and Renshaw cells in the spinal cord.

Neurotransmitters, Receptors and Pathways

The neurotransmitter is released at the synapse and works with a specific protein in the postsynaptic membrane called the receptor. In some synapses the neurotransmitter may also be found to interact with a presynaptic autoreceptor. The PSA acts as a regulator of the amount of transmitter released.

Receptors are normally specific for a particular neurotransmitter. There are several types of receptor. Co-released neurotransmitters may regulate the binding of another transmitter. Receptors for specific neurotransmitters may be either coupled directly to ion channels or to a membrane enzyme where the binding of the neurotransmitter to the receptor either opens an ion channel via an intracellular enzyme cascade or indirectly modulating the probability of other ion channels opening in response to voltage changes. (neuromodulation). Activated receptor can only return to its resting state once the neurotransmitter is removed by the process of enzymatic hydrolysis (uptake) into the presynaptic nerve terminal or into the nearby glial cells.

- Desensitisation/Down regulation: A decrease in affinity of the receptor for the transmitter in the short term, in the longterm, this leads to a decrease in the number of receptors.

- Supersensitivity/Up regulation: An increased affinity of the receptor for the transmitter in the short term can lead to an increase in channels in the longterm.

Receptors

- Ionotropic: N-methyl-D-aspartate(NMDA).

- Non NMDA.

- Metabotropic: G-protein associated glutamate receptors that respond by initiating intracellular biochemical events, modulating synaptic transmission.

There are a large number of Neurotransmitters:

- Excitatory Amino Acids: These are the main excitatory NTs in the CNS. The main NT in this group is Glutamate which acts at a number of receptors.

- Inhibitory Amino Acids: These are the major inhibitory neurotransmitters, the main one of which is GABA, present throughout the CNS. Glycine found mainly in the spinal cord.

- Monoamines: Found in small groups of neurons in the brain stem, projecting widely into the CNS. Found in the autonomic NS. They bind to a host of receptors.

- Acetylcholine: Widely distributed throughout the nervous system, including the neuromuscular junction and autonomic NS.

- Neuropeptides: Found all over the NS. Often released simultaneously with other NTs.

In addition, over 50 neuroactive peptides have been found, and new ones are discovered regularly. Many of these are "co-released" along with a small-molecule transmitter. Nevertheless, in some cases a peptide is the primary transmitter at a synapse. β-endorphin is a relatively well known example of a peptide neurotransmitter because it engages in highly specific interactions with opioid receptors in the central nervous system.

Single ions (such as synaptically released zinc) are also considered neurotransmitters by some, as well as some gaseous molecules such as nitric oxide (NO), carbon monoxide (CO), and hydrogen sulfide (H_2S). The gases are produced in the neural cytoplasm and are immediately diffused through the cell membrane into the extracellular fluid and into nearby cells to stimulate production of second messengers. Soluble gas neurotransmitters are difficult to study, as they act rapidly and are immediately broken down, existing for only a few seconds.

The most prevalent transmitter is glutamate, which is excitatory at well over 90% of the synapses in the human brain. The next most prevalent is Gamma-Aminobutyric Acid, or GABA, which is inhibitory at more than 90% of the synapses that do not use glutamate. Although other transmitters are used in fewer synapses, they may be very important functionally: the great majority of psychoactive drugs exert their effects by altering the actions of some neurotransmitter systems, often acting through transmitters other than glutamate or GABA. Addictive drugs such as cocaine and amphetamines exert their effects primarily on the dopamine system. The addictive opiate drugs exert their effects primarily as functional analogs of opioid peptides, which, in turn, regulate dopamine levels.

Computational Neuroanatomy

In the broadest sense, computational neuroanatomy is the application of computational techniques (e.g. analysis, visualization, modeling, and simulation) to the investigation of neural structure. Within the field of computational neuroscience, computational neuroanatomy is principally considered to aim at creating anatomically accurate models of the nervous system. At the cellular level, computational neuroanatomy is based on the quantitative description of the structure of individual neurons, the density of neuronal elements within specific brain areas, and their interconnectivity. An important goal in computational neuroanatomy is to relate the structure to the function, at both the single cell and network levels. Combining precise morphology and detailed biophysics of single cells within large-scale realistic and data-driven network models allows simulation of emergent properties of neural circuits. Development of databases of neuronal structures and biophysical models enables quantitative data transfer between laboratories and constitutes an essential area of scientific emphasis in contemporary computational neuroanatomy research.

Staining and Imaging Techniques for Morphology and Connectivity

For about a century the Golgi technique has been very successful in staining neurons enabling the semi-automatic reconstruction and the quantitative analysis of their neuronal branching patterns. In combination with other classical staining methods it has been used to achieve a quantitative statistical description of brain tissue in terms of the density of neurons, synapses, and total length of axonal and dendritic arborizations (per cubic millimeter). Further progress in computational neuroanatomy was enabled by the spread of modern imaging techniques that allow digital reconstructions of dendritic and axonal morpohology. In the last few decades, the development of intracellular labeling using biocytin/HRP injections and various visualization methods, including HRP-DAB or fluorescent avidin reaction, has led to a large output of high resolution data about dendritic morphology. Tracer injections are typically performed in single neurons in vivo (anesthetized animal) or in vitro (slice conditions), and microscopy rendering often involves fixing and reslicing the tissue. New visualization approaches, such as GFP expression in specific cell types, allow direct morphology observation in vivo, both at the whole cell and subcellular levels. In addition, cell-class specific GFP expression in conjunction with traditional in vitro microscopy reduces the sampling bias due to limited access to certain neuron type's in vivo and variable cell survival during slice preparation. Finally, in vivo visualization enables observation of developmental and activity-dependent morphological changes, such as individual spine plasticity. McCormick reconstructs neurons and their connections directly from stacks of thin sections, milled off from a block of tissue. Methods of automatic slice production, image capture and digitization play an important role in high-volume reconstructions.

Quantitative Analysis of Dendritic and Axonal Morphology

A fundamental step for computational neuroanatomy is the tracing of the acquired neuronal images into a three-dimensional (3D) digital representation of the branching dendrites and/or axons. Traditionally performed manually, this process is very labor intensive severely limiting the number of available reconstructions. Both commercial (Neurolucida, MicroBrightField) and freeware software systems (Neuromantic, NeuroMorpho, or NeuronStudio) offer some level of automatization of the reconstruction process. These tools considerably simplify data acquisition thus contributing to the increase of the neuron morphology databases. In computer-aided neuromorphological reconstructions, the digital tracing files describe neuronal trees as a series of interconnected cylinders, each represented by diameter, spatial coordinates, and links to other cylinders in the arbor. The number of data points representing a single neuron can be quite large.

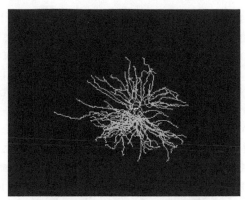

Example of reconstructed neuron.

Digital reconstructions enable quantitative analysis of neuronal shapes by means of morphometric parameters describing the metrical and topological properties and the spatial embedding of the three-dimensional structures. These morphometric parameters make it possible to statistically describe the variability in neuronal morphologies. In more advanced approaches investigators have designed procedures for the computational generation of neuronal morphologies with realistic variabilities in their shapes based on intrinsic correlations between morphometric parameters or based on neuronal growth principles. Both the reconstruction and the growth-model approach are algorithmic procedures, using a limited set of statistical descriptors (basic parameters) or growth rules, respectively, to generate stochastic neuronal structures that are statistically indistinguishable from the real neurons of the same morphological class. Freeware tools for the reconstruction approach are available to measure nearly unlimited structural features from digital reconstruction files (e.g., the L-Measure software program). The ability to characterize neurons with a compact code consisting of a few statistical descriptors represents a valuable compression tool of vast neuroanatomical data.

Potential Synaptic Connectivity between Individual Cells

The number of synapses between two given cells in a brain depends on multiple factors, including partitioning of 3D space by the dendrites of multiple neurons that share it, trajectories of the axons that navigate this 3D neuropil forest, and spatial distribution of chemical factors during axonal growth and neuronal activity. While the reconstruction of dendritic and axonal trees of selected pre- and postsynaptic cells is possible, in fixed adult tissue the neuronal activity pattern and the chemical makeup of the environment during development are obviously unknown. Computational neuroanatomists have developed both theoretical and numerical approaches to tackle this issue. One study suggested that intricate branching of axonal and dendritic trees are optimized to provide a high degree of connectivity between neurons, given the existing geometrical restrictions. In a different attempt to predict individual axon pathways through well-defined structural landmarks, a system was built for simulation of growth and branching of thalamocortical projections on the basis of a voxel-based mouse brain atlas.

The critical underlying question remains: how does the number of synapses between two neurons depend on the overlap between their dendritic and axonal trees? According to "Peters rule", synaptic contacts occur where dendrites and axons happen to be in apposition. These "potential synapses" are required but not sufficient for an actual synapse formation; and the expected number of connections between two neurons is proportional to the product of their dendritic and axonal trees densities. However, a recent study of connectivity between two neurons using glutamate uncaging and dendritic/axonal reconstruction shows that there may be fewer functional synapses than geometrical appositions. Furthermore, the ratio of the number of functional synapses to that of total possible synapses specifically depends on the laminar source of axonal projection as well as dendritic target. In particular, in the somatosensory cortex, this ratio for synapses between layer 5 and layers 2/3 is higher than the ratio for the layer 4 to layer 2/3 projection (but both are significantly less than 1). Therefore, notwithstanding a baseline correlation between potential synaptic connectivity and axo-dendritic overlap, the set of functional synapses effectively expressed at any one time represents only one of a combinatorial multitude of possibilities. On the one hand, this may subserve a greater network capacity for representation diversity. On the other, there is the additional possibility to increase total synaptic strength by recruiting new synapses (for example, as a result of learning).

Structure/Activity Relationship: Dendritic Trees, Input Processing and Firing Patterns

The computational simulation of detailed brain activity at the cellular level requires quantitative knowledge of neuronal class specific distribution of ionic channel and other membrane properties, as well as synaptic connectivity between neurons. Digital reconstructions of neuronal morphology represent a central node for both of these requirements. Furthermore, they have been proven useful to investigate another crucial facet of neuronal activity, namely the effect of dendritic structure on cell function. Numerous modeling reports demonstrated that the neuronal firing patterns simulated with anatomically realistic compartmental representations of the neurons with a specified channel distribution heavily depend on morphology. Several known "cortical spiking patterns" were obtained by distributing the same membrane properties on cell classes such as pyramidal and stellate cells, or only changing the topological asymmetry of the model dendrites. Even more specifically, the whole range of diverse firing observed in hippocampal CA_3 pyramidal cells was reproduced when implementing an identical biophysical model on a set of morphologies which reflected the naturally occurring variability. These findings are particularly striking because they were obtained with simple stimulation corresponding to the experimental protocol of somatic current injection. A more natural activation of synaptic inputs, which are distributed on the dendrites, would be expected to exacerbate the influence of morphology on output patterns. Following these results, extensive efforts are ongoing to correlate dendritic structure and neuronal activity in various cell classes. At the same time, multiple studies indicate that channel distribution can change dendritic processing and neuronal firing properties.

It is clear that static anatomical information may be necessary but not sufficient to predict individual neuron properties. At the very least, the study of dynamic functional properties of neurons in vivo is required. Recent attempts to integrate vast and diverse information on the anatomical, physiological, and molecular characteristics of neurons into a comprehensive, practical, and useful classification system led to the emerging consensus that dendritic morphology is only one of the factors that can aid specific neuronal identification. Axonal projections, laminar distribution of neuronal inputs and outputs, and immunohistochemical markers are other prominent features, especially for interneurons. Noticeably, computational neuroanatomy techniques (and particularly digital reconstructions among them) are contributing substantially to foster progress in many if not all of these aspects.

Stereology, Cell Densities and Brain Region Volumes

Quantification of network connectivity presupposes a robust estimate of cell count. It is important to recognize that the number of neurons in a given brain region is not constant over time, but can change during development, as a consequence of neurodegenerative disease, or in the process of learning, as was suggested in particular for hippocampal areas such as the dentate gyrus (DG). To compute the convergence and/or divergence ratios between cell populations in a normal brain, or to test hypotheses about changes in a specific cell group count associated with a particular neurological disorder, total cell numbers and densities have to be calculated. Earlier anatomical studies counted Nissl-stained cells in two-dimensional (2D) slices. A switch to the 3D volume is not trivial. Stereology techniques developed in the last decades provide unbiased estimates of such quantitative 3D parameters as the number of cells, volumes of brain areas, and cell density. Development of specialized software such as Stereoinvestigator and Neurolucida (MicroBrightField) combines modern stereological tools with a precise control of microscope lateral and depth displacements. These programs automate data collection from 2D slices and significantly speed up and simplify acquiring 3D estimates.

Recent application of stereological techniques together with new cell-specific imaging labels has led to considerable scientific achievements. These include demonstrating a quantitative link between aging in human brain and number of neocortical neurons, changes in Alzheimer's disease, link between the drop in the number of cells in hippocampal areas CA1 and DG and cognitive decline in Alzheimer patients, discovering that a significant proportion (6%) of new DG cells develop each month, finding that decreased amygdala cell numbers but not volumes are associated with autism, alterations in neuronal numbers in Schizophrenia, and no further doubling of number of neurons in Broca's area after birth. An important aspect of testing hypotheses associating changes in brain volume with specific neurological disorders involves parcellation of image stacks (e.g. from MRI scans), into specific areas as a prerequisite for the reliable measurement of corresponding volumes. Significant inter-subject variability, especially in the gyral and sulcal patterns of the human cortex, corroborated the idea of probabilistic brain atlases. Automated techniques have been developed to aid extraction of cortical thickness and boundaries of specific areas. Moreover, computational methods of cortical inflation and flattening exist to switch to a surface-based coordinate system for a more accurate representation of cortical topography. An important component of computational neuroanatomy develops tools for quantitative comparisons between different brain atlases.

Connectivity between Brain Areas and Network Topology

Synaptic connectivity data between pairs of individual cells can be summarized into cell class-specific statistics that will generally be location dependent within a brain area. Another important aspect of computational neuroanatomy involves the analysis of connectivity between different brain regions. Structural connectivity can be assessed by tracer injections in a given area of interest and the subsequent study of fixed tissue. In addition, the recently developed structural MRI technique, Diffusion Tensor Imaging, can be used in vivo. Computational analysis of cortico-cortical connections pointed out the similarities with the small-world network architecture which has a short average path length and relatively high clustering. Network modeling studies demonstrated that changes in the fundamental pattern of network connectivity can contribute to the manifestation of pathological population activity such as epilepsy. Structural connectivity between areas reflects the topological proximity of different areas, but not the total number and strength of the synaptic connections (which, in turn, can be modified during development or in a task-dependent manner). To address that, new modeling techniques estimate functional connectivity between different areas based on the correlation of activity as detected by fMRI, EEG or MEG activation.

Development and Activity-Dependent Plasticity of Neural Connectivity

Neuroanatomical studies in fixed tissue produce a snapshot of neuronal structure and connectivity at a given moment in time. In the living brain, this architecture changes as it develops, or as a result of learning. A key challenge is to characterize the mechanisms contributing to these plastic changes. Sophisticated imaging techniques have been recently established to assess the dynamics of dendritic spine turnover in the mature sensory cortex in vivo. Meanwhile, methods for observing axonal extension, branching and maturation of synaptic contacts, as a consequence of or even during manipulation of the experimental environment, are still being developed. Biophysical models of molecular processes underlying axonal and dendritic elongation and branching give an insight into intracellular and extracellular determinants of neuronal morphology. Computational techniques that relate developmental changes in neural architecture to the functionality of mature neural circuits provide a useful tool and allow testing hypothesized metabolic or activity-dependent constraints.

Numerous computational models explain how columnar structure and feature representation develops in the visual cortex based on cross-correlation and Hebbian learning, elastic self-organizing nets or efficient information coding. These models typically use simplified neural elements, generalized cell populations with uniform properties, and connections with average weights from one cell class to another. The fate of an individual axon distributing synaptic contacts across a complex dendritic tree during development or experience-dependent plasticity remains to be fully explored. A separate class of models addresses effects of chemoattractant, and homeostatic plasticity on neural circuit organization and functionality.

Permissions

Index

Printed in the USA
CPSIA information can be obtained
at www.ICGtesting.com
LVHW081652200324
774517LV00083B/753

9 781639 892235